# 375 SOUTHERN HOME PLANS

M000082205

## TABLE OF CONTENTS

HOMES IN FULL COLOR.................................................................2

MORE SOUTHERN HOMES.........................................................33

OUR COVER HOME...PLAN NO. 10778.......................................199

HIGH WIND LOAD ENGINEERING...............................................339

HERE'S WHAT YOU GET.............................................................340

OPTIONS & EXTRAS..................................................................342

MODIFICATIONS MADE EASY!....................................................343

ZIP QUOTE — HOME COST CALCULATOR.....................................344

LEGAL INFORMATION...............................................................345

ORDERING INFORMATION.........................................................346

INDEX...YOUR NEW HOME AT A GLANCE......................................348

HOW-TO BOOKS.....................................................................350

Library of Congress
Catalogue Card No.: 98-87398
IBSN: 1-58011-061-4

CREATIVE HOMEOWNER
A Division of
Federal Marketing Corp.
24 Park Way,
Upper Saddle River, NJ 07458

Manufactured in the
United States of America

Current Printing (last digit)
1 0 9 8 7 6 5 4 3 2

Cover Photography by
John Ehrenclou

CREATIVE
HOMEOWNER®

COPYRIGHT © 1999
CREATIVE HOMEOWNER®
A Division of Federal Marketing Corp.
Upper Saddle River, NJ

plan no.

# 94220

total living area: **3,477** sq. ft.

# Turret Study

Photography Supplied by The Sater Design Group

An angled garage, raised entry and a turret study help create a visually exciting and unique streetscape. The angled theme is present throughout the design and is useful in view orientation. The entry doors open to the formal living room focusing to the lanai through sliding glass doors and mitered glass corner. A double sided fireplace is shared with the master suite to the right, a wetbar easily serves the living room, dining room and lanai and makes this home perfect for family gatherings or entertaining on a grand scale. An island kitchen easily serves all informal family areas. An octagon nook has windows spanning to all rear views. The leisure room has a fireplace wall with built-ins along the back wall. Optional fixed glass windows above the entertainment center and gas fireplace allow for natural light and a visually exciting detail. The bath resembles a custom design typically seen in master areas. The study has a peaked vaulted ceiling and cove lighting. The spacious master suite includes a fireplace, a morning kitchen bar, and lanai access. A full bath accesses the outdoor area. No materials list is available for this plan. The photographed home may have been modified to suit individual tastes.

## plan info

| | |
|---|---|
| **Main Floor** | **3,477** sq. ft. |
| **Garage** | **771** sq. ft. |
| **Bedrooms** | **Three** |
| **Baths** | **2**(full), **1**(three quarter) |
| **Foundation** | **Slab** |

A cook's delight, this fabulous kitchen makes entertaining a breeze with its spacious layout.

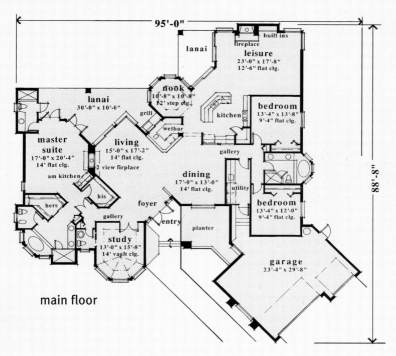

**95'-0"**

lanai

leisure
23'-0" x 17'-8"
12'-6" flat clg.

fireplace
built ins

nook
10'-8" x 10'-8"
12' step clg.

lanai
30'-0" x 10'-0"

grill

kitchen

bedroom
13'-4" x 13'-8"
9'-4" flat clg.

master suite
17'-0" x 20'-4"
14' flat clg.

living
15'-0" x 17'-2"
14' flat clg.

wetbar

am kitchen

2 view firplace

gallery

his

dining
17'-0" x 13'-0"
14' flat clg.

hers

foyer

utility

bedroom
13'-4" x 12'-0"
9'-4" flat clg.

gallery

entry

study
13'-0" x 15'-8"
14' vault clg.

planter

garage
23'-4" x 29'-8"

**88'-8"**

HIGH WIND
LOAD ENGINEERING
AVAILABLE
SEE PAGE 339 FOR DETAILS

main floor

Enjoy expansive views while curled up by a cozy fire.

**plan no.**

**9**
**3**
**2**
**7**
**0**

price code **F**

total living area: **3,656** sq. ft.

# Stucco Opulence

Photography by John Ehrenclou

An open foyer leads to a two-story living room with a great fireplace. The well-appointed kitchen has a cook-top island/snack bar, built-in pantry and desk, and an abundance of cabinet and counter space. The kitchen expands to the breakfast nook and the keeping room creating a feeling of spaciousness. His-n-her walk-in closets, a luxurious bath and private sitting room create a master suite sure to be a personal retreat for the owner of this home. The library is in close proximity to the master suite for those late nights working at home. The additional bedrooms are on the second floor. The children's den gives the children needed space and the two full baths are situated close to the bedrooms. No materials list is available for this plan. The photographed home may have been modified to suit individual tastes.

## plan info

| | |
|---|---|
| **First Floor** | **2,329 sq. ft.** |
| **Second Floor** | **1,259 sq. ft.** |
| **Finished Staircase** | **68 sq. ft.** |
| **Bonus Room** | **420 sq. ft.** |
| **Basement** | **1,806 sq. ft.** |
| **Garage** | **528 sq. ft.** |
| **Bedrooms** | **Four** |
| **Baths** | **3(full), 2(half)** |
| **Foundation** | **Basement** |

This great kitchen, with abundant space, easily accomodates two or more cooks when meal preparation is to be shared.

first floor

77'-0"

*An*
EXCLUSIVE DESIGN
*By Jannis Vann & Associates, Inc.*

second floor

Relax in your private sitting room, giving the Master Suite that "get-away" feeling.

**plan no.**    price code **C**    total living area: 2,085 sq. ft.

**9 3 2 1 3**

# Distinctive Windows

Photography Supplied by Jannis Vann & Associates

The windows of this home give it character and distinction. The formal areas are located at the front of the home. The living room and the dining room enjoy the natural light from the bayed windows. The expansive family room is enhanced by a fireplace and view of the rear yard. A U-shaped kitchen efficiently serves the dining room and the breakfast bay. Both the breakfast bay and the family room have access to the patio. The master suite is elegantly crowned by a decorative ceiling. The private master bath offers a garden tub and a step-in shower. Two large additional bedrooms share a full hall bath. There is a convenient second floor laundry center. This plan is available with a basement or slab foundation. Please specify when ordering. No materials list is available for this plan. The photographed home may have been modified to suit individual tastes.

## plan info

| | |
|---|---|
| **First Floor** | 1,126 sq. ft. |
| **Second Floor** | 959 sq. ft. |
| **Basement** | 458 sq. ft. |
| **Garage** | 627 sq. ft. |
| **Bedrooms** | Three |
| **Baths** | 2(full), 1(half) |
| **Foundation** | Basement or Slab |

◀ The sunny breakfast bay provides not only a delightful dining area, but access to the patio for ease in outdoor entertaining.

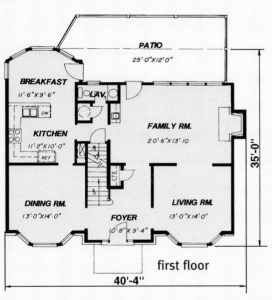

PATIO
25'-0"X12'-0"

BREAKFAST
11'-6"X9'-6"

LAV.

KITCHEN
11'-2"X10'-0"

REF

FAMILY RM.
20'-6"X13'-10

DINING RM.
13'-0"X14'-0"

FOYER
10'-8" X 9'-4"

LIVING RM.
13'-0"X14'-0"

35'-0"

first floor

40'-4"

*An* EXCLUSIVE DESIGN
*By Jannis Vann & Associates, Inc.*

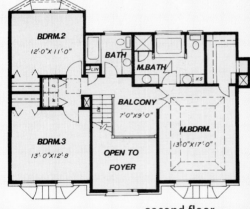

BDRM.2
12'-0"X11'-0"

BATH

M.BATH

BDRM.3
13'-0"X12'-8

BALCONY
7'-0"X9'-0"

OPEN TO FOYER

M.BDRM.
13'-0"X17'-0"

second floor

Built-in bookshelves and a cozy fireplace create an inviting spot for both family and friends. ▶

# 9 3 2 9 4

# For a Family to Grow In

Photography by John Ehrenclou

This attractive stucco home is perfect for modern family living. The formal living room and dining room are located on either side of the foyer. The two secondary bedrooms are at the end of a short hallway to the right of the foyer. The master suite is tucked into its own private rear corner. The family room is at the "heart" of the home, providing a cozy fireplace to gather around in colder weather. The kitchen includes a peninsula counter/breakfast bar and plenty of storage and counter space. There is an optional second floor area that could include a fourth bedroom, a loft, a full bath and storage space. This plan is available with a basement, slab or crawl space foundation. Please specify when ordering. The photographed home may have been modified to suit individual tastes.

## plan info

| | |
|---|---|
| **First Floor** | 2,384 sq. ft. |
| **Second Floor** | 176 sq. ft. |
| **Bonus Room** | 392 sq. ft. |
| **Basement** | 2,384 sq. ft. |
| **Bedrooms** | Three |
| **Baths** | 2(full), 1(half) |
| **Foundation** | Basement, Slab or Crawl Space |

High ceilings and a stone hearth makes this the "heart of the home" for family and guests.

**74' - 0"**

**70' - 0"**

BREAKFAST 13 x 10

KITCHEN 15 x 15

FAMILY ROOM 15 x 16

PATIO

MASTER BEDROOM 14 x 17

M. BATH

BEDROOM 2 11 x 14

BATH

DINING ROOM 14 x 14

FOYER

LIVING ROOM 14 x 14

BEDROOM 3 13 x 12

LAV.

LAUNDRY

DOUBLE GARAGE

first floor

*An*
EXCLUSIVE DESIGN
*By Jannis Vann & Associates, Inc.*

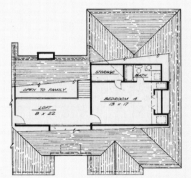

OPEN TO FAMILY

STORAGE

BATH

LOFT 8 x 22

BEDROOM 4 13 x 17

second floor

Retreat to your own private haven in this comfortable Master Suite.

# 98904

# Columned Porch

Photography by John Ehrenclou

The foyer leads into the formal dining room, topped by a decorative ceiling, the library with double door entry, or the master suite. The cooktop island kitchen has direct access to the formal dining room and flows into the breakfast bay and the family room. There is a deck expanding living space outside. Two secondary bedrooms, tucked into the left side of the home, share use of the full bath in the hall. There is room to expand into the second floor. The photographed home may have been modified to suit individual tastes.

## plan info

| | |
|---|---|
| **Main Floor** | 2,614 sq. ft. |
| **Bonus Floor** | 1,681 sq. ft. |
| **Basement** | 2,563 sq. ft. |
| **Garage** | 596 sq. ft. |
| **Bedrooms** | Three |
| **Baths** | 2(full), 1(half) |
| **Foundation** | Basement |

Columns lend style and elegance to the formal dining room. ◄

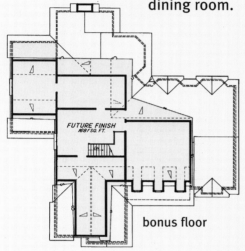

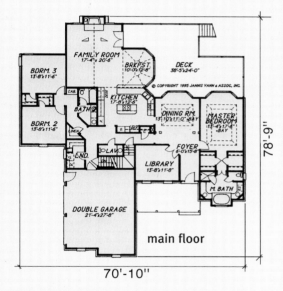

FAMILY ROOM
17'-4"x20'-6"

BRKFST.
10'-0"x12'-6"

DECK
38'-5"x24'-0"

© COPYRIGHT 1995 JANNIS VANN & ASSOC. INC.

BDRM. 3
13'-8"x11'-6"

KITCHEN
17'-8"x12'-6"

CAB.

BATH 2

DINING RM.
13'-10"x11'-0" +BAY

MASTER
BEDROOM
13'-4"x17'-4"
+BAY

BDRM. 2
13'-8"x11'-6"

LINEN

FOYER
6'-0"x15'-8"

LND.

LIBRARY
13'-8"x11'-8"

M. BATH

DOUBLE GARAGE
21'-4"x27'-8"

main floor

78'-9"

70'-10"

FUTURE FINISH
169'/SQ. FT.

bonus floor

*An*
EXCLUSIVE DESIGN
*By Jannis Vann & Associates, Inc.*

The kitchen becomes the center of activity with easy access to both dining and family rooms. ►

plan no.    price code **B**     total living area: **1,772** sq. ft.

# 94203

# Decorative Widows Walk

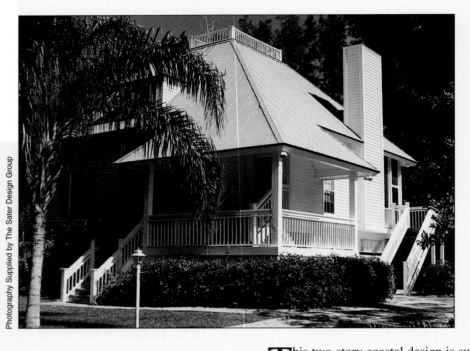

Photography Supplied by The Sater Design Group

This two-story coastal design is sure to please with its warm character and decorative widows walk. The covered entry, with dramatic transom window, leads to a spacious living room highlighted by a warming fireplace. The dining room and kitchen combine to provide a delightful place for mealtimes inside or out, with access to a side deck. A study, a bedroom and a full bath complete the first floor. The luxurious master suite is located on the second floor for privacy and features an oversized walk-in closet and a separate dressing area. The pampering master bath enjoys a whirlpool tub, a double vanity and a compartmented toilet. No materials list is available for this plan. The photographed home may have been modified to suit individual tastes.

**first floor**

41'-9"

down

screened verandah
20'-0" x 7'-8"

kitchen

great room
21'-0" x 14'-0"
vault. clg.

fireplace

dining
12'-6" x 9'-0"
8' clg.

sundeck

45'-0"

up

down

foyer

study
10'-0" x 13'-0"
8' clg.

br. 2
11'-8" x 11'-6"
8' clg.

entry porch

down

**second floor**

open to below

master suite
12'-3" x 20'-0"
8' clg.

down

loft

w.i.c.

**garage**

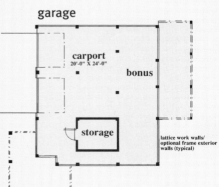

carport
20'-0" X 24'-0"

bonus

storage

lattice work walls/
optional frame exterior
walls (typical)

HIGH WIND
LOAD ENGINEERING
AVAILABLE
SEE PAGE 339 FOR DETAILS

## plan info

| | |
|---|---|
| **First Floor** | **1,136 sq. ft.** |
| **Second Floor** | **636 sq. ft.** |
| **Garage** | **526 sq. ft.** |
| **Bedrooms** | **Two** |
| **Baths** | **2(full)** |
| **Foundation** | **Pier/Post** |

**total living area: 1,861 sq. ft.**  ⚒  **C** price code  **plan no.**

# Windows and Gables

Flanked by columns, the barrel vaulted entrance of this home is echoed in its dramatic arched windows and gables. Interior columns add elegance while visually dividing the foyer from the dining room, and the Great room from the kitchen. The Great room is made even larger by its cathedral ceiling and bank of windows, including an arched clerestory window. A box bay window adds space to the formal dining room, while the kitchen features an angled center island with breakfast counter for the busy family. The master suite, secluded on the first floor, boasts his-n-her walk-in closets and a garden tub with a skylight. This plan is available with a basement or crawl space foundation. Please specify when ordering. The photographed home may have been modified to suit individual tastes.

second floor

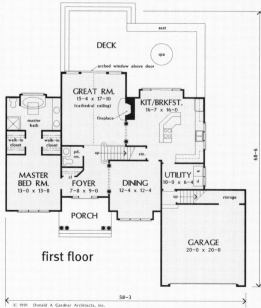

first floor

## plan info

| | |
|---|---|
| **First Floor** | **1,416 sq. ft.** |
| **Second Floor** | **445 sq. ft.** |
| **Bonus Room** | **284 sq. ft.** |
| **Garage & Storage** | **485 sq. ft.** |
| **Bedrooms** | **Three** |
| **Baths** | **2(full), 1(half)** |
| **Foundation** | **Basement or Crawl Space** |

plan no. **93202**

price code **A**

total living area: **1,447** sq. ft.

# Everything in Its Place

Photography by John Ehrenclou

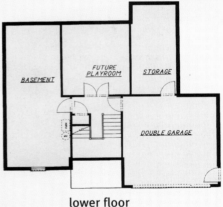

lower floor

Not only is this plan attractive on the outside, it is pleasing on the inside. The central living area is equipped with a fireplace and has access to the wood deck. The well-appointed, U-shaped kitchen flows efficiently into the dining room. The master suite is on the opposite side of the house from the secondary bedrooms to insure privacy. The secondary bedrooms have a full hall bath situated between them. Each bedroom has ample storage space; the master suite features a walk-in closet. The photographed home may have been modified to suit individual tastes.

*An* EXCLUSIVE DESIGN
*By Jannis Vann & Associates, Inc.*

first floor

## plan info

| | |
|---|---|
| **First Floor** | 1,407 sq. ft. |
| **Finished Staircase** | 40 sq. ft. |
| **Bonus** | 224 sq. ft. |
| **Basement** | 732 sq. ft. |
| **Garage** | 400 sq. ft. |
| **Bedrooms** | Three |
| **Baths** | 2(full) |
| **Foundation** | Basement |

**total living area:   2,588 sq. ft.**   ✕   **ⓓ price code**   **plan no.**

# Home Sweet Home

**9 3 2 0 5**

Photography by John Ehrendlou

A house is not a home until the family gives it heart. This plan is ready for your family. The formal areas are placed at the front of the home with a view of the wrap-around porch and the front yard. The informal family areas are located in the center and rear of the home, which include a fireplaced family room. The efficient kitchen has direct access to either the formal dining room or the breakfast room. Upstairs, the family's sleeping quarters give everyone their own private space. The master suite has a decorative ceiling and a walk-in closet. A bonus room can be finished according to the family's needs. This plan is available with a basement, slab or crawl space foundation. Please specify when ordering. The photographed home may have been modified to suit individual tastes.

*An*
EXCLUSIVE DESIGN
*By Jannis Vann & Associates, Inc.*

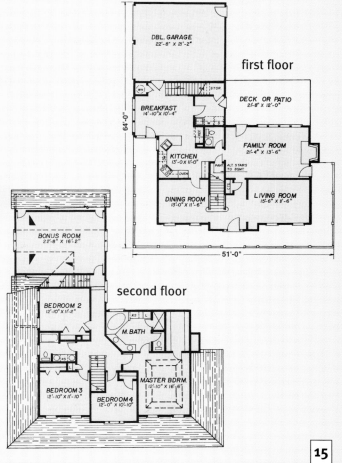

first floor

second floor

## plan info

| | |
|---|---|
| **First Floor** | **1,320 sq. ft.** |
| **Second Floor** | **1,268 sq. ft.** |
| **Bonus** | **389 sq. ft.** |
| **Basement** | **1,320 sq. ft.** |
| **Garage** | **482 sq. ft.** |
| **Bedrooms** | **Four** |
| **Baths** | **2(full), 1(half)** |
| **Foundation** | **Basement, Slab or Crawl Space** |

plan no.

# 93439

price code **E**

total living area: **3,013** sq. ft.

# Victorian Touches

Photography by Joel Whisenant

*An* EXCLUSIVE DESIGN *By Greg Marquis*

The formal foyer is accented by a decorative staircase. The living room and the dining room flow together for ease in entertaining. The family room is enhanced by a fireplace and includes French doors to the front porch and the rear deck. The expansive kitchen flows into the sun room/breakfast area. A built-in pantry and an island with a snack bar highlight the kitchen. The first master suite includes a five-piece private bath and a walk-in closet. The second master suite features a full, private bath and a walk-in closet. The two additional bedrooms share the full bath in the hall. No materials list is available for this plan. The photographed home may have been modified to suit individual tastes.

## plan info

| | |
|---|---|
| **First Floor** | **1,459 sq. ft.** |
| **Second Floor** | **1,554 sq. ft.** |
| **Basement** | **1,459 sq. ft.** |
| **Garage** | **525 sq. ft.** |
| **Bedrooms** | **Four** |
| **Baths** | **3(full), 1(half)** |
| **Foundation** | **Basement** |

total living area:  3,748  sq. ft.          **F** price code          plan no.

# Beautiful Street Presence

Photography Supplied by The Sater Design Group

**9229**

Inside the grand foyer, the plan opens through archways to the formal living spaces. The high stepped ceilings open up the rooms and give it a grand airy feel. An oversized kitchen with a cooktop island and large walk-in pantry makes this area perfect for family cooking or entertaining on a grand scale. A bayed leisure room features large windows. The secondary bedrooms, including one full guest suite, round out the family wing. The master suite area features an extravagant oversized bedroom and a sitting bay. The bath has a walk-in shower, his-n-her vanities and a garden tub. The second floor features a study and a guest suite with private balconies. No materials list is available for this plan. The photographed home may have been modified to suit individual tastes.

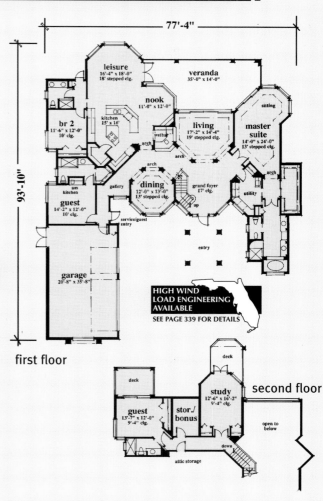

first floor

second floor

## plan info

| | |
|---|---|
| **First Floor** | **3,092 sq. ft.** |
| **Second Floor** | **656 sq. ft.** |
| **Porch** | **479 sq. ft.** |
| **Deck** | **204 sq. ft.** |
| **Garage** | **785 sq. ft.** |
| **Bedrooms** | **Four** |
| **Baths** | **4(full)** |
| **Foundation** | **Slab** |

17

plan no. **9 3 2 1 0**

price code **D**

total living area: **2,394** sq. ft.

# French Distinction

Photography by John Ehrenclou

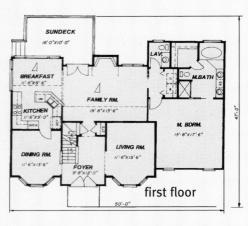

first floor

second floor

The distinctive French door entrance of this home is sure to turn heads. The two-story foyer is flooded with natural light from the arched window above. The living and dining rooms enjoy the sunlight streaming through the attractive bay windows. The well-appointed kitchen includes a peninsula counter and easy access to the formal and informal eating areas. The open layout between the kitchen, breakfast area and family room adds to the spacious feeling. The expansive family room is warmed by a fireplace. The large master suite has a private master bath and a walk-in closet. There are three more bedrooms on the second floor bridged by a hallway that overlooks the family room. The full hall bath has a double vanity. No materials list is available for this plan. The photographed home may have been modified to suit individual tastes.

## plan info

| | |
|---|---|
| **First Floor** | 1,560 sq. ft. |
| **Second Floor** | 834 sq. ft. |
| **Basement** | 772 sq. ft. |
| **Garage** | 760 sq. ft. |
| **Bedrooms** | Four |
| **Baths** | 2(full), 1(half) |
| **Foundation** | Basement |

An
**EXCLUSIVE DESIGN**
By Jannis Vann & Associates, Inc.

total living area: 3,980 sq. ft.   **F** price code   plan no.

# Elegant Traditional

Photography Supplied by The Sater Design Group

The turret stairway, detailed columns and an arched window give this home beautiful curb appeal. Inside the home, the grand foyer opens up to the formal dining room and overlooks the outdoors. Arches and columns grace the staircase area off the foyer. The right wing of the ground floor features the kitchen, nook, leisure room and utility areas. The wonderful leisure room has a wetbar and a built-in entertainment center, perfect for casual entertaining or family relaxing. The owner's suite is on the opposite wing with windows and glass doors to the rear grounds. The bath has a his-n-her walk-in closet, a garden tub and a walk-in shower. The secondary bedrooms are located upstairs with private baths and open to a rear deck. No materials list is available for this plan. The photographed home may have been modified to suit individual tastes.

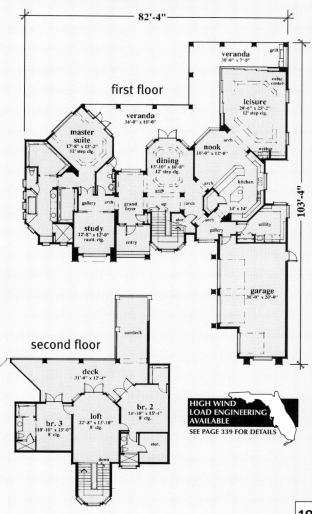

## plan info

| | |
|---|---|
| **First Floor** | 3,035 sq. ft. |
| **Second Floor** | 945 sq. ft. |
| **Garage** | 802 sq. ft. |
| **Bedrooms** | Three |
| **Baths** | 3(full), 1(half) |
| **Foundation** | Slab |

HIGH WIND
LOAD ENGINEERING
AVAILABLE
SEE PAGE 339 FOR DETAILS

plan no. **price code** **E** total living area: 2,875 sq. ft.

# 94247

# Socially Minded

HIGH WIND
LOAD ENGINEERING
AVAILABLE
SEE PAGE 339 FOR DETAILS

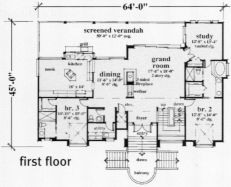

first floor

second floor

bonus floor

If entertaining is your passion, then this is the design for you. With a large, open floor plan and an array of amenities, every gathering will be a success. The foyer embraces the living areas accented by a glass fireplace and a wetbar. The living and dining rooms each access a screened entertainment center for outside enjoyment. The gourmet kitchen delights with its openness to the rest of the house. A morning room also adds a nice touch. Two bedrooms and a den radiate from the first floor living area. Climb up the stairs or use the elevator to reach the lovely master suite. It contains a huge walk-in closet, a whirlpool tub and a private sun deck. No materials list is available for this plan. The photographed home may have been modified to suit individual tastes.

## plan info

| | |
|---|---|
| **First Floor** | 2,066 sq. ft. |
| **Second Floor** | 809 sq. ft. |
| **Bonus** | 1,260 sq. ft. |
| **Garage** | 798 sq. ft. |
| **Bedrooms** | Three |
| **Baths** | 3(full), 1(half) |
| **Foundation** | Pier/Post |

# total living area: 2,509 sq. ft. Reward Yourself

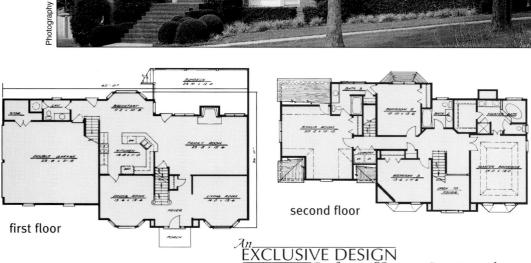

first floor

second floor

*An* EXCLUSIVE DESIGN
*By Jannis Vann & Associates, Inc.*

**D** price code

## plan no. 93254

This house has conveniences and luxurious touches. The expansive family room has a large fireplace flanked by windows. The kitchen, breakfast bay and family room are open to each other. There is a bonus room for future expansion. This plan is available with a basement, slab or crawl space foundation. Please specify when ordering. No materials list is available for this plan. The photographed home may have been modified to suit individual tastes.

### plan info

| | |
|---|---|
| First Flr. | 1,282 sq. ft. |
| Second Flr. | 1,227 sq. ft. |
| Bonus Room | 314 sq. ft. |
| Basement | 1,154 sq. ft. |
| Garage | 528 sq. ft. |
| Bedrooms | Three |
| Baths | 3(full), 1(half) |
| Foundation | Basement, Slab or Crawl |

---

# total living area: 2,421 sq. ft. Stucco and Stone

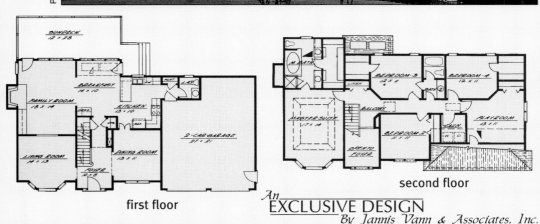

first floor

second floor

*An* EXCLUSIVE DESIGN
*By Jannis Vann & Associates, Inc.*

**D** price code

## plan no. 93208

The formal living room enjoys the sunlight from the bay window. The kitchen has a built-in pantry, double sinks, and a peninsula counter. The fireplace in the family room can be enjoyed from the breakfast room and kitchen. The private master bath and walk-in closet complete the suite. This plan is available with a basement or crawl space foundation. Please specify when ordering. No materials list is available for this plan. The photographed home may have been modified to suit individual tastes.

### plan info

| | |
|---|---|
| First Flr. | 1,090 sq. ft. |
| Second Flr. | 1,331 sq. ft. |
| Basement | 1,022 sq. ft. |
| Garage | 562 sq. ft. |
| Bedrooms | Four |
| Baths | 2(full) 1(half) |
| Foundation | Basement or Crawl Space |

plan no.     price code **C**     total living area: **1,576 sq. ft.**

## 99802

# Traditional Beauty

© Donald A. Gardner Architects, Inc.

This smaller, traditional beauty features large arched windows, round columns, covered porch, brick veneer, and an open floor plan. Clerestory dormers above the covered porch light the foyer which leads to the Great room with a cathedral ceiling and a fireplace. The Great room opens to the island kitchen with a breakfast area and accesses a large deck with optional spa. Columns define the spaces. Tray ceilings create an out-of-the-ordinary master bedroom, dining room and bedroom/study. The luxurious master bath features a double vanity, a separate shower and a whirlpool tub.

main floor

© 1993 Donald A Gardner Architects, Inc.

## plan info

| | |
|---|---|
| **Main Floor** | **1,576 sq. ft.** |
| **Garage** | **465 sq. ft.** |
| **Bedrooms** | **Three** |
| **Baths** | **2(full)** |
| **Foundation** | **Crawl Space** |

# Elegant Brick Exterior

**9 2 5 5 7**

This home exudes elegance and style, using detailing and a covered front porch accented by gracious columns. The den is enhanced by a corner fireplace and adjoins with the dining room. The efficient kitchen is well-appointed and has easy access to the utility room/laundry. The master bedroom is topped by a vaulted ceiling and pampered by a private bath and a walk-in closet. The two secondary bedrooms are located at the opposite end of the home from the master suite and share a full bath located between the rooms. This plan is available with a slab or crawl space foundation. Please specify when ordering.

**WIDTH 67'-4"**
**DEPTH 32'-10"**

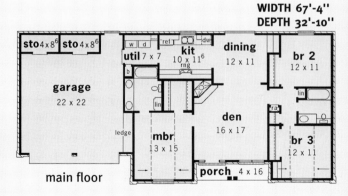

main floor

## plan info

| | |
|---|---|
| **Main Floor** | 1,390 sq. ft. |
| **Garage** | 590 sq. ft. |
| **Porch** | 66 sq. ft. |
| **Bedrooms** | Three |
| **Baths** | 2(full) |
| **Foundation** | Crawl Space or Slab |

# 92502

# Spectacular Traditional

This traditional design is accented by the use of gable roofs and the blend of stucco and brick to form a truly spectacular exterior. Entering the den from the covered front porch, find a high vaulted ceiling with built-in cabinets and a fireplace. The dining room is open to the den creating a Great room feeling in this area. The U-shaped kitchen is adjacent to the dining area and features built-in appliances. Two bedrooms are located on the right of the plan and share a hall bath. The master bedroom, on the opposite side, features a large walk-in closet and a private bath. The ceiling is raised to create a more spacious feel. The split bedroom concept allows for maximum privacy for the master bedroom. This plan is available with a slab or crawl space foundation. Please specify when ordering.

WIDTH 50'-0"
DEPTH 38'-0"

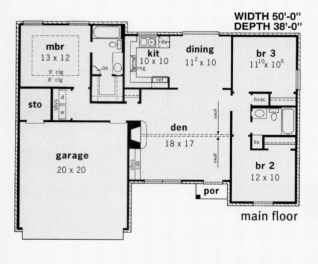

main floor

## plan info

| | |
|---|---|
| **Main Floor** | **1,237 sq. ft.** |
| **Garage** | **436 sq. ft.** |
| **Bedrooms** | **Three** |
| **Baths** | **2(full)** |
| **Foundation** | **Crawl Space or Slab** |

# A Gathering Place

© Donald A. Gardner Architects, Inc.

A feeling of spaciousness pervades the 1,346 square feet of this cozy country plan, thanks to a large, open common area. The Great room, kitchen and breakfast bay share a cathedral ceiling and fireplace (perfect for family gatherings). Located in the back for privacy, the master suite features a soaring cathedral ceiling, direct access to the deck and a well appointed bath with large walk-in closet. At the front of the house, two family bedrooms share a full bath. Note how utility and storage spaces are centrally located for convenience.

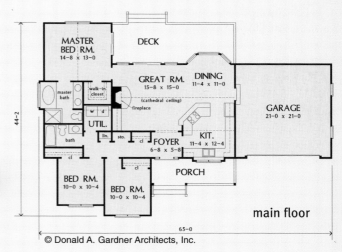

main floor

© Donald A. Gardner Architects, Inc.

## plan info

| | |
|---|---|
| **Main Floor** | **1,346 sq. ft.** |
| **Garage & Storage** | **462 sq. ft.** |
| **Bedrooms** | **Three** |
| **Baths** | **2(full)** |
| **Foundation** | **Crawl Space** |

# Front & Back Porches

If you are looking for Southern country styling, this is the home for you. The dining room is to the right of the foyer and includes direct access to the kitchen and built-in cabinets. The kitchen is made more efficient by the peninsula counter/eating bar extending counter space and provides a perfect place for meals on the go. The den is enhanced by a vaulted ceiling and a lovely fireplace. The master suite is tucked into a private corner and pampered by a five-piece master bath. The two additional bedrooms are on the opposite side of the home and share the full bath located in the hall. This plan is available with a slab or crawl space foundation. Please specify when ordering.

**WIDTH 66'-10''**
**DEPTH 46'-10''**

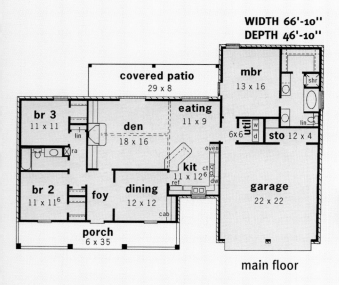

main floor

## plan info

| | |
|---|---|
| **Main Floor** | **1,660 sq. ft.** |
| **Garage** | **544 sq. ft.** |
| **Porch** | **447 sq. ft.** |
| **Bedrooms** | **Three** |
| **Baths** | **2(full)** |
| **Foundation** | **Crawl Space or Slab** |

total living area:  1,253  sq. ft.  ⚔️ 🗺️  **B** price code   plan no.

# Abundant Amenities

© Donald A. Gardner Architects, Inc.

This compact home offers tremendous curb appeal and amenities normally found only in larger houses. A continuous cathedral ceiling in the Great room, kitchen, and dining room gives a spacious feel to this efficient plan. The skylit kitchen features a seven foot high wall by the Great room and a popular plant shelf. The master suite opens up with a cathedral ceiling and contains walk-in and linen closets and a private bath with garden tub and dual vanity. Another cathedral ceiling tops off the front bedroom/study.

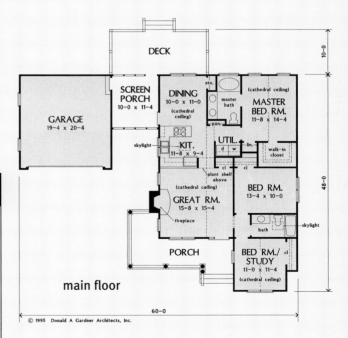

main floor

© 1995  Donald A Gardner Architects, Inc.

## plan info

| | |
|---|---|
| **Main Floor** | **1,253 sq. ft.** |
| **Garage & Storage** | **420 sq. ft.** |
| **Bedrooms** | **Three** |
| **Baths** | **2(full)** |
| **Foundation** | **Crawl Space** |

plan no.

# 96417

price code **C**

total living area: 1,561 sq. ft.

# Casually Elegant

© Donald A. Gardner Architects, Inc.

This country classic offers a casually elegant exterior with arched windows, dormers, and charming front and back porches with columns. Inside, the open, casual mood is continued in the central Great room which features a cathedral ceiling, a fireplace and a clerestory window that splashes the room with natural light. Other special touches include a breakfast bay and interior columns. The master suite with cathedral ceiling is privately located and features a skylit bath with whirlpool tub, shower and a double vanity. Two additional bedrooms share a full bath, and a garage with storage completes the plan.

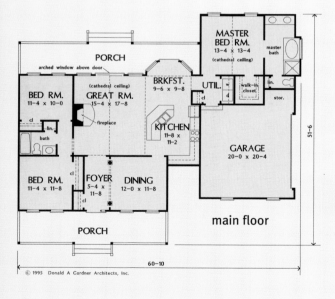

main floor

© 1995 Donald A Gardner Architects, Inc.

## plan info

| | |
|---|---|
| **Main Floor** | 1,561 sq. ft. |
| **Garage & Storage** | 346 sq. ft. |
| **Bedrooms** | Three |
| **Baths** | 2(full) |
| **Foundation** | Crawl Space |

# Southern Traditional

This charming Southern traditional styled home has all the features and looks of a much larger home. The covered front porch with its striking columns, brick quoins, and dentil moulding add a rich elegance to this stately design. Upon entering, you will find the spacious living room with vaulted ceilings, a fireplace, built-in cabinets and an adjoining dining room. The utility room is adjacent to the kitchen and leads to the two-car garage with a storage room. To the right of the entrance is the bedroom wing. The secondary bedrooms each have walk-in closets and a hall bath to serve them. The master bedroom is located to the rear of the home and features a large walk-in closet and compartmentalized bath. This plan is available with a slab or crawl space foundation. Please specify when ordering.

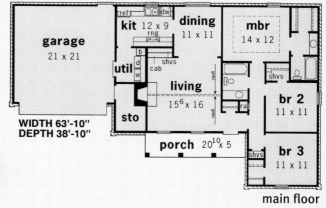

main floor

## plan info

| | |
|---|---|
| **Main Floor** | 1,271 sq. ft. |
| **Garage** | 506 sq. ft. |
| **Bedrooms** | Three |
| **Baths** | 2(full) |
| **Foundation** | Crawl Space or Slab |

plan no.    price code **C**    total living area:  **1,685**  sq. ft.

# 99810

# Dramatic Dormers

© 1996 Donald A. Gardner Architects, Inc.

The foyer is open to the dramatic dormer and is defined by elegant columns, while the dining room is augmented by a tray ceiling. The front room does double duty as a bedroom or a study. A cathedral ceiling and a clerestory window accentuating the rear porch open the Great room. The Great room is further expanded into the open kitchen and breakfast room by a cased opening with accent columns. The master suite, privately removed to one side of the house, features a tray ceiling in the bedroom. A garden tub with a picture window is the focal point of the master bath. Buyers will love the roomy walk-in closet. Two bedrooms on the other side of the home share a full bath and a linen closet.

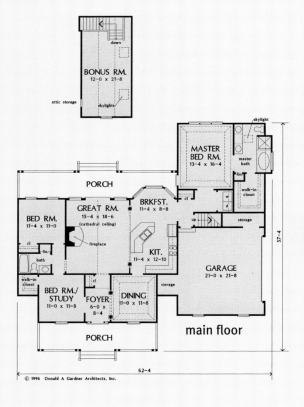

main floor

© 1996  Donald A Gardner Architects, Inc.

## plan info

| | |
|---|---|
| **Main Floor** | **1,685 sq. ft.** |
| **Bonus Room** | **331 sq. ft.** |
| **Garage** | **536 sq. ft.** |
| **Bedrooms** | **Three** |
| **Baths** | **2(full)** |
| **Foundation** | **Crawl Space** |

# total living area: 1,452 sq. ft. Compact Country

## plan no. 96418

© Donald A. Gardner Architects, Inc.

This compact three bedroom country charmer has a contemporary interior punctuated by elegant columns. Dormers above the covered porch light the foyer which leads to the dramatic Great room with a cathedral ceiling and a fireplace. The Great room opens to the island kitchen with a breakfast area. Tray ceilings add interest to the bedroom/study, dining room, and master bedroom. The luxurious master suite features a walk-in closet and a bath with a dual vanity, separate shower, and a whirlpool tub.

**main floor**

© 1990 Donald A. Gardner Architects, Inc.

## plan info

| | |
|---|---|
| Main Flr. | 1,452 sq. ft. |
| Garage | 427 sq. ft. |
| Bedrooms | Three |
| Baths | 2(full) |
| Foundation | Crawl Space |

---

# total living area: 1,322 sq. ft. Full of Charm

## plan no. 99849

© Donald A. Gardner Architects, Inc.

We captured a lot of country charm and excitement in this economical three bedroom plan that belies its compact square footage. Dormers above the covered porch cast light into the foyer. Columns punctuate the entrance to the open Great room/dining room area with a cathedral ceiling. The kitchen, with a breakfast counter, is open to the dining area. The master suite has a tray ceiling and a luxurious bath with operable skylights over the whirlpool tub.

**main floor**

© 1993 Donald A. Gardner Architects, Inc.

## plan info

| | |
|---|---|
| Main Flr. | 1,322 sq. ft. |
| Garage | 413 sq. ft. |
| Bedrooms | Three |
| Baths | 2(full) |
| Foundation | Crawl Space |

# Private Master Suite

A welcoming porch shelters the entrance of this home. The spacious Great room is enhanced by vaulted ceilings, a large fireplace and built-in shelves and cabinets. The well-equipped kitchen has a double sink with a window over it, providing natural light and a view of the rear yard. The master bedroom has a decorative ceiling and a private master bath with a walk-in closet. Its location gives the room a secluded feeling. The laundry area is conveniently located in the hall outside of the master bedroom. Two additional bedrooms are located at the other end of the house and share a full bath. This plan is available with a slab or crawl space foundation. Please specify when ordering.

**WIDTH 51'-10''**
**DEPTH 40'-4''**

**mbr** 12⁶ x 12⁶

**sto** 5⁶ x 6

d w

**garage** 20 x 20

shvs

**kit** 9 x 10   rng   dw

**dining** 11⁴ x 10

ref

**den** 19 x 17

shvs cab

**porch** 19 x 4

**br 3** 11⁸ x 11

hvac

lin

**br 2** 12 x 11

main floor

## plan info

| | |
|---|---|
| **Main Floor** | **1,293 sq. ft.** |
| **Porch** | **76 sq. ft.** |
| **Garage** | **433 sq. ft.** |
| **Bedrooms** | **Three** |
| **Baths** | **2(full)** |
| **Foundation** | **Crawl Space** |

■ *Total living area  2,069 sq. ft.* ■ *Price Code  D* ■

# No. 96505

■ **This plan features:**

– Three bedrooms

– Two full and one half baths

■ Secluded Master Bedroom tucked into the rear left corner of the home with a five-piece bath and two walk-in closets

■ Two additional bedrooms at the opposite side of the home sharing the full bath in the hall

■ Expansive Living Room highlighted by a corner fireplace and access to the rear Porch

■ Kitchen is sandwiched between the bright, bayed Nook and the formal Dining Room providing ease in serving

Main floor — 2,069 sq. ft.
Garage — 481 sq. ft.

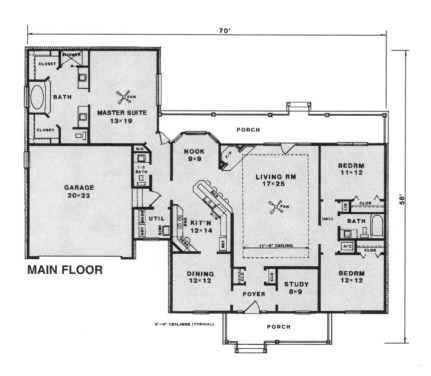

**MAIN FLOOR**

# Cabin in the Country

■ Total living area 928 sq. ft. ■ Price Code A ■

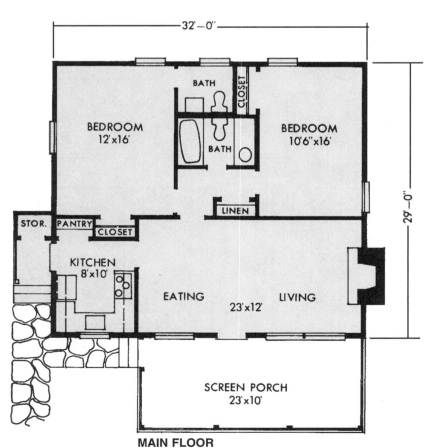

**MAIN FLOOR**

## No. 90433

■ **This plan features:**

— Two bedrooms

— One full and one half baths

■ A screened Porch for enjoyment of your outdoor surroundings

■ A combination Living and Dining area with cozy fireplace for added warmth

■ An efficiently laid out Kitchen with a built-in Pantry

■ Two large bedrooms located at the rear of the home

■ An optional slab or crawl space foundation — please specify when ordering

Main floor — 928 sq. ft.
Screened porch — 230 sq. ft.
Storage — 14 sq. ft.

# Soft Arches Accent Country Design

■ *Total living area 2,527 sq. ft.* ■ *Price Code D* ■

## No. 94233

■ **This plan features:**

— Four or five bedrooms

— Two full and one half baths

■ Entry Porch with double dormers and doors

■ Pillared arches frame Foyer, Dining Room and Great Room

■ Open Great Room with optional built-ins and sliding glass doors to Verandah

■ Kitchen with walk-in pantry and a counter/snackbar which opens to eating Nook and Great Room

■ Master Suite with his-n-her closets and vanities and a garden tub

■ An optional basement or slab foundation — please specify when ordering

■ No materials list is available for this plan

First floor — 1,676 sq. ft.
Second floor — 851 sq. ft.
Garage — 304 sq. ft.

**SECOND FLOOR**

HIGH WIND
LOAD ENGINEERING
AVAILABLE
SEE PAGE 339 FOR DETAILS

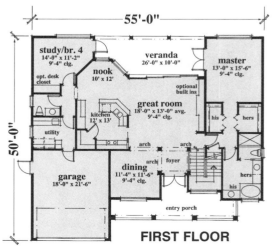

**FIRST FLOOR**

# Split Bedroom Ranch

■ *Total living area 1,804 sq. ft.* ■ *Price Code C* ■

Main floor — 1,804 sq. ft.
Basement — 1,804 sq. ft.
Garage — 506 sq. ft.

## No. 90476

■ **This plan features:**

— Three bedrooms

— Two full baths

■ The formal Foyer opens into the Great room which features a vaulted ceiling and a hearth fireplace

■ The U-shaped Kitchen is located between the Dining Room and the Breakfast nook

■ The secluded Master Bedroom is spacious and includes amenities such as walk-in closets and a full bath

■ Two secondary bedrooms have ample closet space and share a full bath

■ The covered front Porch and rear Deck provide additional space for entertaining

■ An optional basement, slab or a crawl space foundation — please specify when ordering

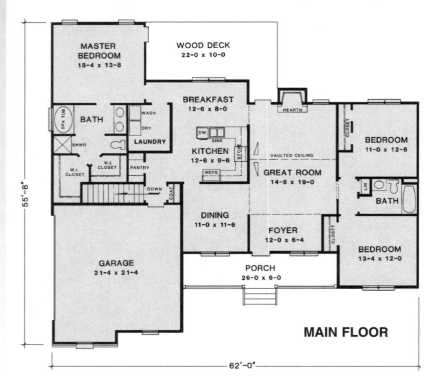

**MAIN FLOOR**

© 1994 Donald A. Gardner Architects, Inc.

*■ Total living area 2,563 sq. ft. ■ Price Code E ■*

# No. 99843 ⚒

**■ This plan features:**

— Four bedrooms

— Two full and one half baths

■ Bay windows and a long, skylit, screened Porch make this four bedroom Country style home a haven for outdoor enthusiasts

■ Foyer is open to take advantage of the light from the central dormer with palladian window

■ Vaulted ceiling in the Great Room adds vertical drama to the room

■ Contemporary Kitchen is open to the Great Room creating a feeling of additional space

■ Master Bedroom is privately tucked away with a large luxurious bath complete with a bay window, corner shower and a garden tub

First floor — 1,907 sq. ft.
Second floor — 656 sq. ft.
Bonus room — 467 sq. ft.
Garage & storage — 580 sq. ft.

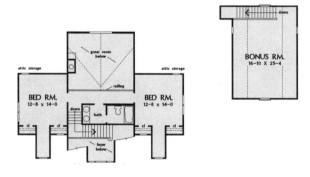

SECOND FLOOR PLAN

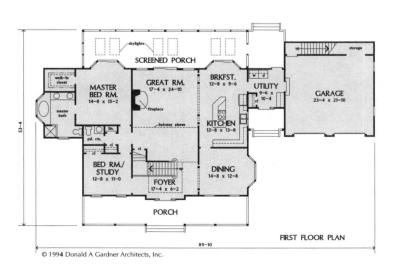

© 1994 Donald A Gardner Architects, Inc.

FIRST FLOOR PLAN

# Timeless Appeal

© Larry E. Belk

■ *Total living area  1,170 sq. ft.* ■ *Price Code  A* ■

WIDTH 51'-10"

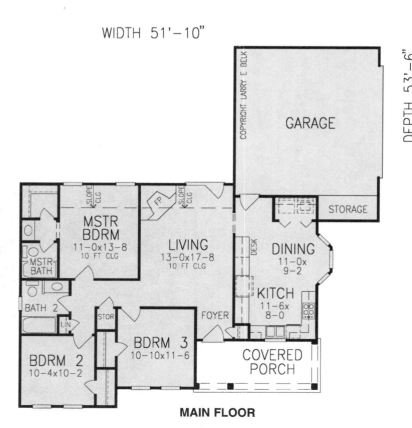

**MAIN FLOOR**

# No. 93075

■ **This plan features:**

— Three bedrooms

— Two full baths

■ Ten foot ceilings give the Living Room an open feel

■ Corner fireplace highlights the Living Room

■ Dining area enhanced by a sunny bay window

■ Master Bedroom features a private bath

■ Garage is located on the rear and not visible from the front

■ An optional crawl space or slab foundation — please specify when ordering

■ No materials list is available for this plan

Main floor — 1,170 sq. ft.
Garage — 478 sq. ft.

# Country Exterior With Formal Interior

■ *Total living area 2,068 sq. ft.* ■ *Price Code C* ■

# No. 90451 ✖

## ■ This plan features:

— Three bedrooms

— Two full and one half baths

■ Wrap-around Porch leads into central Foyer and formal Living and Dining rooms

■ Large Family Room with a cozy fireplace and Deck access

■ Convenient Kitchen opens to Breakfast area with a bay window and built-in Pantry

■ Corner Master Bedroom with walk-in closet and appealing bath

■ An optional basement or crawl space foundation — please specify when ordering

First floor — 1,046 sq. ft.
Second floor — 1,022 sq. ft.
Bonus — 232 sq. ft.
Basement — 1,046 sq. ft.

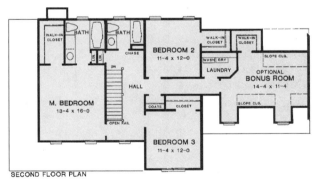

SECOND FLOOR PLAN

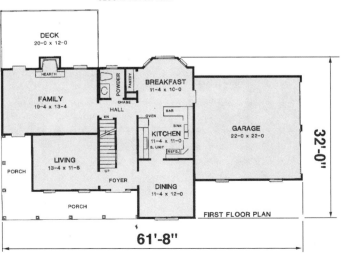

FIRST FLOOR PLAN

# Dressed to Impress

© 1997 Donald A Gardner Architects, Inc.

■ *Total living area  2,121 sq. ft.* ■ *Price Code D* ■

First floor — 1,572 sq. ft.
Second floor — 549 sq. ft.
Bonus room — 384 sq. ft.
Garage & storage — 540 sq. ft.

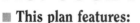

SECOND FLOOR PLAN

FIRST FLOOR PLAN

## No. 99824

### ■ This plan features:

— Three bedrooms

— Two full and one half baths

■ A stone and stucco exterior plus a dramatic entry with square columns provide impressive curb appeal

■ The Great Room has a cathedral ceiling and adjoins the Breakfast Area

■ The Kitchen is enhanced by an angled counter with stovetop, a Pantry and easy access to the formal Dining Room

■ A separate Utility Room with built-in cabinets and a counter top with laundry sink add efficiency

■ Double doors lead into the Master Suite with a box bay window, two walk-in closets and a lavish bath

■ Located upstairs are two more bedrooms, a full bath, linen closet and skylit Bonus Room

# Sprawling Wrap-Around Porch

■ *Total living area 1,985 sq. ft.* ■ *Price Code D* ■

## No. 94812

### ■ This plan features:

— Three bedrooms

— Two full and one half baths

■ Old-fashioned quality with dormers and a Covered Porch leading into this modern floor plan

■ Activity Room has a fireplace for warmth and comfort

■ Efficient, U-shaped Kitchen has a work island, a snack bar and a vaulted Breakfast Room with Sun Deck access

■ First floor Master Bedroom enjoys a plush bath and a walk-in closet

■ Two additional bedrooms on the second floor each have dormer windows and access to a full bath

First floor — 1,426 sq. ft.
Second floor — 559 sq. ft.
Basement — 1,426 sq. ft.
Garage — 500 sq. ft.

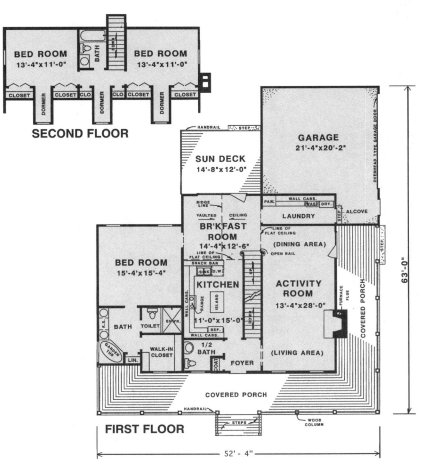

SECOND FLOOR

FIRST FLOOR

# Sophisticated Southern Styling

■ *Total living area  2,858 sq. ft.* ■ *Price Code E* ■

First floor — 2,256 sq. ft.
Second floor — 602 sq. ft.
Bonus — 264 sq. ft.
Garage — 484 sq. ft.

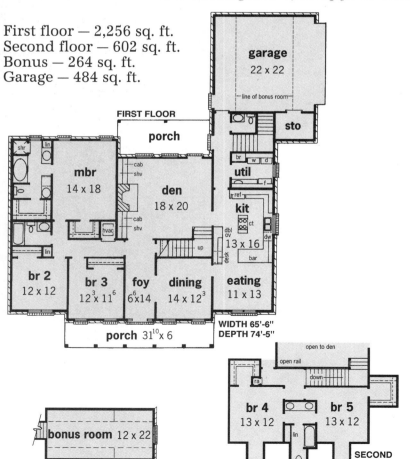

## No. 92576

### ■ This plan features:

— Five bedrooms

— Three full and one half baths

■ Covered front and rear Porches expanding the living space to the outdoors

■ A Den with a large fireplace and built-in cabinets and shelves

■ A cooktop island, built-in desk, and eating bar complete the Kitchen

■ The Master Suite has two walk-in closets and a luxurious bath

■ Four additional bedrooms, two on the main level and two on the upper level, all have easy access to a full bath

■ An optional slab or crawl space foundation — please specify when ordering

■ *Total living area 1,625 sq. ft.* ■ *Price Code B* ■

# No. 93263

## ■ This plan features:

— Four bedrooms

— Two full baths

■ Sheltered entry leads into Living Area with focal point fireplace, Dining Room with lovely bay window and access to Deck

■ Efficient Kitchen with peninsula serving counter for glass Breakfast area, built-in Pantry, Laundry and Garage entry

■ Secluded Master Bedroom with decorative ceiling offers walk-in closet and plush bath with double vanity and window tub

■ Three additional bedrooms with ample closets share a full bath

■ No materials list is available for this plan

Main floor —1,625 sq. ft.
Basement — 1,579 sq. ft.
Garage — 406 sq. ft.

*An*
EXCLUSIVE DESIGN
*By Jannis Vann & Associates, Inc.*

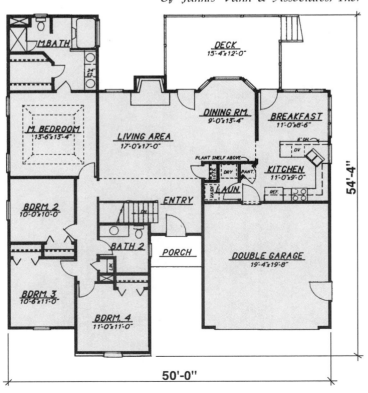

**MAIN FLOOR**

# Luxurious Yet Cozy

■ *Total living area  3,395 sq. ft.* ■ *Price Code F* ■

SECOND FLOOR

FIRST FLOOR

## No. 98403

### ■ This plan features:

— Four bedrooms

— Three full and one half baths

■ Living Room is enhanced by a fieldstone fireplace and vaulted ceiling

■ Inviting fireplace between windows, and a vaulted ceiling enhance Great Room

■ Kitchen with a work island, serving bar, bright Breakfast Area and walk-in Pantry

■ Corner Master Suite includes a cozy fireplace, a vaulted Sitting Room and a lavish Dressing Area

■ Optional basement, crawl space or slab foundation — please specify when ordering

First floor — 2,467 sq. ft.
Second floor — 928 sq. ft.
Bonus — 296 sq. ft.
Basement — 2,467 sq. ft.
Garage — 566 sq. ft.

■ *Total living area 1,770 sq. ft.* ■ *Price Code B* ■

# No. 94716 ⚒

## ■ This plan features:

- Three bedrooms

- Two full and one half baths

■ Formality & function combine in an open & comfortable floor plan

■ Entry Portico leads into a Dining area defined by columns and two-story Great Room with a cozy fireplace and Patio access

■ Convenient Kitchen with a peninsula counter serving bright Breakfast area

■ Secluded Master Suite enhanced by a decorative ceiling, walk-in closet and plush bath with a whirlpool tub

■ Two more bedrooms with walk-in closets and an adjoining bath

First floor — 1,318 sq. ft.
Second floor — 452 sq. ft.
Garage — 431 sq. ft.

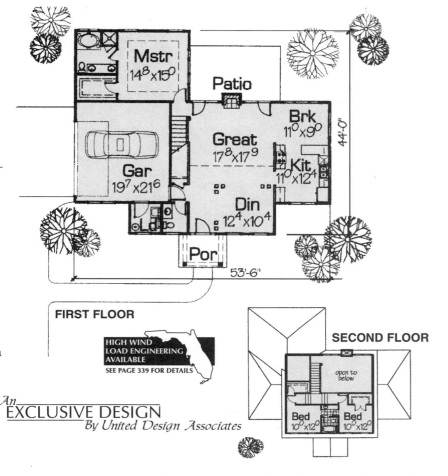

**FIRST FLOOR**

HIGH WIND
LOAD ENGINEERING
AVAILABLE
SEE PAGE 339 FOR DETAILS

**SECOND FLOOR**

*An*
EXCLUSIVE DESIGN
*By United Design Associates*

# Elegant Executive Home

© 1994 Donald A. Gardner Architects, Inc.

B. NATHAN.

■ *Total living area 2,301 sq. ft.* ■ *Price Code D* ■

**SECOND FLOOR PLAN**

BED RM.
11-0 x 11-9

BED RM.
12-4 x 11-2

attic storage

foyer below

BED RM.
11-8 x 12-4

bath

clerestory window with arched top

BONUS RM.
12-11 x 24-4

skylights

down

down

DECK

spa

arched window above door

skylight

GREAT RM.
16-0 x 18-0

fireplace

(cathedral ceiling)

master bath

walk-in closet

walk-in closet

BRKFST.
11-4 x 11-8

stor.

KITCHEN
13-6 x 11-10

up

MASTER BED RM.
13-0 x 14-4

FOYER
7-8 x 7-0

DINING RM.
11-8 x 14-8

UTIL.
8-4 x 9-6

pd. rm.

storage

porch

up

GARAGE
20-0 x 20-8

**FIRST FLOOR PLAN**

12-0

61-6

54-11

## No. 96448

■ **This plan features:**

— Four bedrooms

— Two full and one half baths

■ Understated elegance with arched clerestory window lighting the two-story Foyer

■ With a cathedral ceiling topping it, the Great Room has an arched transom window above the slider to Deck and a fireplace

■ Open and efficient the Kitchen with adjacent Breakfast area accesses the Deck, Dining Room and the Garage

■ First floor Master Bedroom offers twin closets and vanities, plus a skylight over the garden tub

■ Second floor boasts three bedrooms, and a full bath

First floor — 1,639 sq. ft.
Second floor — 662 sq. ft.
Bonus Room — 336 sq. ft.
Garage & storage — 520 sq. ft.

■ *Total living area  1,282 sq. ft.* ■ *Price Code  A* ■

## No. 93021

■ **This plan features:**

- Three bedrooms

- Two full baths

■ An angled Entry creating the illusion of space

■ Two square columns that flank the bar and separate the Kitchen from the Living Room

■ A Dining Room that may service both formal and informal occasions

■ A Master Bedroom with a large walk-in closet

■ A large master bath with double vanity, linen closet and whirlpool tub/shower combination

■ Two additional bedrooms that share a full bath

■ No materials list is available for this plan

Main floor — 1,282 sq. ft.
Garage — 501 sq. ft.

WIDTH 48–10

OPTIONAL BAY WINDOW

FP

LIN

MASTER BATH

DINING
9-8 X 9-6
10 FT CLG

LIVING ROOM
16-0 X 17-6
10 FT CLG

SLOPE

BEDRM 3
10-0 X 10-0

SLOPE

MASTER BEDRM
11-0 X 14-0
10 FT CLG

10 FT CLG
KITCHEN
13-4 X 9-6

ARCH

DEPTH 52–6

FOYER

ARCH

BATH 2

LIN

BEDRM 2
10-0 X 12-0

STORAGE

PORCH

**MAIN FLOOR**

GARAGE

© Larry E. Belk

47

# Family-Sized Accommodations

*Total living area  1,874 sq. ft.* ■ *Price Code C* ■

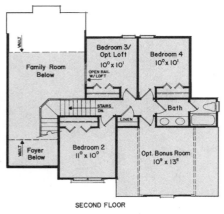

SECOND FLOOR

FIRST FLOOR

# No. 98454

## ■ This plan features:

— Four bedrooms

— Two full and one half baths

■ A spacious feeling provided by a vaulted ceiling in Foyer

■ A fireplace is nestled by an alcove of windows in the Family Room

■ An angled Kitchen with a work island and a Pantry easily serves the Breakfast area and the Dining Room

■ The Master Bedroom is accented by a tray ceiling, a lavish bath and a walk-in closet

■ An optional basement or crawl space foundation — please specify when ordering

First floor — 1,320 sq. ft.
Second floor — 554 sq. ft.
Bonus room — 155 sq. ft.
Basement — 1,320 sq. ft.
Garage — 406 sq. ft.

48

# Brick Opulence and Grandeur

■ *Total living area  3,921 sq. ft.* ■  *Price Code  F* ■

## No. 92248

■ **This plan features:**

— Four bedrooms

— Three full and one half baths

■ Dramatic two-story glass Entry with a curved staircase

■ Both Living and Family rooms offer high ceilings, decorative windows and large fireplaces

■ Large, efficient Kitchen with a cooktop serving island, walk-in pantry, bright Breakfast Area and Patio access

■ Lavish Master Bedroom with a cathedral ceiling, two walk-in closets and large bath

■ Two additional bedrooms with ample closets share a double vanity bath

■ No materials list is available for this plan

First floor — 2,506 sq. ft.
Second floor — 1,415 sq. ft.
Basement — 2,400 sq. ft.
Garage — 660 sq. ft.

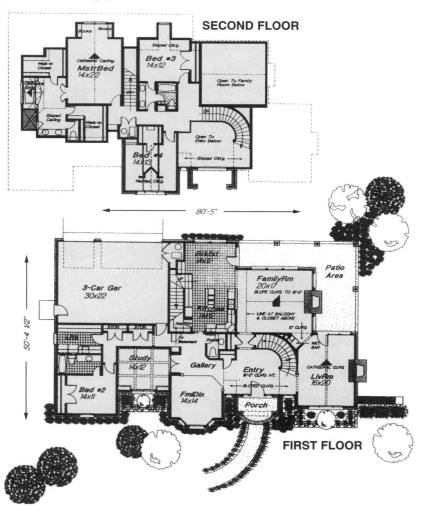

# Country Styled Home

■ *Total living area  1,833 sq. ft.* ■ *Price Code C* ■

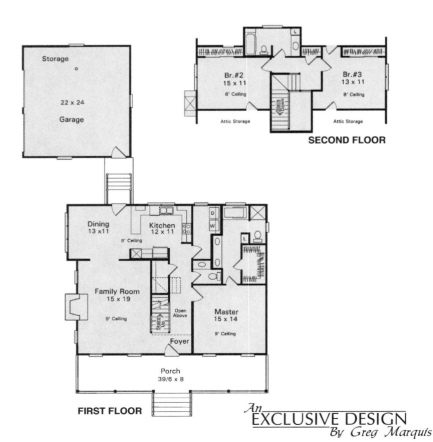

**SECOND FLOOR**

Storage

Garage
22 x 24

Br.#2
15 x 11
8' Ceiling

Br.#3
13 x 11
8' Ceiling

Attic Storage

Attic Storage

Dining
13 x 11
9' Ceiling

Kitchen
12 x 11

Family Room
15 x 19
9' Ceiling

Open Above

Master
15 x 14
9' Ceiling

Foyer

Porch
39/6 x 8

**FIRST FLOOR**

## No. 93432

■ **This plan features:**

— Three bedrooms

— Two full and one half baths

■ A Country style front Porch provides a warm welcome

■ The Family Room is highlighted by a fireplace and front windows

■ The Dining Room is separated from the U-shaped Kitchen by only an extended counter

■ The first floor Master Suite pampers the owners with a walk-in closet and a five-piece bath

■ Two additional bedrooms with a convenient hall bath

First floor — 1,288 sq. ft.
Second floor — 545 sq. ft.
Garage — 540 sq. ft.
Width — 50'-8"
Depth — 74'-0"

*An*
EXCLUSIVE DESIGN
*By Greg Marquis*

# High Ceilings Add Volume

■ *Total living area  1,715 sq. ft.* ■ *Price Code  B* ■

# No. 98456

## ■ This plan features:

- Three bedrooms
- Two full baths
- A covered entry gives way to a 14-foot high ceiling in the Foyer
- An arched opening greets you in the Great Room that also has a vaulted ceiling and a fireplace
- The Dining Room is brightened by triple windows with transoms above
- The Kitchen is a gourmet's delight and is open to the Breakfast Nook
- The Master Suite is sweet with a tray ceiling, vaulted Sitting Area and private bath
- Two bedrooms on the opposite side of the home share a hall bath
- An optional basement, slab or crawl space foundation — please specify when ordering

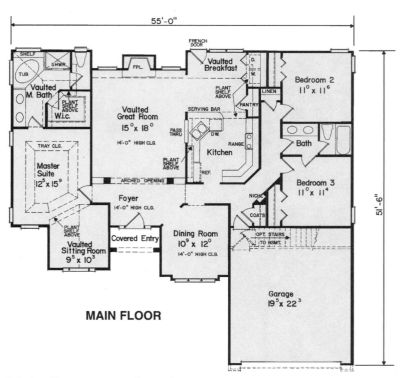

**MAIN FLOOR**

Main floor — 1,715 sq. ft.
Basement — 1,715 sq. ft.
Garage — 450 sq. ft.

# Columns Punctuate the Interior Space

© 1997 Donald A Gardner Architects, Inc.

B. NATHAN

■ *Total living area  2,188 sq. ft.* ■ *Price Code D* ■

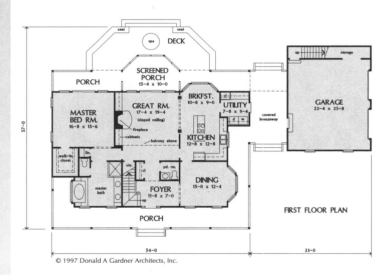

© 1997 Donald A Gardner Architects, Inc.

DECK
seat   spa   seat
SCREENED PORCH 15-4 x 10-0
PORCH
MASTER BED RM. 16-8 x 15-6
GREAT RM. 17-4 x 19-4 (sloped ceiling)
fireplace
cabinets
balcony above
BRKFST. 10-8 x 9-0
UTILITY 7-8 x 9-4
covered breezeway
GARAGE 22-4 x 25-8
up   storage
walk-in closet
lin.
KITCHEN 12-8 x 12-8
master bath
sto.
cl.
pd. rm.
DINING 15-0 x 12-4
FOYER 11-8 x 7-0
up
PORCH
57-0
54-0   33-0
FIRST FLOOR PLAN

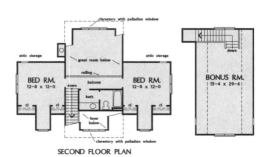

clerestory with palladian window
attic storage
great room below
railing
balcony
attic storage
BED RM. 12-8 x 12-0
down
BED RM. 12-8 x 12-0
cl.   cl.   cl.
bath
foyer below
clerestory with palladian window
BONUS RM. 15-4 x 29-4
down
SECOND FLOOR PLAN

## No. 99801

■ **This plan features:**

— Three bedrooms

— Two full and one half baths

■ A two-story Great Room and Foyer, both with dormer windows

■ Large Kitchen, featuring a center cooking island with counter and large Breakfast Area

■ Columns punctuate interior spaces

■ Master Bedroom suite, privately situated on the first floor, has a dual vanity, garden tub and separate shower

First floor — 1,618 sq. ft.
Second floor — 570 sq. ft.
Bonus room — 495 sq. ft.
Garage & storage — 649 sq. ft.

# Dignified French Country Style

■ *Total living area 1,805 sq. ft.* ■ *Price Code D* ■

# No. 92517

## ■ This plan features:

- Three bedrooms

- Two full baths

■ Sheltered Porch leads into an open Foyer

■ The Great Room is enhanced by raised hearth fireplace

■ Hub Kitchen with a peninsula counter serves Breakfast area and Dining Room

■ Spacious Master Bedroom offers a Sitting Area and bath

■ Two additional roomy bedrooms with oversized closets share a double vanity bath

■ An optional crawl space or slab foundation — please specify when ordering

Main area — 1,805 sq. ft.
Garage & Storage — 524 sq. ft.

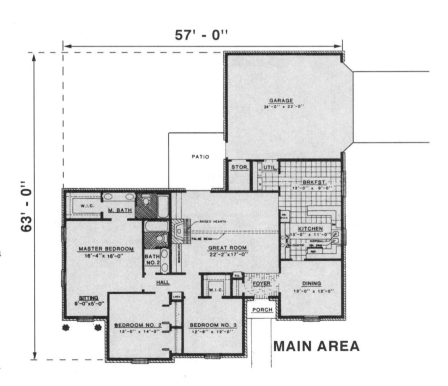

**MAIN AREA**

# Roomy and Rustic Fieldstone

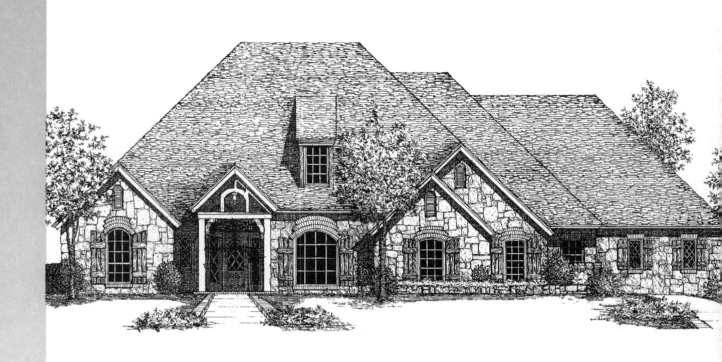

■ *Total living area  3,079 sq. ft.* ■ *Price Code E* ■

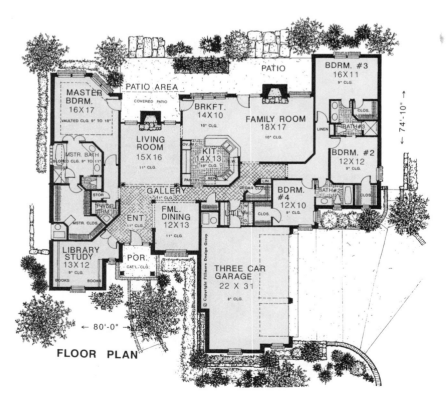

**FLOOR PLAN**

## No. 92279

■ **This plan features:**

— Four bedrooms

— Three full and one half baths

■ Cathedral Porch leads into easy-care Entry and formal Living Room with fieldstone fireplace

■ Hub Kitchen with curved peninsula serving counter convenient to Breakfast area, Covered Patio, Family Room, Utility/Garage entry and Dining Room

■ Corner Master Bedroom enhanced by vaulted ceiling, plush bath and a huge walk-in closet

■ Three additional bedrooms with walk-in closets and private access to a full bath

■ No materials list is available for this plan

Main floor — 3,079 sq. ft.
Garage — 630 sq. ft.

■ *Total living area 4,441 sq. ft.* ■ *Price Code F* ■

# No. 10492

## ■ This plan features:

— Three/four bedrooms

— Three full baths

■ A Television Room, Den, Family Room and an upstairs Sitting Room for many individual activities

■ A well-equipped Kitchen with double bay windows, separate dining Nook, and adjoining the formal Dining Room

■ A fireplace warming the Sitting Room adjacent to the spacious Master Suite

■ A private Deck and Master Bath complete with Roman tub and room-size, walk-in closet enhance the Master Suite

■ Two smaller bedrooms connecting to a walk-through, full bath

First floor — 2,409 sq. ft.
Second floor — 2,032 sq. ft.
Garage — 690 sq. ft.

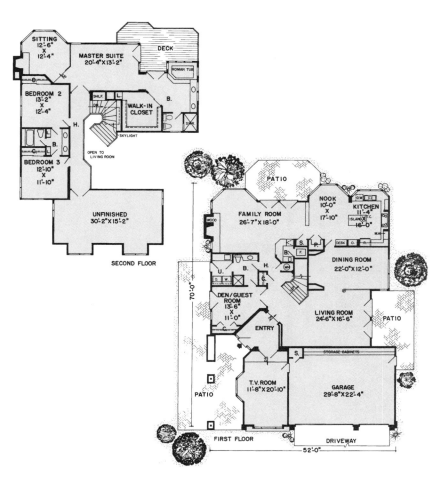

# First Floor Master Suite

■ *Total living area  1,780 sq. ft.* ■ *Price Code B* ■

Attic Storage

32'

BR. # 2
11 x 13

Foyer Below

BR. #3
11 x 13
8' Ceiling

**Second Floor**

63'

Deck

Garage
22 x 24

Kitchen

Dining
13 x 12
9' Ceiling

14 x 13

snack bar

Pass Thru

Balcony Above

Shelves

32'

Drive

Family Room
14 x18
9' Clg.

UP
DN

Master
14 x 16/10
9' Clg.

Foyer

**First Floor**

## No. 93411

### ■ This plan features:

— Three bedrooms

— Two full and one half baths

■ An open layout between the Kitchen and Dining Room

■ The cooktop island/snack bar expands work space in the Kitchen

■ A pass-through into the Family Room offers convenience

■ The Family Room includes a fireplace and views to the front yard

■ No materials list available for this plan

First floor — 1,229 sq. ft.
Second floor — 551 sq. ft.
Basement — 1229 sq. ft.
Garage — 569 sq. ft.

*An*
EXCLUSIVE DESIGN
*By Greg Marquis*

# Perfect for a First Home

■ *Total living area  1,564 sq. ft.* ■  *Price Code  B* ■

## No. 92405

■ **This plan features:**

– Three bedrooms

– Two full baths

■ A spacious Master Suite including a separate master bath with a garden tub and shower

■ A Dining Room and Family Room highlighted by vaulted ceilings

■ An oversized patio accessible from the Master Suite, Family Room and Breakfast Room

■ A well planned Kitchen measuring 12' x 11'

■ No materials list available for this plan

Main area — 1,564 sq. ft.
Garage & Storage — 476 sq. ft.

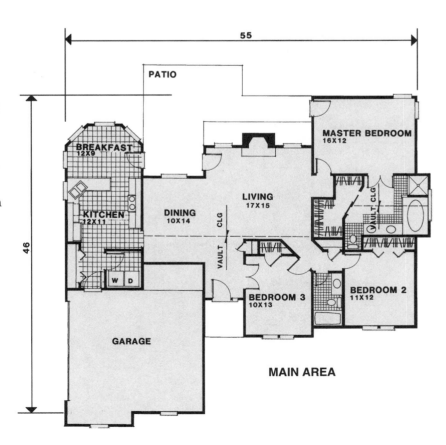

# Welcoming Exterior

© 1995 Donald A. Gardner Architects, Inc.

■ *Total living area 2,832 sq. ft.* ■ *Price Code E* ■

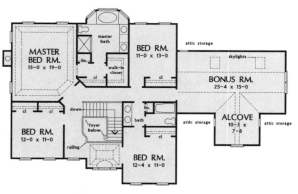

SECOND FLOOR PLAN

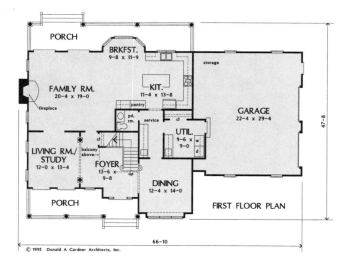

FIRST FLOOR PLAN

© 1995 Donald A Gardner Architects, Inc.

## No. 96403

### ■ This plan features:

— Four bedrooms

— Two full and one half baths

■ Columns between the Foyer and Living Room/Study hint at all the extras in this four bedroom country estate with a warm, welcoming exterior

■ Transom windows over French doors open up the Living Room/Study to the front Porch, while a generous Family Room accesses the covered back Porch

■ Deluxe Master Suite is topped by a tray ceiling and includes a bath with a sunny garden tub bay and ample closet space

■ Bonus Room is accessed from the second floor

First floor — 1,483 sq. ft.
Second floor — 1,349 sq. ft.
Garage — 738 sq. ft.
Bonus — 486 sq. ft.

# Cozy Front Porch

■ *Total living area  1,735 sq. ft.* ■  *Price Code  B* ■

## No. 93269

### ■ This plan features:

– Three bedrooms

– Two full and one half baths

■ A Living Room enhanced by a large fireplace

■ A formal Dining Room that is open to the Living Room

■ An efficient Kitchen that includes ample counter and cabinet space as well as double sinks and pass-thru window

■ Breakfast Area with vaulted ceiling and a door to the Sundeck

■ First floor Master Suite with separate tub & shower stall, plus a walk-in closet

■ Two additional bedrooms that share a full hall bath

First floor — 1,045 sq. ft.
Second floor — 690 sq. ft.
Basement — 465 sq. ft.
Garage — 580 sq. ft.

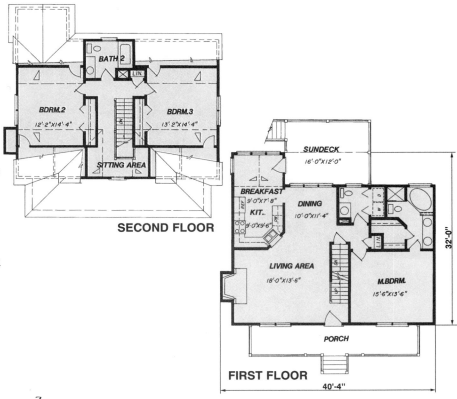

*An* EXCLUSIVE DESIGN
*By Jannis Vann & Associates, Inc.*

# Four Bedroom Stucco

■ *Total living area  1,647 sq. ft.* ■ *Price Code B* ■

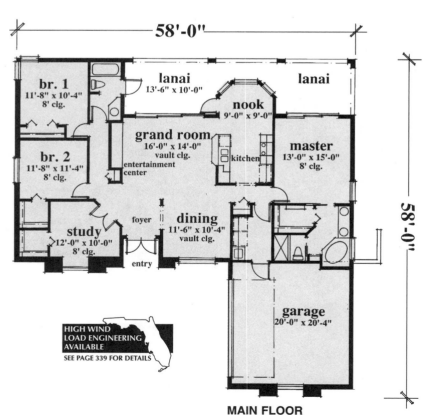

**MAIN FLOOR**

HIGH WIND
LOAD ENGINEERING
AVAILABLE
SEE PAGE 339 FOR DETAILS

## No. 94240

■ **This plan features:**

— Three bedrooms

— Two full baths

■ Fits easily on narrow depth lots

■ Grand Room layout has vaulted ceiling that includes the Foyer and Dining Room

■ Grand Room is highlighted by a built-in entertainment center and access to Lanai

■ Compact Kitchen opens to glass Nook and formal Dining Area

■ Private Master Suite has glass doors to the Lanai Area and a plush bath

■ No materials list is available for this plan

Main floor — 1,647 sq. ft.
Garage — 427 sq. ft.

■ *Total living area 2,747 sq. ft.* ■ *Price Code E* ■

# No. 91109

## ■ This plan features:

– Five bedrooms

– Three full baths

■ A beautiful brick exterior is accentuated by double transoms over double windows

■ Big bedrooms and an oversized Great Room, desirable for a large family

■ Volume ceilings in the Master Suite, Great Room, Dining Room, Kitchen, Breakfast Nook and bedroom four

■ Three bathrooms, including a plush master bath, with a double vanity and knee space

■ Plenty of room to spread out in the Sun Room adjacent to the Great Room and the Game Room above the Garage

■ No materials list is available for this plan

First floor — 2,307 sq. ft.
Second floor — 440 sq. ft.
Garage & Storage — 517 sq. ft.

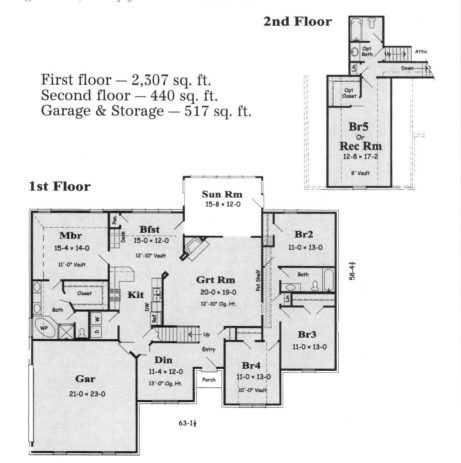

# Clever Use of Interior Space

© 1994 Donald A. Gardner Architects, Inc.

■ *Total living area 1,737 sq. ft.* ■ *Price Code C* ▶

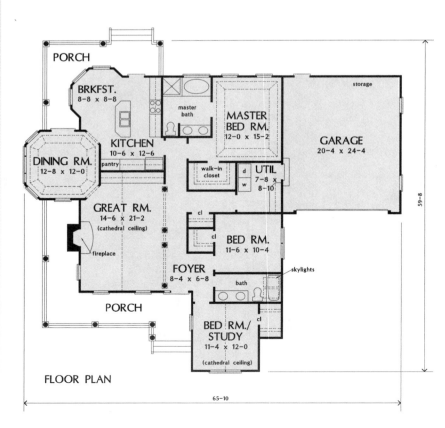

FLOOR PLAN

# No. 99844

## ■ This plan features:

— Three bedrooms

— Two full baths

■ Efficient interior with cathedral and tray ceilings create feeling of space

■ Great Room boasts cathedral ceiling above cozy fireplace, built-in shelves and columns

■ Octagon Dining Room and Breakfast alcove bathed in light and easily accessed Porch

■ Open Kitchen features island counter sink and Pantry

■ Master Bedroom enhanced by tray ceiling and plush bath

Main floor — 1,737 sq. ft.
Garage & storage — 517 sq. ft.

# Elegant Victorian

■ *Total living area 2,455 sq. ft.* ■ *Price Code D* ■

## No. 98518

### This plan features:

– Three bedrooms

– Two full and one half baths

■ Serve guests dinner in the bayed Dining Room and then gather in the Living Room which features a cathedral ceiling

■ The Family Room is accented by a fireplace

■ The Master Bedroom has a Sitting Area, walk-in closet, and a private bath

■ There is a Bonus Room upstairs for future expansion

■ An optional basement or slab foundation — please specify when ordering

■ No materials list is available for this plan

First floor — 1,447 sq. ft.
Second floor — 1,008 sq. ft.
Garage — 756 sq. ft.

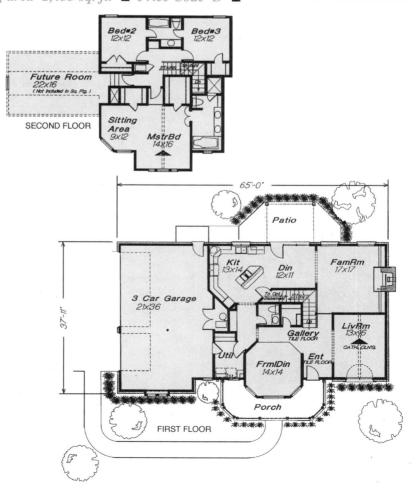

SECOND FLOOR

Bed#2 12x12
Bed#3 12x12
Future Room 22x16 ( Not Included In Sq. Ftg. )
STAIRS
Sitting Area 9x12
MstrBd 14x16

FIRST FLOOR

65'-0"
37'-11"
Patio
Kit 13x14
Din 12x11
FamRm 17x17
3 Car Garage 21x36
To Opt. Basement
Gallery TILE FLOOR
LivRm 13x16 CATH. CLNG.
Util
FrmlDin 14x14
Ent TILE FLOOR
Porch

# Traditional Brick with Detailing

■ *Total living area  1,869 sq. ft.* ■ *Price Code D* ■

## No. 92536

■ **This plan features:**

— Three bedrooms

— Two full baths

■ Covered entry leads into the Foyer, the formal Dining Room and the Den

■ Expansive Den with a decorative ceiling over a hearth fireplace and sliding glass doors to the rear yard

■ Country Kitchen with a built-in pantry, double ovens and a cooktop island easily serves the Breakfast Area and Dining Room

■ Private Master Suite with a decorative ceiling, a walk-in closet, a double vanity and a whirlpool tub

■ Two additional bedrooms share a full bath

■ An optional slab or crawl space foundation — please specify when ordering

Main floor — 1,869 sq. ft.
Garage — 561 sq. ft.

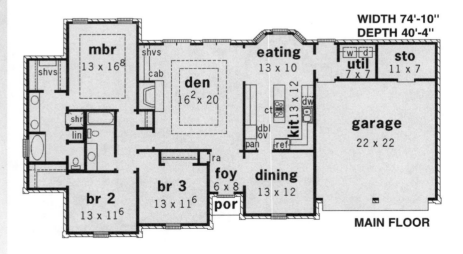

**WIDTH 74'-10"**
**DEPTH 40'-4"**

mbr
13 x 16$^8$

shvs
cab

eating
13 x 10

w d
util
7 x 7

sto
11 x 7

den
16$^2$ x 20

kit 13 x 12

garage
22 x 22

shr
lin

br 2
13 x 11$^6$

br 3
13 x 11$^6$

foy
6 x 8

por

dining
13 x 12

**MAIN FLOOR**

■ *Total living area  1,670 sq. ft.* ■ *Price Code  B* ■

# No. 90409 ✖

■ **This plan features:**

– Three bedrooms

– Two full baths

■ A massive fireplace separating Living and Dining rooms

■ An isolated Master Suite with a walk-in closet and handy compartmentalized bath

■ A galley-type Kitchen between the Breakfast Room and Dining Room

■ An optional basement, slab or crawl space foundation — please specify when ordering

Main area — 1,670 sq. ft.

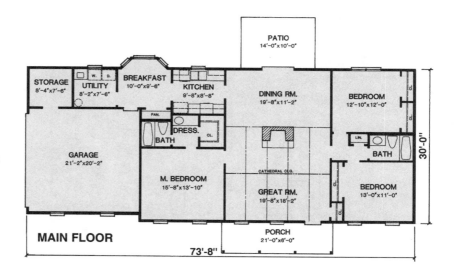

# Casual Country Charmer

© 1997 Donald A. Gardner Architects, Inc.

B. NATHAN

■ *Total living area  1,770 sq. ft.* ■ *Price Code C* ■

attic storage

down

**BONUS RM.**
13-6 x 24-0

PORCH

**DINING**
11-4 x 12-0

(dormers above)

PORCH

master bath

lin.

walk-in closet  walk-in closet

d w

**UTIL.**
7-0 x 10-0

**KIT.**
13-0 x 12-0

fireplace

(cathedral ceiling)

**MASTER BED RM.**
13-0 x 14-8

pan.

storage

up

**GREAT RM.**
17-8 x 20-4

shelves

cl

cl

lin.

57-4

**GARAGE**
22-0 x 24-0

**FOYER**
8-0 x 9-3

cl

**BED RM.**
11-4 x 11-8

bath

**PORCH**

**BED RM.**
11-0 x 11-0

cl

**FLOOR PLAN**

54-0

© 1997  Donald A Gardner Architects, Inc.

# No. 96493

■ **This plan features:**

— Three bedrooms

— Two full baths

■ Columns and arches frame the front Porch

■ The open floor plan combines the Great Room, Kitchen and Dining Rooms

■ The Kitchen offers a convenient breakfast bar for meals on the run

■ The Master Suite features a private bath oasis

■ Secondary bedrooms share a full bath with a dual vanity

Main floor — 1,770 sq. ft.
Bonus — 401 sq. ft.
Garage — 630 sq. ft.

# Compact Southern Traditional

■ *Total living area 2,545 sq. ft.* ■ *Price Code D* ■

# No. 93035

■ **This plan features:**

- Four bedrooms

- Two full and one half baths

■ An entrance flanked by columns and imposing gables, accented with dentil molding

■ An angled Foyer, drawing the eye to an arched passage in the Living Room

■ A large Kitchen/Family Room combination with an octagonal shaped breakfast area

■ A Master Bedroom that is entered through angled double doors and has a cathedral ceiling

■ A Master Bath with his-and-her vanities and walk-in closets

■ No materials list is available for this plan

Main floor — 2,545 sq. ft.
Garage — 436 sq. ft.

© Larry E. Belk

MAIN FLOOR

# Exquisite Detail

■ *Total living area 3,262 sq. ft.* ■ *Price Code F* ■

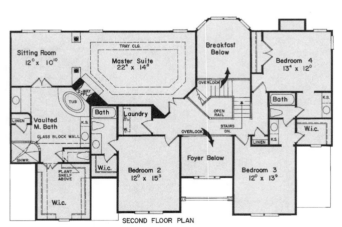

SECOND FLOOR PLAN

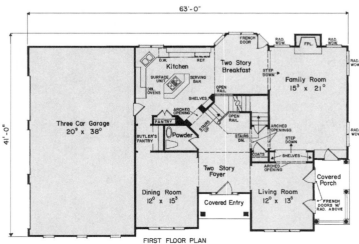

FIRST FLOOR PLAN

# No. 98400

## ■ This plan features:

— Four bedrooms

— Three full and one half baths

■ Formal Living Room with access to Covered Porch

■ Radius windows and arches, huge fireplace enhance spacious Family Room

■ Kitchen has a Pantry, cooktop/serving bar and a two-story Breakfast Area

■ Expansive Master Bedroom offers a tray ceiling, a cozy Sitting Room, a luxurious bath and huge walk-in closet

■ An optional basement or crawl space foundation — please specify when ordering

First floor — 1,418 sq. ft.
Second floor — 1,844 sq. ft.
Basement — 1,418 sq. ft.
Garage — 820 sq. ft.

# Spacious Elegance

■ *Total living area 2,349 sq. ft.* ■ *Price Code D* ■

# No. 98455

## ■ This plan features:

— Four bedrooms

— Three full baths

■ The two-story Foyer with palladian window illuminates a lovely staircase and the Dining Room entry way

■ The Family Room has a vaulted ceiling and an inviting fireplace

■ Vaulted ceiling and a radius window highlight the Breakfast area and the efficient Kitchen

■ The Master Suite boasts a tray ceiling, luxurious bath and a walk-in closet

■ An optional basement or crawl space foundation — please specify when ordering

First floor — 1,761 sq. ft.
Second floor — 588 sq. ft.
Bonus Room — 267 sq. ft.
Basement — 1,761 sq. ft.
Garage — 435 sq. ft.

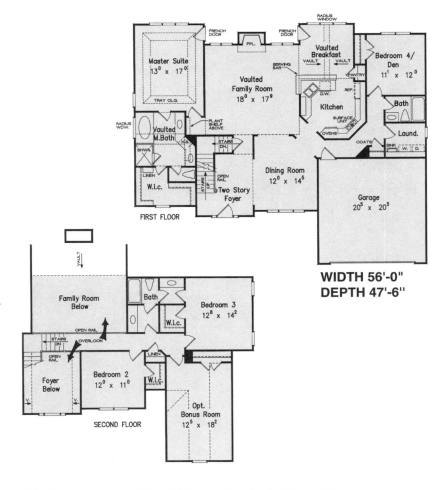

**WIDTH 56'-0"**
**DEPTH 47'-6"**

# Your Classic Hideaway

■ *Total living area  1,773 sq. ft.* ■ *Price Code B* ■

## No. 90423 ⚒

■ **This plan features:**

— Three bedrooms

— Two full baths

■ A lovely fireplace in the Living Room which is both cozy and a source of heat for the core area

■ An efficient country Kitchen, connecting the large Dining and Living rooms

■ A lavish Master Suite enhanced by a step-up sunken tub, more than ample closet space, and separate shower

■ A screened Porch and Patio area for outdoor living

■ An optional basement, slab or crawl space foundation — please specify when ordering

Main area — 1,773 sq. ft.
Screened porch — 240 sq. ft.

### MAIN AREA

PATIO
16-0x10-0

GARAGE
21-0x21-0

SCR. PORCH
12-0x20-4

DINING
12-0x13-4

KITCHEN
10x13

UTILITY

PANTRY

BEDROOM
11-0x13-4

CLOSET

STEP

CLOSET

M. BATH

SEAT

CLOSET

M. BEDROOM
12-0x18-0

LIVING ROOM
15-6x17-8

DOWN

COATS

CLOSET

BEDROOM
12-0x11-4

LINEN

DRESSING

LINEN

BATH

FOYER

PORCH
26-0x6-0

88'-8"

43'-8"

# Unique and Desirable

© 1996 Donald A Gardner Architects, Inc.

■ *Total living area  1,977 sq. ft.* ■ *Price Code  C* ■

# No. 99803

### ■ This plan features:

— Three bedrooms

— Two full baths

■ Private Master Bedroom has a walk-in closet and a skylit bath

■ Two additional bedrooms, one with a possible use as a study, share a full bath

■ From the Foyer columns lead into the Great Room with a cathedral ceiling and a fireplace

■ In the rear of the home is a skylit screen Porch and a Deck that features built-in seats and a spa

■ The Kitchen is conveniently located between the Dining Room and the skylit Breakfast Area

■ An optional basement or crawl space foundation — please specify when ordering

Main floor — 1,977 sq. ft.
Bonus room — 430 sq. ft.
Garage & storage — 610 sq. ft.

# Southern Hospitality

■ *Total living area  1,830 sq. ft.* ■ *Price Code C* ■

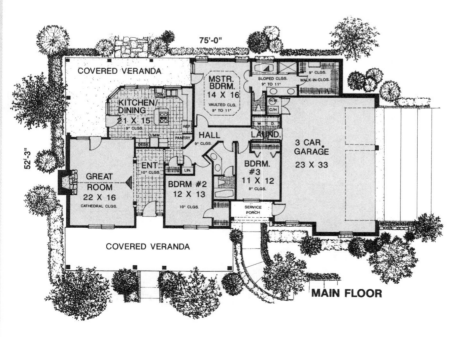

**MAIN FLOOR**

## No. 92220

### ■ This plan features:

— Three bedrooms

— Two full baths

■ Covered Veranda catches breezes

■ Tiled Entry leads into Great Room with fieldstone fireplace, a cathedral ceiling and atrium door to another Covered Veranda

■ A bright Kitchen/Dining Room includes a stovetop island/ snackbar, built-in Pantry and desk

■ Vaulted ceiling crowns Master Bedroom that offers a plush bath and huge walk-in closet

■ Two additional bedrooms with ample closets share a double vanity bath

■ No materials list is available for this plan

Main floor — 1,830 sq. ft.
Garage — 759 sq. ft.

*Total living area  2,400 sq. ft.* ■ *Price Code  D* ■

# No. 94641

■ **This plan features:**

— Four bedrooms

— Two full baths

■ Four columns accentuating the warm Southern welcome alluded to by the front Porch

■ Kitchen includes a peninsula counter, plenty of counter and storage space and an easy flow into the Breakfast Room

■ Master Bedroom topped by a decorative ceiling treatment and a compartmental master bath with a whirlpool tub

■ Two additional bedrooms with walk-in closets share a double vanity bath in the hall

■ No materials list is available for this plan

Main floor — 2,400 sq. ft.
Garage — 534 sq. ft.

WIDTH 61'-10"
DEPTH 66'-6"

MAIN FLOOR

# Rustic Three Bedroom

© 1992 Donald A. Gardner Architects, Inc.

B·NATHAN

■ *Total living area  1,622 sq. ft.* ■ *Price Code C* ■

**SECOND FLOOR**

BED RM.
12-6 x 13-8

bath

walk-in closet

closet

down

railing

great room below

BED RM.
12-0 x 15-8

PORCH
34-6 x 8-0

KIT./ DINING
10-10 x 17-8

walk-in closet

w   d

MASTER BED RM.
12-0 x 17-0

bedroom above

sto.

GREAT RM.
17-4 x 17-2

fireplace

up

cl

master bath

44-8

PORCH
34-6 x 8-0

37-9

**FIRST FLOOR**

# No. 96436

## ■ This plan features:

— Three bedrooms

— Two full baths

■ Spacious covered Porches on the front of the home and on the rear of the home

■ Openness in the Great Room to the Kitchen/Dining area provides a spacious feeling of a much larger home

■ Cooktop island Kitchen includes L-shaped counter for ample work space

■ Master Suite, with a generous walk-in closet and pampering master bath

■ Two second floor bedrooms, one overlooking the Great Room for added drama

First floor — 1,039 sq. ft.
Second floor — 583 sq. ft.

# Whimsical Two-story Farmhouse

© 1993 Donald A. Gardner Architects, Inc.

B. NATHAN

■ *Total living area  2,182 sq. ft.* ■  *Price Code  D* ■

# No. 96442 ✂

## ■ This plan features:

– Four bedrooms

– Three full and one half baths

■ Double gable with palladian, clerestory window and wrap-around Porch provide country appeal

■ First floor enjoys nine foot ceilings throughout

■ Palladian windows flood two-story Foyer and Great Room with natural light

■ Both Master Bedroom and Great Room access covered, rear Porch

■ One upstairs bedroom offers a private bath and walk-in closet

First floor — 1,346 sq. ft.
Second floor — 836 sq. ft.

SECOND FLOOR PLAN

FIRST FLOOR PLAN

© Donald A. Gardner Architects, Inc.

# One Floor Convenience

■ *Total living area 1,359 sq. ft.* ■ *Price Code A* ■

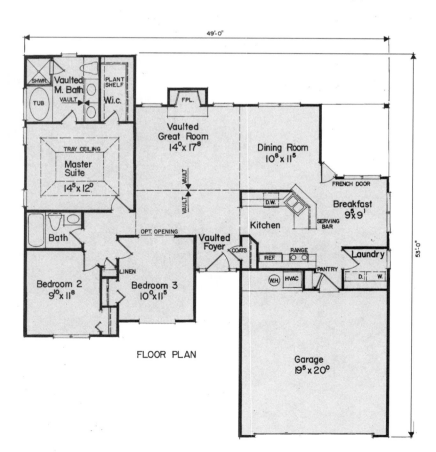

49'-0"

53'-0"

**SHWR.** **Vaulted M. Bath** **VAULT** **PLANT SHELF** **TUB** **Wi.c.**

**TRAY CEILING**

**Master Suite** 14⁸ x 12⁰

**FPL.**

**Vaulted Great Room** 14' x 17⁸

**VAULT** **VAULT**

**Dining Room** 10⁸ x 11⁵

**FRENCH DOOR**

**Bath**

**OPT. OPENING**

**Vaulted Foyer**

**COATS**

**LINEN**

**Bedroom 2** 9¹⁰ x 11⁸

**Bedroom 3** 10⁰ x 11⁵

**D.W.**

**Kitchen**

**SERVING BAR**

**Breakfast** 9⁵ x 9¹

**REF.** **RANGE**

**PANTRY**

**Laundry**

**W.H.** **HVAC**

**D.** **W.**

**FLOOR PLAN**

**Garage** 19⁵ x 20⁰

## No. 98443

■ **This plan features:**

— Three bedrooms

— Two full baths

■ Vaulted Foyer blending with the vaulted Great Room giving a larger feeling to the home

■ Formal Dining Room opening into the Great Room

■ Kitchen including a serving bar, flowing into the Breakfast Room

■ Master Suite topped by a decorative tray ceiling and a vaulted ceiling in the Master Bath

■ Two additional bedrooms sharing the full bath in the hall

■ An optional crawl space or slab foundation available — please specify when ordering

■ No materials list is available for this plan

Main floor — 1,359 sq. ft.
Garage — 439 sq. ft.

■ *Total living area  1,208 sq. ft.* ■ *Price Code  A* ■

# No. 98915 ✗

## This plan features:

- Three bedrooms

- Two full baths

■ Porch shelters Entry into Living
  Area with an inviting fireplace
  topped by a vaulted ceiling

■ Convenient Dining area opens to
  Living Room, Kitchen and
  Sundeck

■ Efficient, U-shaped Kitchen serves
  Dining area and Sundeck beyond

■ Pampering Master Bedroom with
  a vaulted ceiling, two closets and
  a double vanity bath

■ Two additional bedrooms share a
  full bath and convenient laundry
  center

Main floor — 1,208 sq. ft.
Basement — 728 sq. ft.
Garage — 480 sq. ft.

*An*
EXCLUSIVE DESIGN
*By Jannis Vann & Associates, Inc.*

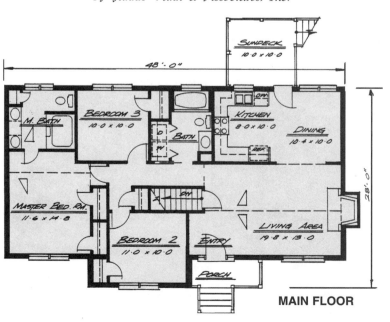

**MAIN FLOOR**

# Impressive Fieldstone Facade

■ *Total living area 3,110 sq. ft.* ■ *Price Code E* ■

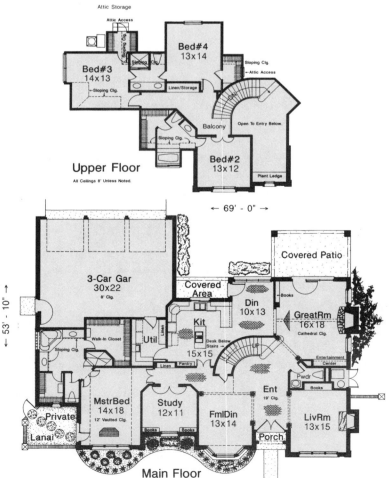

**Upper Floor**

Attic Storage
Attic Access
Bed#4 13x14
Bed#3 14x13
Sloping Clg.
Sloping Clg.
Attic Access
Linen/Storage
Sloping Clg.
Balcony
Open To Entry Below.
Bed#2 13x12
Plant Ledge
All Ceilings 8' Unless Noted.

← 69' - 0" →

← 53' - 10" →

3-Car Gar 30x22
8' Clg.
Covered Patio
Covered Area
Din 10x13
Books
GreatRm 16x18
Cathedral Clg.
Walk-In Closet
Util
Linen
Kit 15x15
Desk Below Stairs
UP
Entertainment Center
Sloping Clg.
Linen
Pantry
Pwdr
MstrBed 14x18
12' Vaulted Clg.
Study 12x11
FmlDin 13x14
Ent 19' Clg.
Books
LivRm 13x15
Private
Lanai
Porch

**Main Floor**

## No. 92277

### ■ This plan features:

— Four bedrooms

— Three full and one half baths

■ Double door leads into two-story entry with an exquisite curved staircase

■ Formal Living Room features a marble hearth fireplace, triple window and built-in book shelves

■ Formal Dining Room defined by columns and a lovely bay window

■ Expansive Great Room with entertainment center, fieldstone fireplace and cathedral ceiling

■ Vaulted ceiling crowns Master Bedroom suite offering a plush bath and two walk-in closets

■ No materials list is available for this plan

Main floor — 2,190 sq. ft.
Upper floor — 920 sq. ft.
Garage — 624 sq. ft.

# Out of the English Countryside

■ *Total living area  2,524 sq. ft.* ■ *Price Code  D* ■

## No. 98519

■ **This plan features:**

- Four bedrooms

- Three full and one half baths

■ From the Entry, is the Living Room/Study with a cozy fireplace, or left into the Dining Room, both rooms have lovely bay windows

■ The Family Room has a fireplace and a door that leads out onto a covered patio

■ The Breakfast Area is adjacent to the Family Room and the Kitchen which features a center island

■ The first floor Master Bedroom has two walk-in closets and an attached bath with a spa tub

■ Upstairs bedrooms each have walk-in closets and use of two full baths

■ Also located upstairs is a Bonus Room that would be a perfect Playroom

■ No materials list is available for this plan

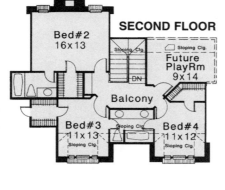

First floor — 1,735 sq. ft.
Second floor — 789 sq. ft.
Bonus — 132 sq. ft.
Garage — 482 sq. ft.

# Turret Adds Appeal

■ *Total living area 2,214 sq. ft.* ■ *Price Code D* ■

## No. 94206

■ **This plan features:**

— Three bedrooms

— Two full baths

■ A double door garden Entry leads to the Foyer and Great Room

■ Vaulted ceilings above a decorative window in the Dining area and sliding glass doors to the Veranda in the Great Room

■ A private Study with double door and turret windows

■ Kitchen featuring a walk-in Pantry and a glassed Nook with skylights

■ A Master Suite with a vaulted ceiling, walk-in closets, a private bath and sliding glass doors to the Veranda

■ Two bedrooms with oversized closets sharing a full bath

■ No materials list is available for this plan

Main floor — 2,214 sq. ft.
Garage — 652 sq. ft.

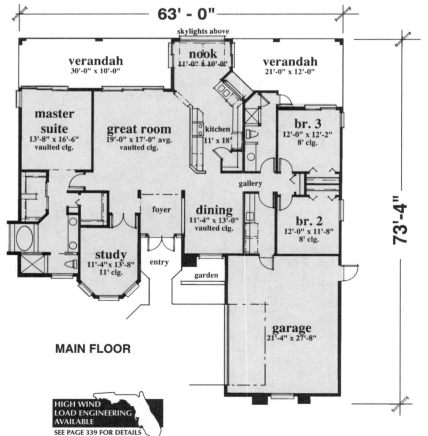

**MAIN FLOOR**

63' - 0"

73'-4"

skylights above

verandah
30'-0" x 10'-0"

nook
11'-0" x 10'-0"

verandah
21'-0" x 12'-0"

master suite
13'-8" x 16'-6"
vaulted clg.

great room
19'-0" x 17'-0" avg.
vaulted clg.

kitchen
11' x 18'

br. 3
12'-0" x 12'-2"
8' clg.

gallery

foyer

dining
11'-4" x 13'-0"
vaulted clg.

br. 2
12'-0" x 11'-8"
8' clg.

study
11'-4" x 13'-8"
11' clg.

entry

garden

garage
21'-4" x 27'-8"

HIGH WIND
LOAD ENGINEERING
AVAILABLE
SEE PAGE 339 FOR DETAILS

# Family Room at the Heart of the Home

■ *Total living area  2,073 sq. ft.* ■ *Price Code  C* ■

## No. 93436

■ **This plan features:**

– Four bedrooms

– Two full and one half baths

■ Formal Foyer opening into the formal Dining Room with grand front window and direct access to the Kitchen

■ Family Room with a vaulted ceiling and a fireplace

■ Kitchen/Breakfast area has been laid out for ultimate efficiency

■ First floor Master Suite is topped by a vaulted ceiling and pampered by a five-piece private bath

■ No materials list is available for this plan

First floor — 1,441 sq. ft.
Second floor — 632 sq. ft.
Basement — 1,441 sq. ft.
Garage — 524 sq. ft.

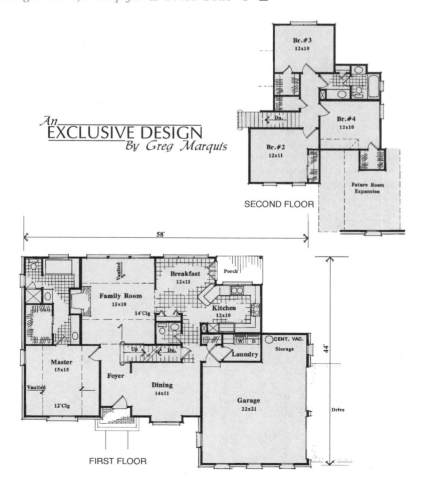

*An*
EXCLUSIVE DESIGN
*By Greg Marquis*

SECOND FLOOR

FIRST FLOOR

# Covered Porch with Columns

Total living area 1,856 sq. ft. ■ Price Code C ■

## No. 98408

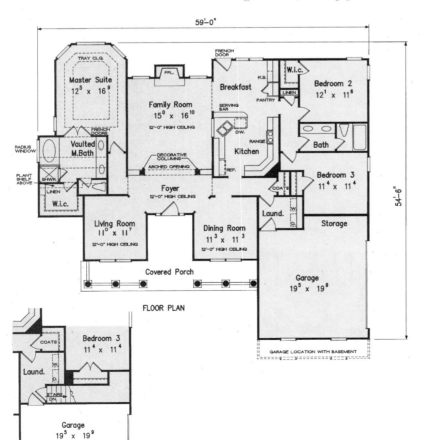

FLOOR PLAN

OPT. BASEMENT STAIR LOCATION

### ■ This plan features:

— Three bedrooms

— Two full baths

■ The foyer with 12' ceiling leads past decorative columns into the Family Room with a center fireplace

■ The Living and Dining Rooms are linked by Foyer and have windows overlooking the front Porch

■ The Kitchen has a serving bar and is adjacent to the Breakfast Nook which has a French door that opens to the backyard

■ The private Master Suite has a tray ceiling and a vaulted bath with a double vanity

■ An optional basement, slab or a crawl space foundation — please specify when ordering

Main floor — 1,856 sq. ft.
Basement — 1,856 sq. ft.
Garage — 429 sq. ft.

# Country Living in Any Neighborhood

■ *Total living area 2,181 sq. ft.* ■ *Price Code C* ■

## No. 90436

■ **This plan features:**

– Three bedrooms

– Two full and two half baths

■ An expansive Family Room with fireplace

■ A Dining Room and Breakfast Nook lit by flowing natural light from bay windows

■ A first floor Master Suite with a double vanity bath that wraps around his-n-her closets

■ An optional basement, slab or crawl space foundation — please specify when ordering

First floor — 1,477 sq. ft.
Second floor — 704 sq. ft.
Basement — 1,374 sq. ft.
Garage — 528 sq. ft.

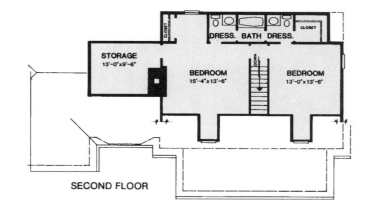

SECOND FLOOR

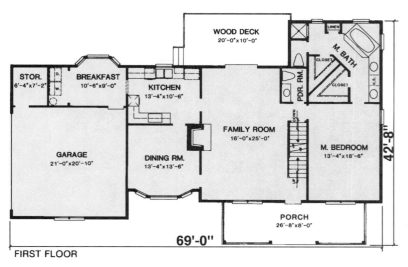

FIRST FLOOR

# Flexible Spaces

B. NATHAN
©1994 Donald A. Gardner Architects, Inc.

■ *Total living area  1,843 sq. ft.* ■ *Price Code C* ■

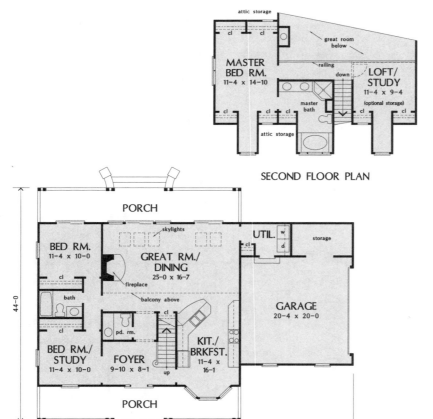

attic storage

cl    cl

**MASTER BED RM.**
11-4 x 14-10

cl    cl    cl

attic storage

great room below

railing

down

master bath

**LOFT/ STUDY**
11-4 x 9-4

(optional storage)

cl    cl

**SECOND FLOOR PLAN**

PORCH

**BED RM.**
11-4 x 10-0

cl

bath

cl

**BED RM./ STUDY**
11-4 x 10-0

44-0

skylights

**GREAT RM./ DINING**
25-0 x 16-7

fireplace

balcony above

cl

pd. rm.

**FOYER**
9-10 x 8-1

up

**KIT./ BRKFST.**
11-4 x 16-1

UTIL.    w  d

cl

storage

**GARAGE**
20-4 x 20-0

PORCH

58-0

**FIRST FLOOR PLAN**

© 1994 Donald A Gardner Architects, Inc.

## No. 96457 ⚒

■ **This plan features:**

— Three bedrooms

— Two full and one half baths

■ The large common area combines the Great Room and the Dining Room under a vaulted ceiling that is punctuated with skylights

■ The Kitchen/Breakfast Bay includes a peninsula counter/snack bar

■ From the Great Room extend entertaining outdoors to the covered back porch

■ The Master Suite has a generous bath and ample closet space

■ The front bedroom/study doubles as a Guest Room

■ On the second floor the loft/study makes a terrific office or play room

First floor — 1,234 sq. ft.
Second floor — 609 sq. ft.
Garage — 496 sq. ft.

# Stylish Bay Window

■ *Total living area 1,260 sq. ft.* ■ *Price Code A* ■

## No. 93004

■ **This plan features:**

– Three bedrooms

– Two Full baths

■ A stylish bay window and a covered Porch highlight the exterior elevation

■ The Great Room has a corner fireplace and a ten foot ceiling

■ The Breakfast Bay is brightened by three windows

■ The Kitchen is set up in a convenient U-shape and features a walk-in Pantry

■ The large Master Bedroom has its own bath and a walk-in closet with built-in shelves

■ Two additional bedrooms share a full bath in the hall.

■ No materials list is available for this plan

Main floor —1,260 sq. ft.

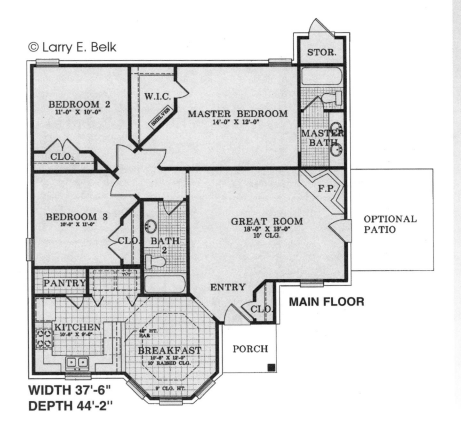

© Larry E. Belk

**MAIN FLOOR**

**WIDTH 37'-6"**
**DEPTH 44'-2"**

# Luxurious Masterpiece

■ *Total living area 3,818 sq. ft.* ■ *Price Code F* ■

## No. 92265

■ **This plan features:**

— Four bedrooms

— Three full and one half baths

■ An elegant and distinguished exterior

■ An expansive formal Living Room with a 14' ceiling and a raised hearth fireplace

■ Informal Family Room offers another fireplace, wetbar and a cathedral ceiling

■ A hub Kitchen with a cooktop island, peninsula counter, and a bright breakfast area

■ Private Master Bedroom with a pullman ceiling, lavish his-n-her baths and a garden window tub

■ Three additional bedrooms with walk-in closets and private access to a full bath

■ No materials list is available for this plan

Main floor — 3,818 sq. ft.
Garage — 816 sq. ft.

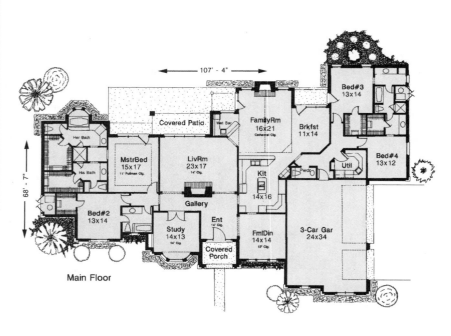

Main Floor

■ *Total living area  1,600 sq. ft.*  ■  *Price Code  B*  ■

# No. 98406 ✖

## ■ This plan features:

— Three bedrooms

— Two full and one half baths

■ Kitchen, Breakfast Bay, and Family Room blend into a spacious open living area

■ Convenient Laundry Center is tucked into the rear of the Kitchen

■ Luxurious Master Suite is topped by a tray ceiling while a vaulted ceiling is in the bath

■ Two roomy secondary bedrooms share the full bath in the hall

■ An optional basement, crawl space or slab foundation — please specify when ordering

First floor — 828 sq. ft.
Second floor — 772 sq. ft.
Basement — 828 sq. ft.
Garage — 473 sq. ft.

FIRST FLOOR

SECOND FLOOR

# European Style

■ *Total living area  2,727 sq. ft.* ■ *Price Code F* ■

## No. 92501 ⚒

### ■ This plan features:

— Four bedrooms

— Three full and one half baths

■ Central Foyer between spacious Living and Dining rooms with arched windows

■ Hub Kitchen with extended counter and nearby Utility/Garage entry, easily serves Breakfast Area and Dining Room

■ Spacious Den with a hearth fireplace between built-ins and sliding glass doors to Porch

■ Master Bedroom wing with decorative ceiling, plush bath with two walk-in closets

■ Three additional bedrooms with ample closets and private access to a full bath

■ An optional slab or crawl space foundation — please specify when ordering

**WIDTH 70'-10"**
**DEPTH 64'-5"**

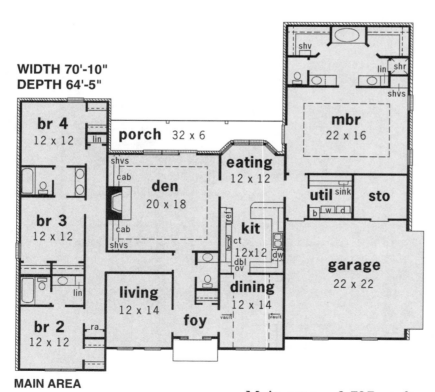

**MAIN AREA**

Main area — 2,727 sq. ft.
Garage — 569 sq. ft.

# A Home for Today's Lifestyle

■ *Total living area 2,787 sq. ft.* ■ *Price Code E* ■

## No. 92902

### ■ This plan features:

– Four bedrooms

– Three full baths

■ Family living area comprised of a family room, breakfast area, and island Kitchen

■ Formal Dining Room with easy access from the Kitchen

■ Pampering Master Suite with private master bath and an abundance of storage space

■ Screened Porch and covered Patio extending living space outdoors

■ No materials list is available for this plan

Main floor — 2,787 sq. ft.
Garage — 685 sq. ft.

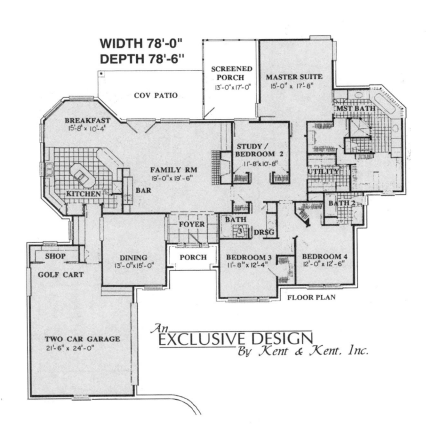

WIDTH 78'-0"
DEPTH 78'-6"

SCREENED PORCH 13'-0"x 17'-0"

MASTER SUITE 15'-0" x 17'-8"

COV PATIO

MST BATH

BREAKFAST 15'-8" x 10'-4"

STUDY / BEDROOM 2 11'-8"x 10'-8"

UTILITY

FAMILY RM 19'-0"x 19'-6"

KITCHEN

BAR

BATH 2

FOYER

BATH 3

DRSG

SHOP

DINING 13'-0"x15'-0"

PORCH

BEDROOM 3 11'-8" x 12'-4"

BEDROOM 4 12'-0" x 12'-6"

GOLF CART

FLOOR PLAN

TWO CAR GARAGE 21'-6" x 24'-0"

*An* EXCLUSIVE DESIGN *By Kent & Kent, Inc.*

# Luxuriant Living

■ *Total living area  2,869 sq. ft.* ■ *Price Code E* ■

## FIRST FLOOR PLAN

PATIO

SITTING
9-4 x 4-4

MASTER
BED RM.
14-0 x 16-0

FAMILY RM.
21-8 x 19-10
(two story ceiling)
fireplace

BRKFST.
9-4 x 10-4

KITCHEN
16-4 x 10-4

BED RM./
OFFICE
12-4 x 12-0

master bath

walk-in closet

lin.

balcony above.

UTIL.
7-0 x
8-8

pd. rm.

storage

bath

up

pan.

(two story ceiling)

FOYER
8-6 x
9-8

DINING
12-8 x 13-4

GARAGE
24-4 x 23-0

LIVING RM./
STUDY
14-0 x 12-0
fireplace

PORCH

52-0

69-6

FIRST FLOOR PLAN

© 1997 Donald A Gardner Architects, Inc.

First floor — 2,249 sq. ft.
Second floor — 620 sq. ft.
Bonus — 308 sq. ft.
Garage — 642 sq. ft.

family room below

railing

balcony

down

foyer below

BED RM.
12-8 x 13-4

walk-in closet shelf

attic storage

BED RM.
14-0 x 14-8

walk-in closet

bath

down

attic storage

BONUS RM.
14-4 x 17-0

attic storage

SECOND FLOOR PLAN

# No. 99825

## ■ This plan features:

— Four bedrooms

— Three full and one half baths

■ French doors, windows and a high gabled Entry make a dramatic entrance

■ Living Room features a box bay window and a fireplace

■ Dining Room is illuminated by a bank of windows

■ Family Room has a two-story ceiling, a fireplace and access to the rear Patio

■ Kitchen and Nook adjoin handy Home Office

■ The Master Suite features a private bath and a Sitting Area

■ Upstairs find two bedrooms, each with a walk-in closet, a full bath and a Bonus Room

# Covered Porches Front and Back

© 1993 Donald A. Gardner Architects, Inc.

■ *Total living area  2,301 sq. ft.* ■ *Price Code  D* ■

## No. 96404

■ **This plan features:**

– Three bedrooms

– Two full and one half baths

■ Open floor plan plus Bonus Room, great for today's family needs

■ Two-story Foyer with palladian, clerestory window and balcony overlooking Great Room

■ Great Room with cozy fireplace provides perfect gathering place

■ Columns visually separate Great Room from Breakfast Area and smart, U-shaped Kitchen

■ Privately located Master Bedroom accesses Porch and luxurious Master Bath with separate shower and double vanity

First floor — 1,632 sq. ft.
Second floor — 669 sq. ft.
Bonus room — 528 sq. ft.
Garage & storage — 707 sq. ft.

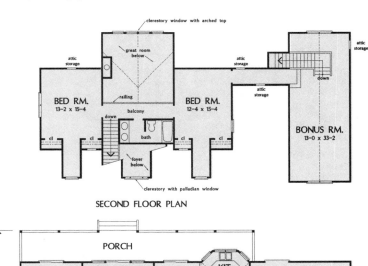

SECOND FLOOR PLAN

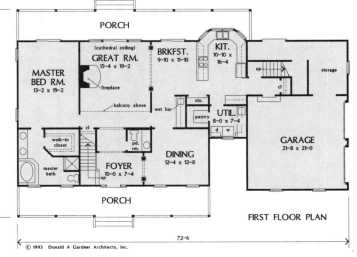

FIRST FLOOR PLAN

© 1993 Donald A Gardner Architects, Inc.

# Compact Victorian Ideal for Narrow Lot

■ *Total living area  1,737 sq. ft.* ■ *Price Code  B* ■

**FIRST FLOOR**

STUDY OR BEDROOM
11'-6"X12'-0"

BATH

WASH DRY

BREAKFAST
9'-0"X11'-8"

PANT.

CLOSET

FURN.

COATS

REFG.

STOOP

RAIL

PARLOR
18'-0"X13'-0"

RANGE

KITCHEN
8'-0"X12'-0"

SINK

RAIL

UP

D.W.

PORCH
18'-0"X6'-0"

RAIL

DINING ROOM
11'-4"X12'-8"

30' - 0"

**SECOND FLOOR**

BEDROOM
9'-4"X9'-6"

CLOSET

BEDROOM
11'-2"X9'-6"

CLOSET

CLOSET

LINEN

BATH

FLUE

DN

RAIL

MASTER SUITE
12'-0"X12'-4"

WHIRLPOOL

BATH

CLOSET

37' - 6"

CATHEDRAL CEILING

CEILING FAN

SITTING ROOM
11'-4"X12'-4"

# No. 90406

## ■ This plan features:

— Three bedrooms

— Three full baths

■ A large, front Parlor with a raised hearth fireplace

■ A Dining Room with a sunny bay window

■ An efficient galley Kitchen serving the formal Dining Room and informal Breakfast Room

■ A beautiful Master Suite with two closets, an oversized tub and double vanity, plus a private sitting room with a bayed window and vaulted ceiling

■ An optional basement, slab or crawl space foundation — please specify when ordering

First floor — 954 sq. ft.
Second floor — 783 sq. ft.

# Grand Design Highlighted by Turrets

■ *Total living area  4,759 sq. ft.* ■ *Price Code  F* ■

## No. 94230

■ **This plan features:**

- Four bedrooms

- Two full, one three-quarter and one half baths

■ Triple arches at entry lead into Grand Foyer and Gallery with arched entries to all areas

■ Triple French doors catch the breeze and access to rear grounds in Living and Leisure rooms

■ Spacious Kitchen with large walk-in Pantry, cooktop/work island and angled serving counter/snack bar, glass Nook, Utility Room and Garage entry

■ Master Suite wing offers Veranda access, two closets and vanities, and a garden window tub

■ Three second floor bedrooms with walk-in closets, balcony and full bath access

■ No materials list is available for this plan

HIGH WIND
LOAD ENGINEERING
AVAILABLE
SEE PAGE 339 FOR DETAILS

First floor — 3,546 sq. ft.
Second floor — 1,213 sq. ft.
Garage — 822 sq. ft.

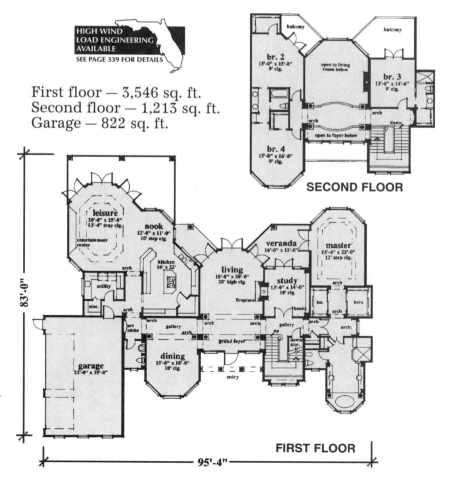

93

# Mixture of Traditional and Country Charm

© 1994 Donald A. Gardner Architects, Inc

■ *Total living area 1,954 sq. ft.* ■ *Price Code C* ■

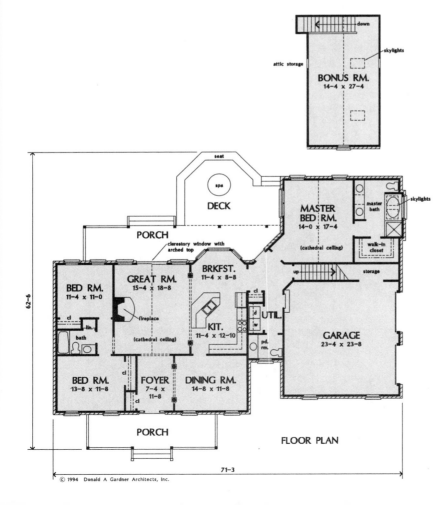

## No. 99845

■ **This plan features:**

— Three bedrooms

— Two full and one half baths

■ Stairs to the skylit Bonus Room located near the Kitchen and Master Suite

■ Master Suite crowned in cathedral ceilings has a skylit bath that contains a whirlpool tub and dual vanity

■ Great Room, topped by a cathedral ceiling and highlighted by a fireplace, is adjacent to the Country Kitchen

■ Two additional bedrooms share a hall bath

Main floor — 1,954 sq. ft.
Bonus area — 436 sq. ft.
Garage — 649 sq. ft.

© 1994 Donald A Gardner Architects, Inc.

■ *Total living area  3,034 sq. ft.* ■ *Price Code  E* ■

# No. 91111

■ **This plan features:**

- Four bedrooms

- Two full and one half baths

■ Dramatic roof lines and a seven foot tall arched transom above front door

■ Columns, arches, angled stairs, a high ceiling and a large plant ledge in the Foyer

■ High vaulted ceilings and an abundance of windows in the Sun Room, Breakfast Nook and Living Room

■ The Master Bedroom has a lavish whirlpool bath and a large walk-in closet

■ No materials list is available for this plan

First floor — 2,123 sq. ft.
Second floor — 911 sq. ft.
Garage & storage — 565 sq. ft.

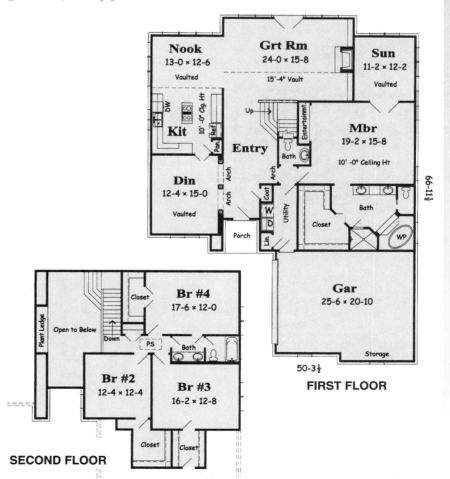

# Steep Pitched Roof with Quoins

■ *Total living area  1,556 sq. ft.*  ■ *Price Code C* ■

## No. 92556

■ **This plan features:**

— Three bedrooms

— Two full baths

■ Classic brick exterior features a steep pitched roof and decorative quoins

■ The Foyer leads into the Den which is highlighted by a fireplace

■ The Kitchen is centered between the Dining room and the Eating nook

■ The isolated Master Bedroom has a walk-in closet and a full bath

■ There is a Bonus Room over the two-car garage for future expansion

■ An optional slab or crawl space foundation — please specify when ordering

Main floor — 1,556 sq. ft.
Bonus — 282 sq. ft.
Garage — 565 sq. ft.

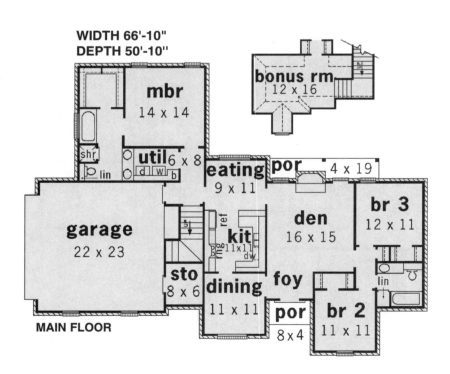

WIDTH 66'-10"
DEPTH 50'-10"

bonus rm
12 x 16

mbr
14 x 14

shr

util 6 x 8

d w b

lin

eating
9 x 11

por
4 x 19

garage
22 x 23

ref

kit
11x11

mg

dw

den
16 x 15

br 3
12 x 11

lin

sto
8 x 6

dining
11 x 11

foy

por
8 x 4

br 2
11 x 11

MAIN FLOOR

# Style and Convenience

■ *Total living area  1,653 sq. ft.* ■ *Price Code  B* ■

# No. 92283

## ■ This plan features:

- Three bedrooms

- Two full baths

■ A sheltered Porch leads into an easy-care tile Entry

■ Spacious Living Room offers a cozy fireplace, triple window and access to Patio

■ An efficient Kitchen with a skylight, work island, Dining area, walk-in pantry and Utility/Garage entry

■ Secluded Master Bedroom highlighted by a vaulted ceiling, access to Patio and a lavish bath

■ Two additional bedrooms, one with a cathedral ceiling, share a full bath

■ No materials list is available for this plan

Main floor — 1,653 sq. ft.
Garage — 420 sq. ft.

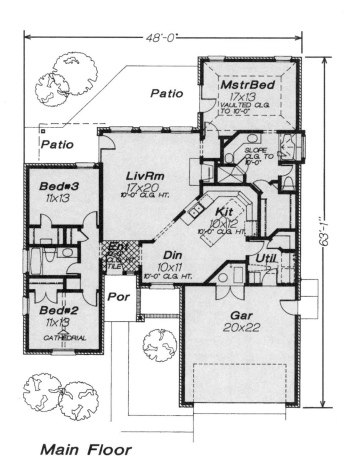

**Main Floor**

# Demonstrative Detail

■ *Total living area 1,854 sq. ft.* ■ *Price Code C* ■

*An* EXCLUSIVE DESIGN
*By Greg Marquis*

2nd Floor

1st Floor

## No. 93410 ✂

■ **This plan features:**

— Three bedrooms

— Two full and one half baths

■ Keystone arched windows, stone and stucco combine with shutters and a flower box to create an eye-catching elevation

■ The Foyer accesses the Dining Room, Family Room or the Master Suite

■ The Family Room has a sloped ceiling and a fireplace with windows to either side

■ The Kitchen/Breakfast area has access to the rear Porch

■ An optional Bonus Area over the Garage offers possibilities for future expansion

First floor — 1,317 sq. ft.
Second floor — 537 sq. ft.
Bonus — 312 sq. ft.
Basement — 1,317 sq. ft.
Garage — 504 sq. ft.

# Brick Abounds

■ *Total living area  1,528 sq. ft.* ■ *Price Code  B* ■

## No. 98522

■ **This plan features:**

– Three bedrooms

– Two full baths

■ The covered front Porch opens into the entry that has a 10-foot ceiling and a coat closet

■ The large Living Room is distinguished by a fireplace and a front window wall

■ The Dining Room features a 10-foot ceiling and access to the rear covered Patio

■ The Kitchen is angled and has a pantry and a cooktop island

■ The Master Bedroom is located in the rear for privacy and boasts a triangular walk-in closet, plus a private bath

■ No materials list is available for this plan

Main floor — 1,528 sq. ft.
Garage — 440 sq. ft.

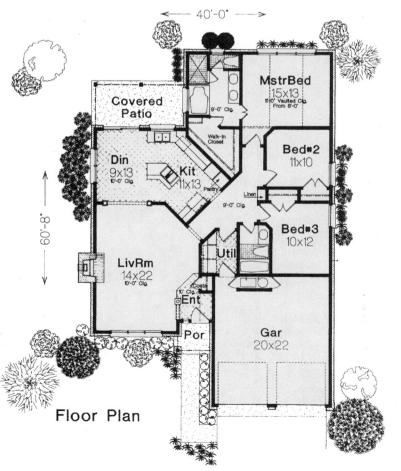

Floor Plan

# Stately Home

© 1992 Donald A. Gardner Architects, Inc.

■ *Total living area  2,526 sq. ft.* ■  *Price Code E* ■

Main floor — 2,526 sq. ft.
Garage — 611 sq. ft.

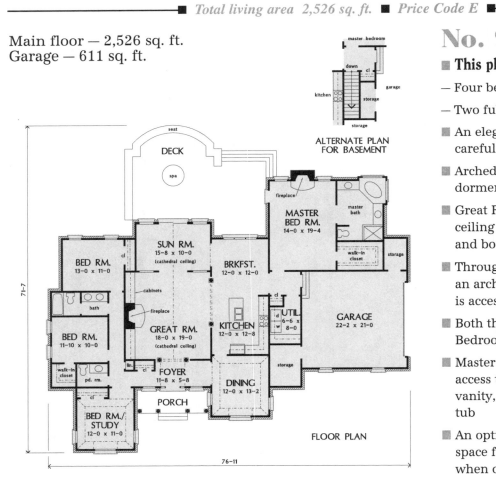

ALTERNATE PLAN
FOR BASEMENT

FLOOR PLAN

# No. 96435 ✗ ℝR

## ■ This plan features:

— Four bedrooms

— Two full and one half baths

■ An elegant brick exterior and careful detailing

■ Arched window in the clerestory dormer above the foyer

■ Great Room topped by a cathedral ceiling boasting built-in cabinets and bookshelves

■ Through glass doors, capped by an arched window, the Sun Room is accessed from the Great Room

■ Both the Dining Room and the Bedroom/Study have tray ceilings

■ Master Suite includes a fireplace, access to the deck, his-n-her vanity, a shower and a whirlpool tub

■ An optional basement or crawl space foundation — please specify when ordering

# Distinguished Look

■ *Total living area  1,906 sq. ft.* ■ *Price Code  C* ■

# No. 98429

## ■ This plan features:

– Three bedrooms

– Two full and one half baths

■ The Family Room, Breakfast Room and the Kitchen are presented in an open layout

■ A fireplace in the Family Room provides a warm atmosphere

■ The plush Master Suite pampers the owner and features a trapezoid glass above the tub

■ Two additional bedrooms share the use of the double vanity bath in the hall

■ An optional basement, crawl space or slab foundation available — please specify when ordering

First floor — 1,028 sq. ft.
Second floor — 878 sq. ft.
Bonus room — 315 sq. ft.
Basement — 1,028 sq. ft.
Garage — 497 sq. ft.

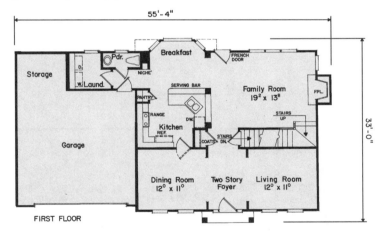

FIRST FLOOR

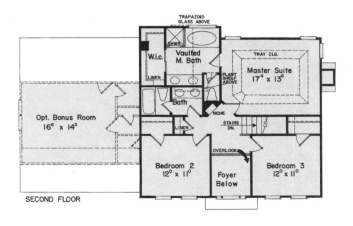

SECOND FLOOR

# Compact Country Cottage

© 1991 Donald A. Gardner Architects, Inc.

■ *Total living area  1,310 sq. ft.* ■ *Price Code B* ■

## No. 99856

### ■ This plan features:

— Three bedrooms

— Two full baths

■ Foyer opening to a large Great Room with a fireplace and a cathedral ceiling

■ Efficient U-shaped Kitchen with peninsula counter extending work space and separating it from the Dining Room

■ Two front bedrooms, one with a bay window, the other with a walk-in closet, sharing a full bath in the hall

■ Master Suite located to the rear with a walk-in closet and a private bath with a double vanity

■ Partially covered deck with skylights accessible from the Dining Room, Great Room and the Master Bedroom

Main floor — 1,310 sq. ft.
Garage & storage — 455 sq. ft.

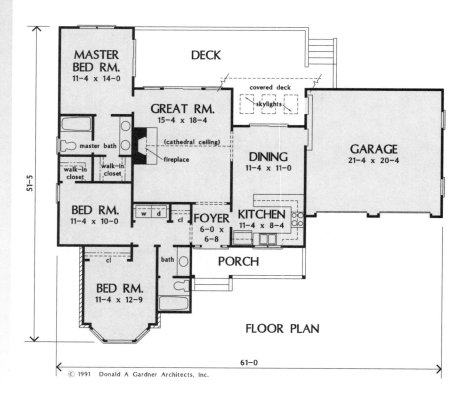

© 1991  Donald A Gardner Architects, Inc.

# Distinctive Brick with Room to Expand

■ *Total living area  2,645 sq. ft.* ■ *Price Code  E* ■

## No. 93206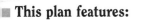

### ■ This plan features:

— Four bedrooms

— Two full and one half baths

■ Arched entrance with decorative glass leads into two-story Foyer

■ Formal Dining Room with tray ceiling above decorative window

■ Efficient Kitchen with island cooktop, built-in desk and Pantry

■ Master Bedroom topped by tray ceiling with French door to Patio, huge private bath with garden tub and two walk-in closets

■ Optional space for Storage and Future Bedroom with full bath

■ An optional basement, crawl space or slab foundation — please specify when ordering

First Floor — 2,577 sq. ft.
Future Second Floor — 619 sq. ft.
Bridge — 68 sq. ft.
Basement — 2,561 sq. ft.
Garage — 560 sq. ft.

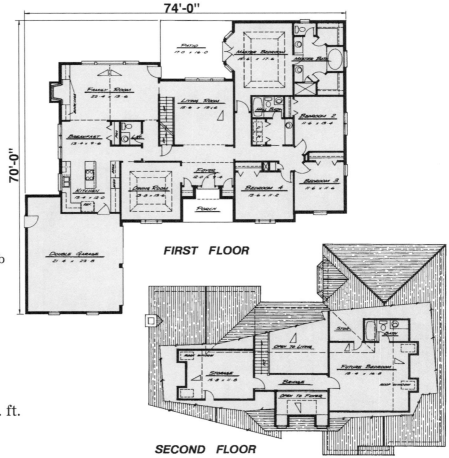

**FIRST FLOOR**

**SECOND FLOOR**

*An*
EXCLUSIVE DESIGN
*By Jannis Vann & Associates, Inc.*

# Columned Keystone Arched Entry

■ Total living area 2,256 sq. ft. ■ Price Code D ■

## No. 96503

■ **This plan features:**

— Three bedrooms

— Two full baths

■ Keystone arches and arched transoms above the windows

■ Formal Dining Room and Study flank the Foyer

■ Fireplace in Great Room

■ Efficient Kitchen with a peninsula counter and bayed Nook

■ A step ceiling in the Master Suite and interesting master bath with a triangular area for the oval tub

■ The secondary bedrooms share a full bath in the hall

Main floor — 2,256 sq. ft.
Garage — 514 sq. ft.

**Main floor**

# Modern Luxury

■ *Total living area  2,686 sq. ft.* ■ *Price Code E* ■

# No. 98457 ✕

## ■ This plan features:

— Four bedrooms

— Three full and one half baths

■ A feeling of spaciousness is created by the two-story Foyer in this home

■ Arched openings and decorative windows enhance the Dining and Living rooms

■ The efficient Kitchen has a work island, Pantry and a Breakfast area

■ The plush Master Suite features a tray ceiling, an alcove of windows and a whirlpool bath

■ An optional basement or a crawl space foundation — please specify when ordering

First floor — 1,883 sq. ft.
Second floor — 803 sq. ft.
Basement — 1,883 sq. ft.
Garage — 495 sq. ft.

# Country Victorian

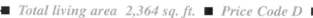

■ *Total living area  2,364 sq. ft.* ■ *Price Code D* ■

## No. 93283

■ **This plan features:**

— Four bedrooms

— Two full and one half baths

■ Victorian accent on a Country Porch with an octagonal Sitting Area

■ A central Foyer area highlighted by a decorative staircase

■ A formal Living Room

■ A large country Kitchen with a central work island

■ An expansive Family Room equipped with a cozy fireplace and two sets of French doors

■ A grand Master Suite with a sitting alcove, a walk-in closet, a bath and a private balcony

First floor — 1,155 sq. ft.
Second floor — 1,209 sq. ft.
Basement — 549 sq. ft.
Garage — 576 sq. ft.

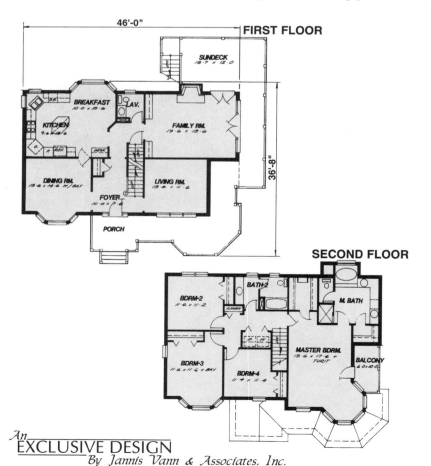

**FIRST FLOOR**

46'-0"

36'-8"

SUNDECK
18'7 x 12'0

BREAKFAST
10'0 x 15'6

KITCHEN
9'6 x 15'6

FAMILY RM.
19'6 x 13'6

DINING RM.
13'6 x 14'6 w/BAY

LIVING RM.
13'6 x 11'6

FOYER
10'0 x 11'6

PORCH

**SECOND FLOOR**

BDRM-2
11'6 x 11'2

BATH-2

M. BATH

BDRM-3
11'6 x 11'6 w/BAY

BDRM-4
11'4 x 11'4

MASTER BDRM.
13'6 x 17'6 +
TURRET

BALCONY
6'0 x 10'0

*An*
EXCLUSIVE DESIGN
*By Jannis Vann & Associates, Inc.*

# Traditional That Has It All

■ *Total living area 2,759 sq. ft.* ■ *Price Code E* ■

## No. 90443

■ **This plan features:**

– Three bedrooms

– Three full and two half baths

■ A Master Suite with two closets and bath with separate shower, corner tub and dual vanity

■ A large Dining Room with a bay window, adjacent to the Kitchen

■ A formal Living Room for entertaining and a cozy Family Room with fireplace

■ Two upstairs bedrooms with walk-in closets and private baths

■ A Bonus Room to allow the house to grow with your needs

■ An optional basement or crawl space foundation — please specify when ordering

First floor — 1,927 sq. ft.
Second floor — 832 sq. ft.
Bonus room — 624 sq. ft.
Basement — 1,674 sq. ft.

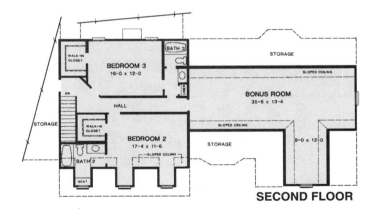

**SECOND FLOOR**

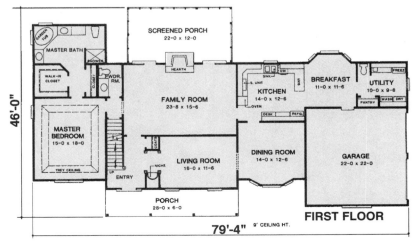

**FIRST FLOOR**

# Amenity-Packed Affordability

■ *Total living area  1,484 sq. ft.* ■ *Price Code B* ■

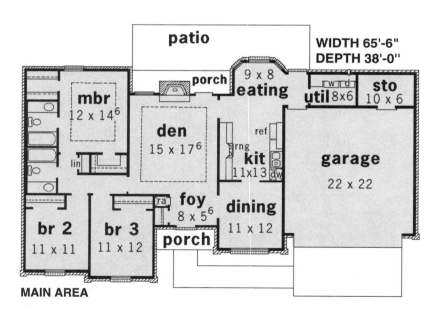

**patio**

**porch**

9 x 8
**eating**

**WIDTH 65'-6"**
**DEPTH 38'-0"**

**mbr**
12 x 14<sup>6</sup>

w d
**util** 8x6

**sto**
10 x 6

lin

**den**
15 x 17<sup>6</sup>

ref

rng

**kit**
11x13

dw

**garage**
22 x 22

br 2
11 x 11

br 3
11 x 12

ra

**foy**
8 x 5<sup>6</sup>

**dining**
11 x 12

**porch**

**MAIN AREA**

## No. 92525

■ **This plan features:**

— Three bedrooms

— Two full baths

■ A sheltered entrance inviting your guests onward

■ A fireplace in the Den offering a focal point, while the decorative ceiling adds definition to the room

■ A well-equipped Kitchen flowing with ease into the Breakfast bay or Dining Room

■ A Master Bedroom, having two closets and a private master bath

■ An optional crawl space or slab foundation — please specify when ordering

Main area — 1,484 sq. ft.
Garage — 544 sq. ft.

# Country Farmhouse

© 1991 Donald A. Gardner Architects, Inc.

■ *Total living area  1,898 sq. ft.* ■ *Price Code  C* ■

# No. 99852 ⚒

## ■ This plan features:

– Three bedrooms

– Two full and one half baths

■ Ready, set, grow with this lovely Country home enhanced by wrap-around Porch and rear Deck

■ Palladian window in clerestory dormer bathes two-story Foyer in natural light

■ Private Master Bedroom offers everything; walk-in closet, whirlpool tub, shower and double vanity

■ Two upstairs bedrooms with dormers and storage access share a full bath

■ An optional basement or crawl space foundation — please specify when ordering

First floor — 1,356 sq. ft.
Second floor — 542 sq. ft.
Bonus room — 393 sq. ft.
Garage & storage — 543 sq. ft.

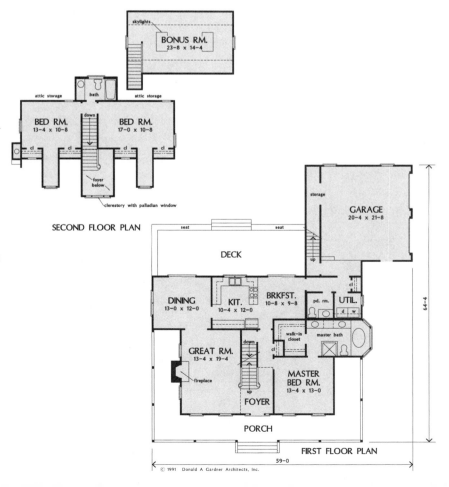

© 1991  Donald A Gardner Architects, Inc.

# Windows Distinguish Design

■ *Total living area  3,525 sq. ft.* ■ *Price Code F* ■

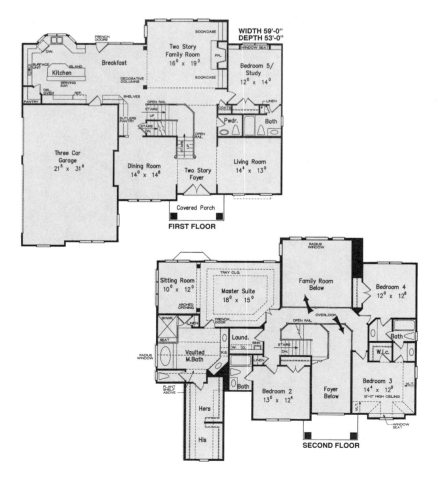

## No. 98438

### ■ This plan features:

— Five bedrooms

— Four full and one half baths

■ Light shines into the Dining Room and the Living Room through their respective elegant windows

■ A hall through the Butler's Pantry leads the way into the Breakfast Nook

■ The two-story Family Room has a fireplace with built-in bookcases on either side

■ The upstairs Master Suite has a Sitting Room and a French door that leads into the vaulted master bath

■ An optional basement or crawl space foundation — please specify when ordering

First floor — 1,786 sq. ft.
Second floor — 1,739 sq. ft.
Basement — 1,786 sq. ft.
Garage — 704 sq. ft.

# Arched Windows Add Natural Light

■ *Total living area  2,060 sq. ft.* ■ *Price Code  C* ■

## No. 94609

■ **This plan features:**

- Four bedrooms

- Three full baths

■ Porch shelters entry into Foyer

■ Dining Room highlighted by alcove of windows

■ Living Room enhanced by a hearth fireplace

■ U-shaped Kitchen with a Breakfast Area with access to Porch

■ Bedroom one offers a large walk-in closet and double vanity bath

■ An optional crawl space or slab foundation — please specify when ordering

■ No materials list is available for this plan

First floor — 1,505 sq. ft.
Second floor — 555 sq. ft.
Garage — 400 sq. ft.

**WIDTH 39'-6"**
**DEPTH 78'-3"**

# An Air of Refinement

© 1993 Donald A. Gardner Architects, Inc.

■ *Total living area 2,130 sq. ft.* ■ *Price Code D* ■

SECOND FLOOR PLAN

FIRST FLOOR PLAN

© 1993 Donald A Gardner Architects, Inc.

BASEMENT PLAN

© 1993 Donald A Gardner Architects, Inc.

# No. 96438

## ■ This plan features:

— Four bedrooms

— Three full baths

■ Hip roof, brick veneer and arched windows catch attention

■ Foyer, flanked by Dining Room and Bedroom/Study, opens to the Great room with cozy fireplace and wall of windows

■ Cathedral ceilings and arched windows bathe Dining Room and Breakfast area in natural light

■ Private Master Bedroom suite has cathedral ceiling and sumptuous bath with whirlpool tub, shower and dual vanity

■ An optional basement or crawl space foundation available — please specify when ordering

First floor — 1,694 sq. ft.
Second floor — 436 sq. ft.
Bonus room — 345 sq. ft.
Garage & storage — 567 sq. ft.

■ *Total living area  1,346 sq. ft.* ■ *Price Code  A* ■

# No. 98434

## This plan features:

- Three bedrooms

- Two full baths

■ Vaulted ceiling crowns spacious Living Room highlighted by a fireplace

■ Built-in pantry and direct access from the garage adding to the conveniences of the Kitchen

■ Walk-in closet and a private five piece bath topped by a vaulted ceiling in the Master Bedroom

■ Proximity to the full bath in the hall from the secondary bedrooms

■ An optional basement, slab or crawl space foundation available — please specify when ordering

Main floor — 1,346 sq. ft.
Basement — 1,358 sq. ft.
Garage — 395 sq. ft.

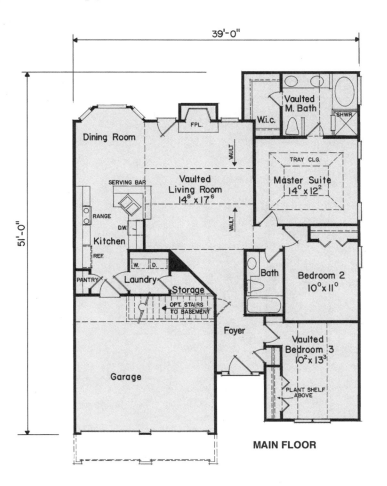

**MAIN FLOOR**

# Distinctive Detailing

© 1995 Donald A. Gardner Architects, Inc.

■ *Total living area 1,972 sq. ft.* ■ *Price Code C* ■

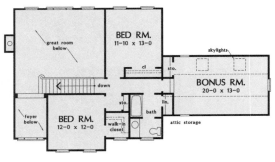

SECOND FLOOR PLAN

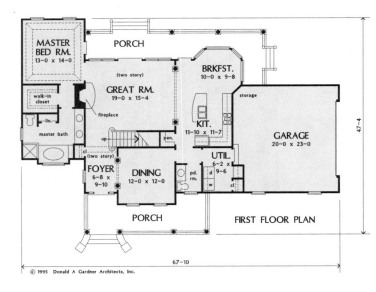

FIRST FLOOR PLAN

© 1995 Donald A Gardner Architects, Inc.

## No. 99829 ⚒

### ■ This plan features:

— Three bedrooms

— Two full and one half baths

■ Interior columns distinguishing the inviting two-story Foyer from the Dining Room

■ Spacious Great Room set off by two-story windows and opening to the Kitchen and Breakfast Bay

■ Nine foot ceilings adding volume and drama to the first floor

■ Secluded Master Suite topped by space amplifying tray ceiling and enhanced by a plush bath

■ Two generous additional bedrooms with ample closet and storage space

■ Skylit Bonus Room enjoying second floor access

First floor — 1,436 sq. ft.
Second floor — 536 sq. ft.
Bonus room — 296 sq. ft.
Garage & storage — 520 sq. ft.

# Rustic Warmth

■ *Total living area 1,764 sq. ft.* ■ *Price Code B* ■

# No. 90440

## ■ This plan features:

- Three bedrooms

- Two full baths

■ A fireplaced Living Room with built-in bookshelves

■ A fully-equipped Kitchen with an island

■ A sunny Dining Room with glass sliders to a wood deck

■ A first floor Master Suite with walk-in closet and lavish master bath

■ An optional basement or crawl space foundation — please specify when ordering

Main floor — 1,100 sq. ft.
Second floor — 664 sq. ft.
Basement — 1,100 sq. ft.

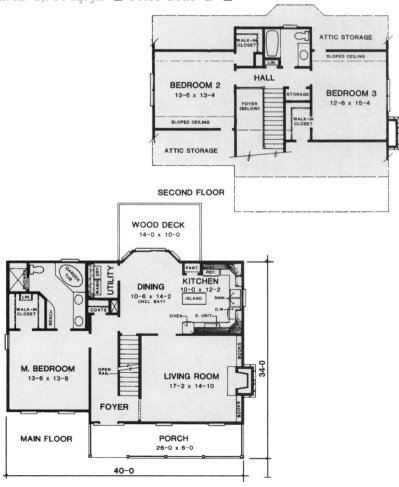

# Charming with Drama

© 1997 Donald A. Gardner Architects, Inc.

■ *Total living area 2,203 sq. ft.* ■ *Price Code D* ■

walk-in closet

lin.

seat

(optional handicapped accessible bath)

PORCH

BRKFST.
11-0 x 9-0

MASTER
BED RM.
14-0 x 17-4

master bath

skylights

walk-in closet

walk-in closet

BED RM.
12-4 x 15-4
(optional 2nd master)

GREAT RM.
16-4 x 19-6
(cathedral ceiling)

fireplace

KIT.
11-0 x
10-10

UTIL.
7-0 x
7-8

up

storage

GARAGE
23-4 x 21-0

bath

lin.

bath

lin.

cl

w d

FOYER
6-4 x
8-2

DINING
11-0 x 13-0

58-8

(optional door location)

BED RM.
11-0 x 11-0

sto.

cl

cl

d

PORCH

FLOOR PLAN

BED RM.
11-0 x 12-0

79-8

© 1997 Donald A Gardner Architects, Inc.

attic storage

down

down

attic storage

BONUS RM.
14-6 x 21-0

skylights

## No. 96478

■ **This plan feature:**

— Four bedrooms

— Three full baths

■ Transom windows and gables charm the exterior

■ Decorative columns and dramatic ceiling treatments highlighting the interior

■ Sharing a cathedral ceiling, the Great Room and Kitchen are open to each other as well as the Breakfast Bay

■ A sliding pocket door separates the Kitchen from the formal Dining Room, topped by a tray ceiling

■ Master Suite also includes a tray ceiling and a luxurious bath with a skylit garden tub and a walk-in closet

Main floor — 2,203 sq. ft.
Garage & storage — 551 sq. ft.
Bonus room — 395 sq. ft.

# Country Style Home With Corner Porch

© 1997 Donald A Gardner Architects, Inc.

■ *Total living area 1,815 sq. ft.* ■ *Price Code C* ■

## No. 99804

■ **This plan features:**

– Three bedrooms

– Two full baths

■ Dining Room has four floor-to-ceiling windows that overlook front Porch

■ Great Room topped by a cathedral ceiling, enhanced by a fireplace, and sliding doors to the back Porch

■ Utility Room located near Kitchen and Breakfast Nook

■ Master Bedroom has a walk in closet and private bath

■ Two additional bedrooms with ample closet space share a full bath

■ A skylight Bonus Room over the two-car Garage

Main floor — 1,815 sq. ft.
Garage — 522 sq. ft.
Bonus — 336 sq. ft.

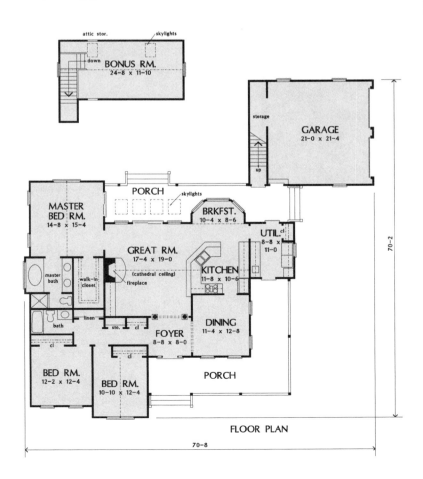

**BONUS RM.**
24-8 x 11-10
attic stor.
skylights
down

**GARAGE**
21-0 x 21-4
storage
up

PORCH   skylights

**MASTER BED RM.**
14-8 x 15-4

**BRKFST.**
10-4 x 8-6

**UTIL.**
8-8 x 11-0

**GREAT RM.**
17-4 x 19-0
(cathedral ceiling)
fireplace

master bath
walk-in closet

**KITCHEN**
11-8 x 10-6

linen
bath
sto.

**FOYER**
8-8 x 8-0

**DINING**
11-4 x 12-8

**BED RM.**
12-2 x 12-4

**BED RM.**
10-10 x 12-4

PORCH

70-2

70-8

FLOOR PLAN

# Stately Stone and Stucco

■ *Total living area 3,027 sq. ft.* ■ *Price Code F* ■

FIRST FLOOR PLAN

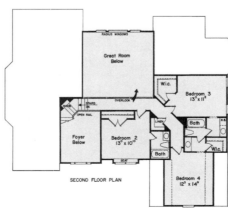

SECOND FLOOR PLAN

# No. 98402

## ■ This plan features:

— Four bedrooms

— Three full and one half baths

■ Two-story Foyer with angled staircase welcomes all

■ Large Great Room has a fireplace, wetbar and French doors

■ Kitchen with a cooktop island, pantry and Breakfast alcove

■ Open Keeping Room accented by a wall of windows

■ Master Suite wing offers a tray ceiling, a plush bath and roomy walk-in closet

■ An optional basement, slab or crawl space foundation — please specify when ordering

First floor — 2,130 sq. ft.
Second floor — 897 sq. ft.
Garage — 494 sq. ft.
Basement — 2,130 sq. ft.

# Stately Elegance

1990 Donald A. Gardner Architects, Inc.

B·NATHAN

■ *Total living area  2,692 sq. ft.* ■ *Price Code  E* ■

# No. 99853

## ■ This plan features:

– Four bedrooms

– Three full and one half baths

■ Impressive double gable roof with front and rear palladian windows and wrap-around Porch

■ Vaulted ceilings in two-story Foyer and Great Room accommodates Loft/Study area

■ Spacious, first floor Master Bedroom offers walk-in closet and luxurious bath

■ Living space extended outdoors by wrap-around Porch and large Deck

■ Upstairs, one of three bedrooms could be a second Master Suite

First floor — 1,734 sq. ft.
Second floor — 958 sq. ft.

SECOND FLOOR PLAN

FIRST FLOOR PLAN

© 1990 Donald A Gardner Architects, Inc.

119

# Street Appeal

■ *Total living area  1,990 sq. ft.* ■ *Price Code  C* ■

Main floor — 1,990 sq. ft.
Basement — 1,415 sq. ft.
Garage — 484 sq. ft.

## No. 90465

### ■ This plan features:

— Three bedrooms

— Two full baths

■ A bay window, arched windows and entrance, plus dormers

■ The Foyer is topped by an eleven foot ceiling with arched glass

■ A large Master Bedroom that has a walk-in closet and a private bath

■ The Great Room has a fireplace, and built-in bookshelves

■ The formal Dining Room is conveniently located

■ The Breakfast area has large windows

■ Two other bedrooms and a full bath complete this split bedroom design

■ An optional basement or crawl space foundation — please specify when ordering

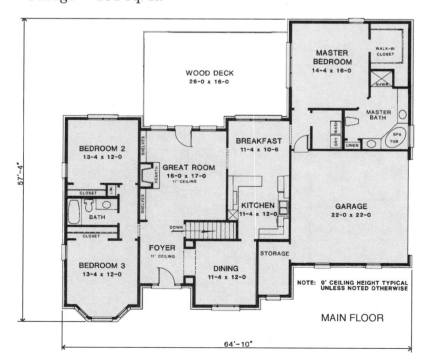

MAIN FLOOR

# Elegant Residence

■ Total living area 3,870 sq. ft. ■ Price Code F ■

# No. 92274

■ **This plan features:**

– Four bedrooms

– Three full and one half baths

■ Two-story glass Entry enhanced by a curved staircase

■ Open Living/Dining Room with decorative windows makes entertaining easy

■ Large, efficient Kitchen with cooktop/work island, huge walk-in Pantry, Breakfast Area, butler's Pantry and Utility/Garage entry

■ Comfortable Family Room with hearth fireplace, built-ins and access to covered Patio

■ Cathedral ceiling tops luxurious Master Bedroom offering a private Lanai, skylit bath, double walk-in closet and adjoining Study

■ No materials list is available for this plan

Main floor — 2,807 sq. ft.
Upper floor — 1,063 sq. ft.
Garage — 633 sq. ft.

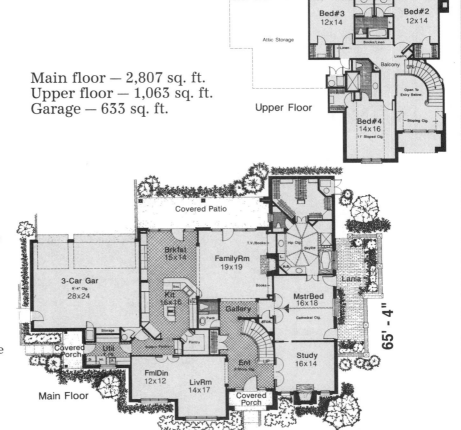

# Style and Convenience

■ *Total living area  1,373 sq. ft.* ■ *Price Code A* ■

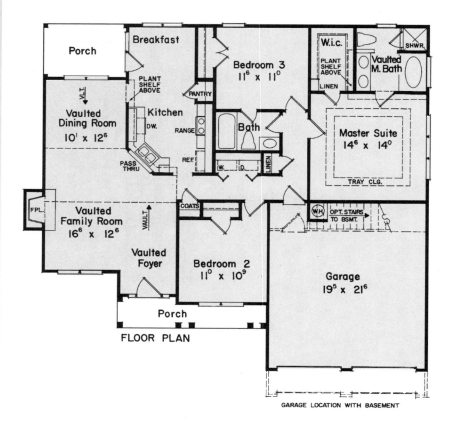

**FLOOR PLAN**

GARAGE LOCATION WITH BASEMENT

## No. 98411

### This plan features:

— Three bedrooms

— Two full baths

■ Large front windows, dormers and an old-fashioned Porch

■ A vaulted ceiling in the Foyer

■ A Formal Dining Room crowned in an elegant vaulted ceiling

■ An efficient Kitchen enhanced by a Pantry, and a pass-through to the Family Room

■ A decorative tray ceiling, a five-piece private bath and a walk-in closet in the Master Suite

■ An optional basement or crawl space foundation available — please specify when ordering

Main floor — 1,373 sq. ft.
Basement — 1,386 sq. ft.
Width — 50'-4"
Depth — 45'-0"

■ *Total living area  1,388 sq. ft.* ■ *Price Code A* ■

# No. 93279

■ **This plan features:**

- Three bedrooms

- Two full baths

■ A central, double fireplace adding warmth and atmosphere to the Family Room, Kitchen and the Breakfast Area

■ An efficient Kitchen highlighted by a peninsula counter that doubles as a snack bar

■ A Master Suite that includes a walk-in closet, a double vanity, separate shower and tub in the bath

■ Two additional bedrooms sharing a full hall bath

■ A wooden Deck that can be accessed from the Breakfast Area

■ An optional crawl space or slab foundation – please specify when ordering

Main floor — 1,388 sq. ft.
Garage — 400 sq. ft.

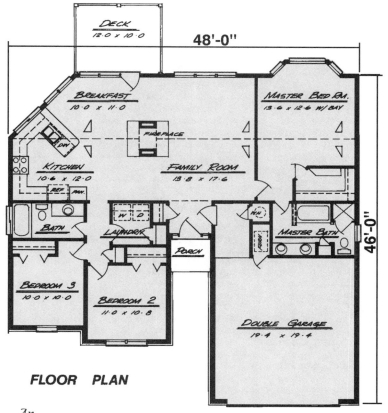

**FLOOR PLAN**

*An*
EXCLUSIVE DESIGN
*By Jannis Vann & Associates, Inc.*

# Relaxed Country Living

© 1997 Donald A. Gardner Architects, Inc.

■ *Total living area  2,027 sq. ft.* ■ *Price Code D* ■

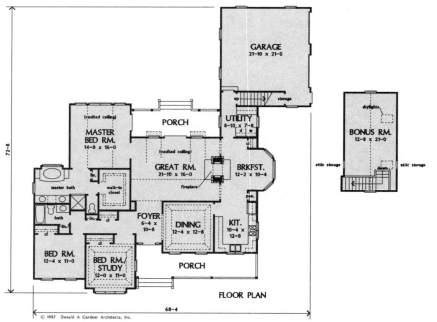

FLOOR PLAN

© 1997 Donald A Gardner Architects, Inc.

## No. 96402

### ■ This plan features:

— Three bedrooms

— Two full baths

■ Comfortable country home with deluxe Master Suite, front and back Porches and dual-sided fireplace

■ Vaulted Great Room brightened by two clerestory dormers and fireplace shared with Breakfast bay

■ Dining Room and front Bedroom/ Study dressed up with tray ceilings

■ Master Bedroom features vaulted ceiling, and luxurious bath with oversized, walk-in closet

■ Skylit Bonus Room over Garage provides extra room for family needs

Main floor — 2,027 sq. ft.
Bonus room — 340 sq. ft.
Garage & storage — 532 sq. ft.

# Ideal for Formal Entertaining

■ *Total living area  1,940 sq. ft.* ■ *Price Code  C* ■

# No. 90421

## This plan features:

- Three bedrooms
- Two full baths
- A lovely French Provincial design
- A large Family Room with a raised hearth fireplace and double doors to the patio
- An L-shaped, island Kitchen with a Breakfast Bay and open counter to the Family Room
- A Master Suite including one double closet and a compartmentalized bath with walk-in closet, step-up garden tub, double vanity and linen closet
- Two front bedrooms sharing a full hall bath with a linen closet
- An optional basement, slab or crawl space foundation — please specify when ordering
- Main floor — 1,940 sq. ft.

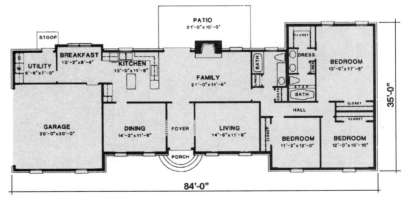

**MAIN FLOOR**

# Cozy Traditional

■ *Total living area  1,862 sq. ft.* ■ *Price Code C* ■

© Larry E. Belk

WIDTH 65-0

DEPTH 46-2

**MAIN FLOOR**

MASTER BATH

BRKFST RM
11-4 X 11-6

UTIL

STORAGE

GREAT ROOM
16-10 X 15-6

KITCHEN
11-4 X 13-6

PAN

GARAGE

MASTER BEDROOM
14-6 X 15-6

BATH 2

ENTRY

BEDROOM 2
12-4 X 13-2

DINING ROOM
11-6 X 12-0

BEDROOM 3
11-4 X 12-0

PORCH

NOTE: ALL CEILINGS 10 FT

# No. 93000

■ **This plan features:**

— Three bedrooms

— Two full baths

■ An angled eating bar separating the Kitchen, Breakfast Room and Great Room, while leaving these areas open for easy entertaining

■ An efficient, well-appointed Kitchen that is convenient to both the formal Dining Room and the sunny Breakfast Room

■ A spacious Master Suite with oval tub, step-in shower, double vanity and walk-in closet

■ Two additional bedrooms with ample closet space that share a full hall bath

■ No materials list is available for this plan

Main floor — 1,862 sq. ft.
Garage — 520 sq. ft.

© 1995 Donald A Gardner Architects, Inc.

■ *Total living area  1,417 sq. ft.* ■ *Price Code  B* ■

# No. 99809

## This plan features:

- Three bedrooms

- Two full baths

■ Cathedral ceiling expanding the Great Room, Dining Room and Kitchen

■ A versatile bedroom or Study topped by a cathedral ceiling accented by double arched windows

■ Master Suite complete with a cathedral ceiling, including a bath with a garden tub, linen closet and a walk-in closet

Main floor — 1,417 sq. ft.
Garage — 441 sq. ft.

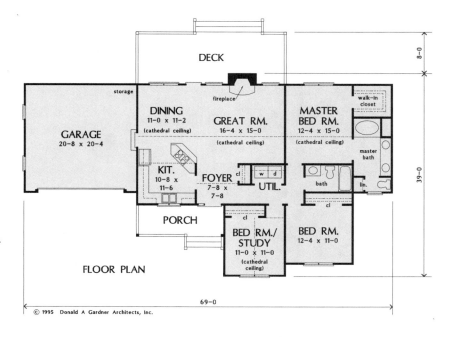

DECK

storage

DINING
11-0 x 11-2
(cathedral ceiling)

fireplace

GREAT RM.
16-4 x 15-0
(cathedral ceiling)

MASTER
BED RM.
12-4 x 15-0
(cathedral ceiling)

walk-in
closet

GARAGE
20-8 x 20-4

master
bath

KIT.
10-8 x
11-6

FOYER
7-8 x
7-8

UTIL.

w  d

bath

lin.

cl

PORCH

BED RM./
STUDY
11-0 x 11-0
(cathedral
ceiling)

BED RM.
12-4 x 11-0

FLOOR PLAN

8-0

39-0

69-0

© 1995  Donald A Gardner Architects, Inc.

# Pleasing to the Eye

© Larry E. Belk

■ *Total living area  1,202 sq. ft.* ■ *Price Code A* ■

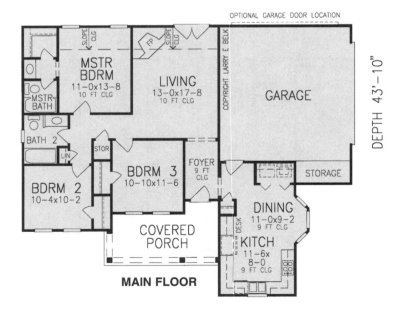

WIDTH 51'–10"

OPTIONAL GARAGE DOOR LOCATION

DEPTH 43'–10"

MSTR BDRM
11–0x13–8
10 FT CLG

LIVING
13–0x17–8
10 FT CLG

GARAGE

MSTR BATH

BATH 2

STOR

LIN

BDRM 3
10–10x11–6

FOYER
9 FT CLG

STORAGE

BDRM 2
10–4x10–2

DINING
11–0x9–2
9 FT CLG

COVERED PORCH

DESK

KITCH
11–6x
8–0
9 FT CLG

**MAIN FLOOR**

Main floor — 1,202 sq. ft.
Garage — 482 sq. ft.

## No. 93073

■ **This plan features:**

— Three bedrooms

— Two full baths

■ A large covered front Porch opening to a Foyer with nine foot ceilings

■ Kitchen with a built-in desk, sunny window over the sink and dining area with a bay window

■ Living Room with a corner fireplace and ten foot ceilings

■ Master Suite topped by a sloped ceiling

■ Two-car Garage with optional door locations located at the rear of the home

■ An optional crawl space or slab foundation available — please specify when ordering

■ No materials list is available for this plan

# European Styling with a Georgian Flair

■ *Total living area  1,873 sq. ft.* ■ *Price Code  D* ■

## No. 92552

### This plan features:

- Four bedrooms

- Two full baths

■ Elegant European styling spiced with Georgian styling

■ Arched windows, quoins and shutters on the exterior, a columned covered front and a rear Porch

■ Formal foyer gives access to the Dining Room to the left and spacious Den straight ahead

■ Kitchen flows into the informal eating area and is separated from the Den by an angled extended counter eating bar

■ An optional crawl space or slab foundation — please specify when ordering

Main floor — 1,873 sq. ft.
Bonus area — 145 sq. ft.
Garage — 613 sq. ft.

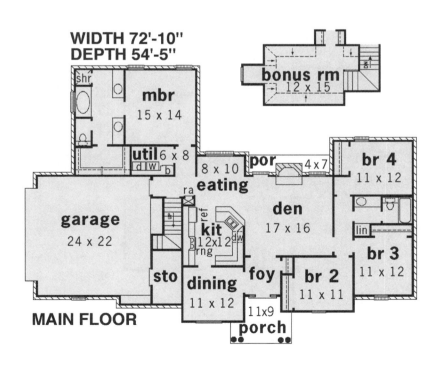

WIDTH 72'-10"
DEPTH 54'-5"

bonus rm 12 x 15

mbr 15 x 14

util 6 x 8

8 x 10

por 4x7

br 4 11 x 12

garage 24 x 22

eating

kit 12x12

den 17 x 16

lin

sto

dining 11 x 12

foy

br 2 11 x 11

br 3 11 x 12

11x9

porch

**MAIN FLOOR**

# Highly Unpretentious

■ *Total living area 2,060 sq. ft.* ■ ● *Price Code C* ■

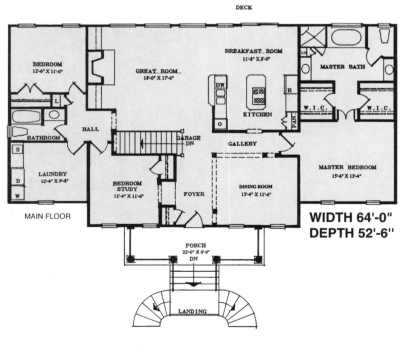

DECK

BEDROOM
12'-6" X 11'-0"

GREAT ROOM
18'-0" X 17'-6"

BREAKFAST ROOM
11'-8" X 8'-0"

MASTER BATH

DW

KITCHEN

W.I.C.    W.I.C.

HALL

BATHROOM

LAUNDRY
12'-4" X 9'-8"

GARAGE
DN

GALLERY

MASTER BEDROOM
15'-6" X 13'-4"

BEDROOM
STUDY
11'-4" X 11'-6"

FOYER

DINING ROOM
13'-4" X 11'-6"

MAIN FLOOR

**WIDTH 64'-0"**
**DEPTH 52'-6"**

PORCH
22'-0" X 6'-0"
DN

LANDING

*An*
EXCLUSIVE DESIGN
*By Garrell Associates Inc.*

## No. 93608

■ **This plan features:**

— Three bedrooms

— Two full baths

■ A graceful front portico leads past the Foyer to the open Grand Room beyond

■ Flat ten-foot ceilings and three large, full radius windows draw in the sunlight

■ A large Kitchen with an island opens to the Breakfast Room and an optional Porch in the rear

■ An oversized Laundry/Sewing Room that is rarely seen in a home of this size

■ A drive under Garage has plenty of room for three vehicles, or two vehicles and a boat

■ No materials list is available for this plan

Main floor — 2,060 sq. ft.
Garage — 1,000 sq. ft.

# High Ceilings and Arched Windows

■ *Total living area  1,502 sq. ft.* ■ *Price Code  B* ■

## No. 98441

### ■ This plan features:

- Three bedrooms

- Two full baths

■ Natural illumination streaming into the Dining Room and Sitting Area of the Master Suite

■ Kitchen with convenient pass-through to the Great Room and a serving bar for the Breakfast Room

■ Great Room topped by a vaulted ceiling accented by a fireplace and a French door

■ Decorative columns accenting the entrance of the Dining Room

■ Tray ceiling over the Master Suite and a vaulted ceiling over the sitting room and the master bath

■ An optional basement or crawl space foundation — please specify when ordering

■ No materials list is available for this plan

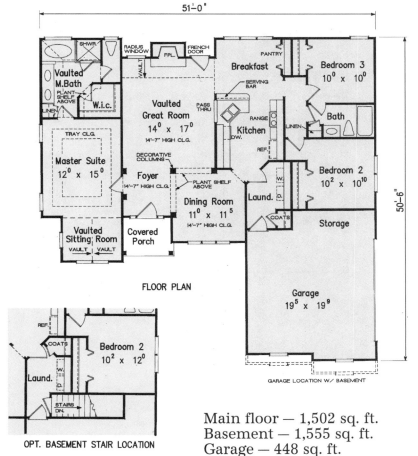

Main floor — 1,502 sq. ft.
Basement — 1,555 sq. ft.
Garage — 448 sq. ft.

# Victorian Charm

© 1997 Donald A. Gardner Architects, Inc.

■ *Total living area  1,903 sq. ft.* ■ *Price Code D* ■

## No. 96405

■ **This plan features:**

— Four bedrooms

— Two full baths

■ This home combines Victorian charm with today's lifestyle needs

■ Ceilings vaulted in Great Room and ten feet high in Foyer, Dining Room, Kitchen/Breakfast Bay and Bedroom/Study

■ Secluded Master Bedroom features tray ceiling, walk-in closet and private, skylit bath

■ Two additional bedrooms, located in separate wing, share a full bath

■ Front and rear Porches extend living area outdoors

Main floor — 1,903 sq. ft.
Garage & storage — 531 sq. ft.

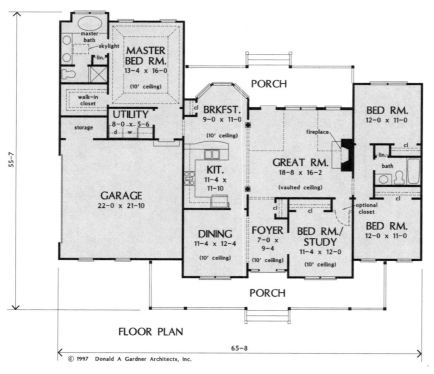

FLOOR PLAN

# Appealing Master Suite

■ *Total living area 1,198 sq. ft.* ■ *Price Code A* ■

## No. 92239

■ **This plan features:**

– Three bedrooms

– Two full baths

■ Sheltered Entry into spacious Living Room with a corner fireplace and Patio access

■ Efficient Kitchen with a serving counter for Dining area and nearby Utility/Garage entry

■ Private Master Bedroom offers a vaulted ceiling and pampering bath with two vanities and walk-in closets and a garden window tub

■ Two additional bedrooms with ample closets share a full bath

■ No materials list is available for this plan

Main floor — 1,198 sq. ft.

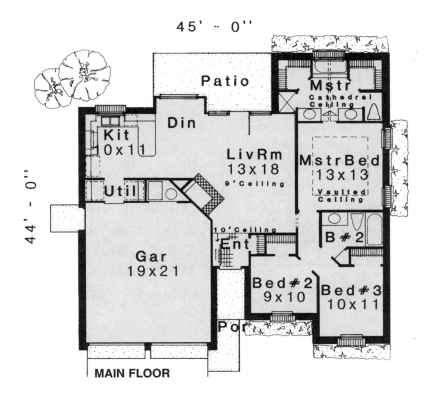

**MAIN FLOOR**

# Sophisticated European Stucco

■ *Total living area  1,856 sq. ft.* ■ *Price Code C* ■

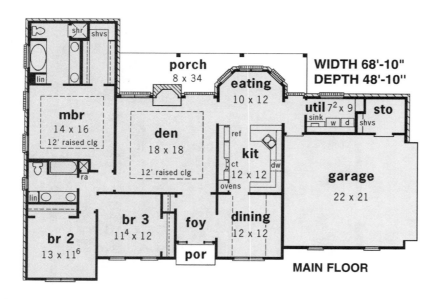

Main floor — 1,856 sq. ft.
Garage & storage — 521 sq. ft.

**WIDTH 68'-10"**
**DEPTH 48'-10"**

**MAIN FLOOR**

## No. 92562

■ **This plan features:**

— Three bedrooms

— Two full baths

■ A raised ceiling in Master Suite and in the Den add architectural interest to the plan

■ A spacious Kitchen serves the Breakfast Area and Dining Room with efficiency and ease

■ A Breakfast Bar for snacks or meals on the go

■ The vaulted ceiling in the Dining Room adds elegance to the room

■ The luxurious master bath with a separate tub and shower pampers you in the Master Suite

■ Secondary bedrooms are in close proximity to the full bath in the hall

■ An optional crawl space or slab foundation — please specify when ordering

© 1993 Donald A. Gardner Architects, Inc.

B. NATHAN

■ *Total living area 1,713 sq. ft.* ■ *Price Code C* ■

# No. 96440 ⚒

■ **This plan features:**

– Three bedrooms

– Two full baths

■ Covered porches, front and back, with an open interior capped by a cathedral ceiling

■ Cathedral ceiling timing the Great Room, Kitchen/Dining and loft/study into an impressive living space

■ Kitchen equipped with an island cooktop and counter opening to both the Great Room and the Dining Room

■ A cathedral ceiling tops the front bedroom/study

■ A large bay cozies up the rear bedroom

■ Luxurious Master Suite located upstairs for extra privacy

First floor — 1,146 sq. ft.
Second floor — 567 sq. ft.

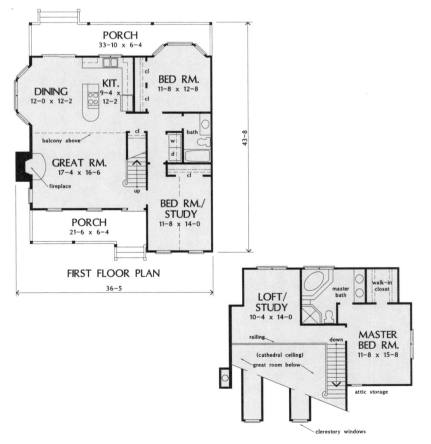

FIRST FLOOR PLAN

SECOND FLOOR PLAN

135

# European Flair

**Total living area 1,544 sq. ft.** ■ **Price Code B**

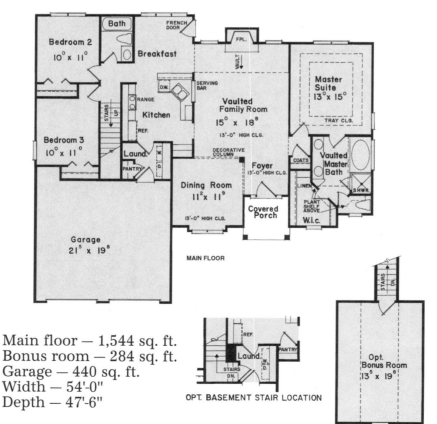

Bedroom 2
10⁰ x 11⁰

Bath

FRENCH DOOR

Breakfast

FPL.

VAULT

Master Suite
13⁰ x 15⁰

TRAY CLG.

D.W.

SERVING BAR

RANGE

Kitchen

Vaulted Family Room
15⁰ x 18⁸

13'-0" HIGH CLG.

STAIRS UP

REF.

Bedroom 3
10⁰ x 11⁰

Laund.

W. D.

PANTRY

DECORATIVE COLUMN

Foyer
13'-0" HIGH CLG.

COATS

Vaulted Master Bath

SHWR.

LINEN

PLANT SHELF ABOVE

Dining Room
11² x 11⁹

13'-0" HIGH CLG.

Covered Porch

W.i.c.

Garage
21⁵ x 19⁸

**MAIN FLOOR**

Main floor — 1,544 sq. ft.
Bonus room — 284 sq. ft.
Garage — 440 sq. ft.
Width — 54'-0"
Depth — 47'-6"

REF.

Laund.

STAIRS DN.

W. D.

PANTRY

**OPT. BASEMENT STAIR LOCATION**

STAIRS DN.

Opt. Bonus Room
13⁵ x 19⁸

**OPTIONAL BONUS ROOM**

## No. 98460

■ **This plan features:**

— Three bedrooms

— Two full baths

■ Large fireplace serving as an attractive focal point for the vaulted Family Room

■ Decorative column defining the elegant Dining Room

■ Kitchen including a serving bar for the Family Room and a Breakfast Area

■ Master Suite topped by a tray ceiling over the bedroom and a vaulted ceiling over the five-piece master bath

■ Optional Bonus Room for future expansion

■ An optional basement or crawl space foundation — please specify when ordering

■ No materials list is available for this plan

# With Room to Expand

■ *Total living area   1,675 sq. ft.* ■ *Price Code   B* ■

# No. 98431

## ■ This plan features:

– Three bedrooms

– Two full and one half baths

■ An impressive two-story Foyer

■ The Kitchen is equipped with ample cabinet and counter space

■ Spacious Family Room flows from the Breakfast Bay and is highlighted by a fireplace and a French door to the rear yard

■ The Master Suite is topped by a tray ceiling and is enhanced by a vaulted, five-piece master bath

■ An optional basement, crawl space or slab foundation available — please specify when ordering

First floor — 882 sq. ft.
Second floor — 793 sq. ft.
Bonus room — 416 sq. ft.
Basement — 882 sq. ft.
Garage — 510 sq. ft.

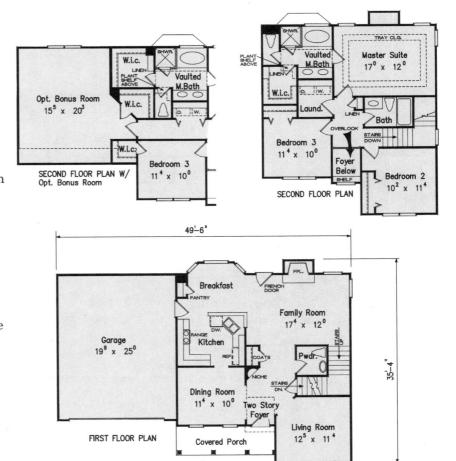

# Elegant and Efficient

■ *Total living area 1,959 sq. ft.* ■ *Price Code D* ■

## No. 92515

■ **This plan features:**

— Three bedrooms

— Two full baths

■ Spacious Den with a decorative ceiling above a hearth fireplace, and French doors

■ Decorative window and ceiling highlight the formal Dining Room

■ Large Kitchen with double ovens, a cooktop and a peninsula snackbar

■ Master Suite with a decorative ceiling, a walk-in closet and a plush bath with a double vanity and a whirlpool tub

■ Two additional bedrooms with walk-in closets share a full bath

■ An optional slab or crawl space foundation — please specify when ordering

Main floor — 1,959 sq. ft.
Garage — 512 sq. ft.

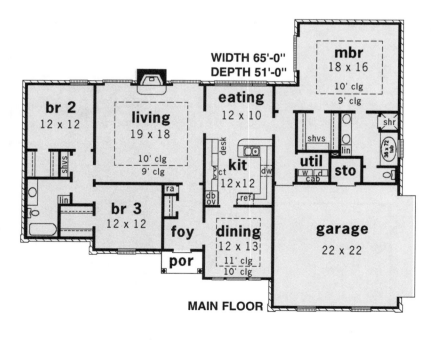

WIDTH 65'-0''
DEPTH 51'-0''

**br 2** 12 x 12

**living** 19 x 18
10' clg
9' clg

**eating** 12 x 10

**mbr** 18 x 16
10' clg
9' clg

shvs
lin
shr

**util**
w d cab

**sto**

**kit** 12 x 12
desk
ct
db ov
ref

**br 3** 12 x 12

**foy**

**dining** 12 x 13
11' clg
10' clg

**garage** 22 x 22

lin
ra

**por**

**MAIN FLOOR**

138

■ *Total living area  2,290 sq. ft.* ■ *Price Code  D* ■

# No. 90467

## This plan features:

– Three bedrooms

– Two full and one half baths

■ The foyer leads to the Living and Dining rooms

■ Large informal area includes the Kitchen, Gathering, and Breakfast rooms

■ The Kitchen features an island bar, Pantry, and a wall oven

■ The home has two fireplaces, in the Great Room and in the Gathering Room

■ The Master Suite features dual walk-in closets and a five-piece bath

■ Two additional bedrooms share a linen closet and a full bath

■ An optional basement or crawl space foundation — please specify when ordering

Main floor — 2,290 sq. ft.
Basement — 2,290 sq. ft.
Bonus — 304 sq. ft.
Garage — 544 sq. ft.

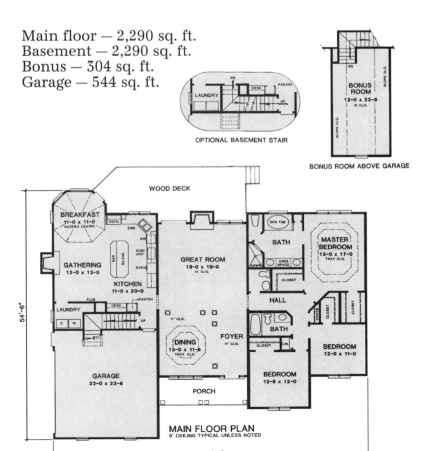

MAIN FLOOR PLAN
9' CEILING TYPICAL UNLESS NOTED

# Colonial Facade Disguises Split Foyer

■ *Total living area  1,704 sq. ft.* ■ *Price Code B* ■

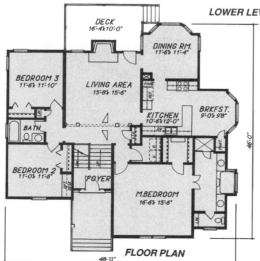

**FLOOR PLAN**

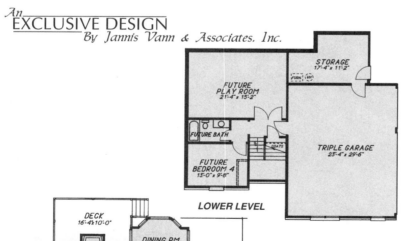

**LOWER LEVEL**

*An*
## EXCLUSIVE DESIGN
*By Jannis Vann & Associates, Inc.*

# No. 93297

■ **This plan features:**

— Three bedrooms

— Two full baths

■ Spacious Kitchen offering all the amenities including a built-in Pantry

■ Bright Breakfast Area and formal Dining Room for informal and formal gatherings

■ Split bedroom design giving Master Suite privacy

■ Spacious Master Bedroom includes a large walk-in closet and a dual vanity master bath

■ Split Foyer design offering an expandable lower level for a growing family

Main floor — 1,672 sq. ft.
Bonus room — 576 sq. ft.
Finished staircase — 32 sq. ft.
Lower level — 192 sq. ft.
Garage — 720 sq. ft.

# Classic Styling

■ *Total living area 2,464 sq. ft.* ■ *Price Code D* ■

## No. 93209

### This plan features:

- Four bedrooms

- Two full and one half baths

■ A wrap-around Porch adding a cozy touch to this classic style

■ A two-story Foyer area that is open to the formal Dining and Living rooms

■ A large Family Room accentuated by columns and a fireplace

■ A sunny Breakfast area with direct access to the Sun Deck, Screen Porch and Kitchen

■ A convenient Kitchen situated between the formal Dining Room and informal Breakfast Area has a Laundry Center and a Pantry

■ A private Deck highlights the Master Suite which includes a luxurious bath and a walk-in closet

*An*
## EXCLUSIVE DESIGN
*By Jannis Vann & Associates, Inc.*

**SECOND FLOOR**

DECK

BEDROOM·4
13'-6" X 11'-6"

MASTER BR.
12'-4" X 17'-6"

M. BATH

BATH·2

BEDROOM·3
13'-6" X 11'-6"

OPEN TO FOYER

BEDROOM·2
13'-6" X 11'-6"

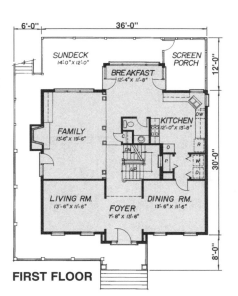

6'-0"    36'-0"

SUNDECK
14'-0" X 12'-0"

BREAKFAST
12'-4" X 11'-8"

SCREEN PORCH

12'-0"

FAMILY
13'-6" X 19'-6"

KITCHEN
12'-0" X 13'-8"

30'-0"

LIVING RM.
13'-6" X 11'-6"

DINING RM.
13'-6" X 11'-6"

FOYER
7'-8" X 13'-6"

8'-0"

**FIRST FLOOR**

First floor — 1,250 sq. ft.
Second floor — 1,166 sq. ft.
Finished stairs — 48 sq. ft.
Basement — 448 sq. ft.
Garage — 706 sq. ft.

# Flexibility to Expand

■ *Total living area  1,831 sq. ft.* ■ *Price Code C* ■

First floor — 1,289 sq. ft.
Second floor — 542 sq. ft.
Bonus room — 393 sq. ft.
Garage & storage — 521 sq. ft.

## No. 99859

■ **This plan features:**

— Three bedrooms

— Two full and one half baths

■ Three-bedroom Country cottage has lots of room to expand

■ Two-story Foyer contains palladian window in a clerestory dormer

■ Efficient Kitchen opens to Breakfast Area and Deck for outdoor dining

■ Columns separating the Great Room and Dining Room which have nine foot ceilings

■ Master Bedroom on the first level features a skylight above the whirlpool tub

■ An optional basement or crawl space foundation — please specify when ordering

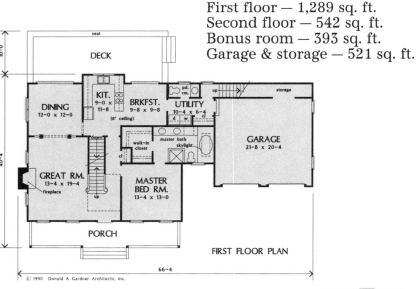

DECK

DINING
12-0 x 12-0

KIT.
9-0 x
11-8
(8' ceiling)

BRKFST.
9-8 x 9-8

pd. rm.

UTILITY
10-4 x 6-4

up

storage

GARAGE
21-8 x 20-4

master bath
skylight

walk-in
closet

GREAT RM.
13-4 x 19-4
fireplace

MASTER
BED RM.
13-4 x 13-0

PORCH

FIRST FLOOR PLAN

seat

10-0

40-4

66-4

© 1990  Donald A Gardner Architects, Inc.

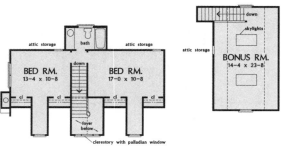

attic storage

bath

attic storage

BED RM.
13-4 x 10-8

BED RM.
17-0 x 10-8

down

cl

cl

cl

cl

foyer
below

clerestory with palladian window

SECOND FLOOR PLAN

down

attic storage

skylights

BONUS RM.
14-4 x 23-8

# Exciting Three-Bedroom

© 1994 Donald A Gardner Architects, Inc.

■ *Total living area 1,787 sq. ft.* ■ *Price Code C* ■

## No. 99805

### This plan features:

- Three bedrooms

- Two full baths

- A Great Room enhanced by a fireplace, cathedral ceiling and built-in bookshelves

- A Kitchen designed for efficiency with a food preparation island and a Pantry

- A Master Suite topped by a cathedral ceiling and pampered by a luxurious bath and a walk-in closet

- Two additional bedrooms, one with a cathedral ceiling and a walk-in closet, sharing a skylit bath

- A second floor Bonus Room, perfect for a Study or a Play Area

- An optional basement or crawl space foundation — please specify when ordering

Main floor — 1,787 sq. ft.
Garage & storage — 521 sq. ft.
Bonus room — 326 sq. ft.

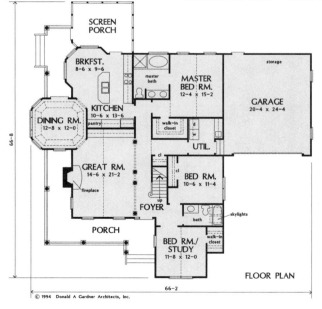

© 1994 Donald A Gardner Architects, Inc.

143

# Compact Plan

© 1996 Donald A. Gardner Architects, In

■ *Total living area 1,372 sq. ft.* ■ *Price Code B* ■

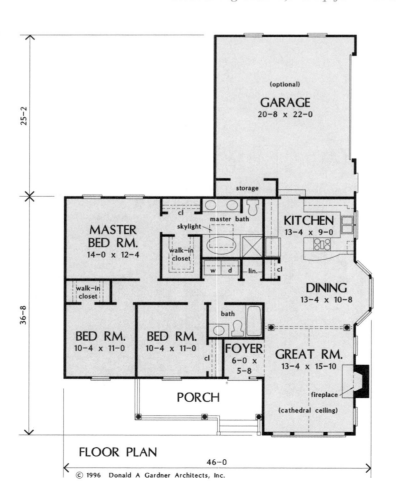

## No. 99830

■ **This plan features:**

— Three bedrooms

— Two full baths

■ A Great Room topped by a cathedral ceiling, combining with the openness of the adjoining Dining Room and Kitchen, to create a spacious living area

■ A bay window enlarging the Dining Room and a palladian window allowing ample light into the Great Room

■ An efficient U-shaped Kitchen leading directly to the Garage, convenient for unloading groceries

■ A Master Suite highlighted by ample closet space and a private skylit bath enhanced by a dual vanity and a separate tub and shower

Main floor — 1,372 sq. ft.
Garage & Storage — 537 sq. ft.

# A Lovely Small Home

■ *Total living area  1,402 sq. ft.* ■ *Price Code  A* ■

## No. 93026

■ **This plan features:**

- Three bedrooms

- Two full baths

■ A large Living Room with a 10'
ceiling

■ A Dining Room with a distinctive
bay window

■ A Breakfast Room located off the
Kitchen

■ A Kitchen with an angled eating
bar that opens the room to the
Living Room

■ A Master Suite with ten foot
ceiling and his-n-her vanities, a
combination whirlpool tub and
shower, plus a huge walk-in closet

■ Two additional bedrooms that
share a full bath

■ No materials list is available for
this plan

Main floor — 1,402 sq. ft.
Garage — 437 sq. ft.

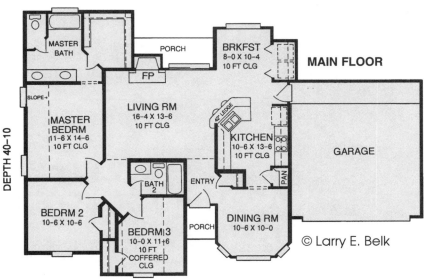

WIDTH 59–10

MAIN FLOOR

DEPTH 40–10

MASTER BATH

PORCH

BRKFST
8-0 X 10-4
10 FT CLG

FP

SLOPE→

MASTER BEDRM
11-6 X 14-6
10 FT CLG

LIVING RM
16-4 X 13-6
10 FT CLG

42" LEDGE

KITCHEN
10-6 X 13-6
10 FT CLG

GARAGE

PAN

BATH 2

BEDRM 2
10-6 X 10-6

ENTRY

BEDRM 3
10-0 X 11-6
10 FT
COFFERED
CLG

PORCH

DINING RM
10-6 X 10-0

© Larry E. Belk

145

# Essence of Style & Grace

■ *Total living area  2,902 sq. ft.* ■ *Price Code E* ■

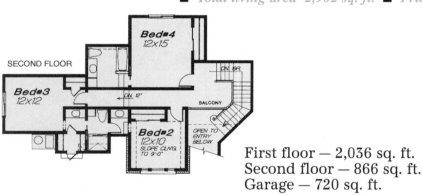

SECOND FLOOR

Bed#4
12x15

Bed#3
12x12

Bed#2
12x10
SLOPE CLNG.
TO 9'-0"

BALCONY

OPEN TO
ENTRY
BELOW

First floor — 2,036 sq. ft.
Second floor — 866 sq. ft.
Garage — 720 sq. ft.

## No. 98524

### ■ This plan features:

— Four bedrooms

— Three full and one half baths

■ French doors introduce Study and
columns define the Gallery and
formal areas

■ The expansive Family Room with
an inviting fireplace and a
cathedral ceiling opens to the
Kitchen

■ The Kitchen features a cooktop
island, butler's Pantry, Breakfast
Area and Patio access

■ The first floor Master Bedroom
offers a private Patio, vaulted
ceiling, twin vanities and a walk-
in closet

■ No materials list is available for
this plan

■ An optional basement or slab
foundation — please specify when
ordering

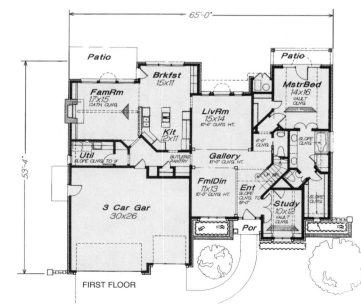

FIRST FLOOR

# Country Living in a Doll House

## No. 90410

**This plan features:**

- Three bedrooms
- Two full and one half baths
- An eat-in country Kitchen with an island counter and bay window
- A spacious Great Room with a fireplace flowing easily into the Dining area
- A first floor Master Suite including a walk-in closet and a private compartmentalized bath
- Two additional bedrooms sharing a full bath with a double vanity
- An optional basement or crawl space foundation — please specify when ordering

First floor — 1,277 sq. ft.
Second floor — 720 sq. ft.

*Total living area  1,997 sq. ft.*  ■  *Price Code  C*

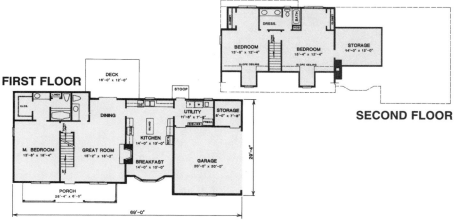

**FIRST FLOOR**

**SECOND FLOOR**

# Luxurious One Floor Living

## No. 92273

**This plan features:**

- Four bedrooms
- Three full baths
- Decorative windows enhance front entrance of elegant home
- Formal Living Room accented by fireplace between windows overlooking rear yard
- Formal Dining Room highlighted by decorative window
- Breakfast bar, work island, and an abundance of storage and counter space featured in Kitchen
- Bright alcove for informal Dining and Family Room with access to covered Patio adjoin Kitchen
- Spacious Master Bedroom with access to covered Patio, a lavish bath and huge walk-in closet
- Three additional bedrooms with large closets and private access to a full bath
- No materials list is available for this plan

Main floor — 3,254 sq. ft.
Garage — 588 sq. ft.

*Total living area  3,254 sq. ft.*  ■  *Price Code  F*

Main Floor

# Rich Elegance

■ *Total living area 2,045 sq. ft.* ■ *Price Code D* ■

**MAIN FLOOR**

## No. 92514 ✕

■ **This plan features:**

— Three bedrooms

— Two full baths

■ A popular split bedroom floor plan affording maximum privacy

■ The formal Dining Room is found to the right of the entrance and accesses the Kitchen

■ The Great Room in the rear features a vaulted ceiling, a fireplace and cabinets with book shelves on the right

■ There are two oversized secondary bedrooms with walk-in closets and access to a bath

■ The Master Bedroom comes with his-n-her walk-in closets and a compartmentalized bath

■ An optional crawl space or slab foundation — please specify when ordering

Main floor — 2,045 sq. ft.
Garage — 541 sq. ft.

# A Touch of Victorian Styling

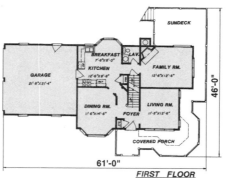

■ *Total living area 1,764 sq. ft.* ■ *Price Code B* ■

**SECOND FLOOR**

**FIRST FLOOR**

## No. 93230

■ **This plan features:**

— Three bedrooms

— Two full and one half baths

■ A covered Porch and a pointed roof on the sitting alcove of the Master Suite giving this home a Victorian look

■ A formal Living Room directly across from the Dining Room for ease in entertaining

■ An efficient Kitchen with a bright bayed Breakfast Area

■ The Family Room has a cozy fireplace nestled in a corner

■ A large Master Suite with a cozy sitting alcove and double vanity bath

■ Two additional bedrooms serviced by a full hall bath

■ No materials list is available for this plan

First floor — 887 sq. ft.
Second floor — 877 sq. ft.
Basement — 859 sq. ft.
Garage — 484 sq. ft.

*An* **EXCLUSIVE DESIGN**
*By Jannis Vann & Associates, Inc.*

# A Modern Look At Colonial Styling

■ *Total living area 2,024 sq. ft.* ■ *Price Code C* ■

## No. 93287

### ■ This plan features:

— Three bedrooms

— Two full and one half baths

■ Brick detailing and keystones highlight elevation

■ Two-story Foyer opens to formal Living and Dining rooms

■ Expansive Family Room with a hearth fireplace between built-in shelves and Deck access

■ U-shaped Kitchen with serving counter, Breakfast alcove, and nearby Garage entry

■ Elegant Master Bedroom with a decorative ceiling, large walk-in closet and a double vanity bath

■ Two additional bedrooms share a full bath, laundry and Bonus area

First floor — 987 sq. ft.
Second floor — 965 sq. ft.
Finished staircase — 72 sq. ft.
Bonus — 272 sq. ft.
Basement — 899 sq. ft.

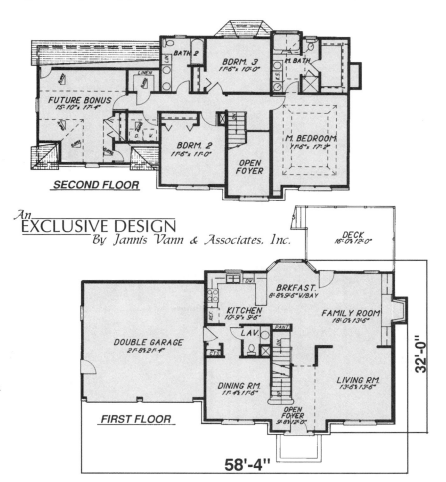

*An* EXCLUSIVE DESIGN *By Jannis Vann & Associates, Inc.*

149

# Three Bedroom Ranch

■ *Total living area  1,575 sq. ft.* ■ *Price Code B* ■

## No. 98414

### ■ This plan features:

— Three bedrooms

— Two full baths

■ Formal Dining Room enhanced by a plant shelf and a side window

■ Wetbar located between the Kitchen and the Dining Room

■ Built-in Pantry, a double sink and a snack bar highlight the Kitchen

■ Breakfast Room containing a radius window and a French door to the rear yard

■ Large cozy fireplace framed by windows in the Great Room

■ Master Suite with a vaulted ceiling over the sitting area, a Master Bath and a walk-in closet

■ An optional basement or crawl space foundation available — please specify when ordering

Main floor — 1,575 sq. ft.
Garage — 459 sq. ft.
Basement — 1,658 sq. ft.

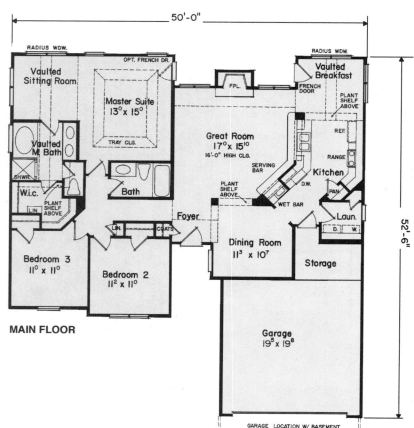

# A Home with Tremendous Appeal

## No. 98535

**This plan features:**

- Four bedrooms

- Three full and one half baths

- A European country exterior with a modern American interior

- The circular stairway highlights the entry

- The formal Dining Room has a bay window and easy access to the Kitchen

- A private Study with a double door entry

- Formal Living Room has a fireplace and elegant columns

- The large Family Room boasts a large brick fireplace and a built-in TV cabinet

- An angled Kitchen contains all the conveniences that the cook demands

- A large informal dining area that is adjacent to the Kitchen

- The Master Suite occupies one wing of the house with a bath and a huge walk-in closet

- No materials list is available for this plan

Main floor — 2,658 sq. ft.
Upper floor — 854 sq. ft.
Garage — 660 sq. ft.

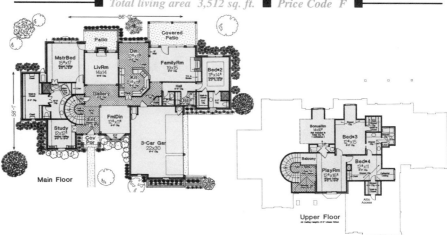

■ *Total living area  3,512 sq. ft.* ■ *Price Code  F* ■

Main Floor

Upper Floor

# Design is Clean and Convenient

## No. 93231

**This plan features:**

- Three bedrooms

- Two full baths

- Arched entrance into Foyer and central Living Area with fireplace and access to Patio/Sundeck

- Kitchen with peninsula counter/snackbar, convenient to formal Dining Room, Breakfast alcove, Laundry and Garage entry

- Private Master Bedroom with decorative ceiling, walk-in closet and lavish bath with corner whirlpool tub and two vanities

- Two additional bedrooms share a double vanity bath

- An optional crawl space or slab foundation — please specify when ordering

- No materials list is available for this plan

Main floor — 1,781 sq. ft.
Garage — 558 sq. ft.

■ *Total living area  1,781 sq. ft.* ■ *Price Code  B* ■

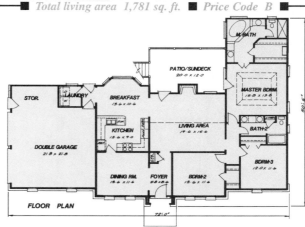

FLOOR PLAN

# Comfortable Family Living

■ *Total living area 1,553 sq. ft.* ■ *Price Code B*

**WIDTH 44'-0"**
**DEPTH 40'-0"**

**FIRST FLOOR**

**LOWER FLOOR**

*An* EXCLUSIVE DESIGN
*By Jannis Vann & Associates. Inc.*

## No. 93280

■ **This plan features:**

— Three bedrooms

— Two full baths

■ A terrific Master Suite with two walk-in closets and a private master bath

■ Two additional bedrooms that are at the opposite end of the house and share a full hall bath

■ A future lower level plan for a bedroom, bath and Playroom

■ A large Living Area sporting a focal point fireplace and access to the wood Deck

■ A bay window adding elegance to the formal Dining Room

■ A modern, well-appointed Kitchen that includes a peninsula counter/eating bar and a Breakfast Nook

First floor — 1,521 sq. ft.
Finished staircase — 32 sq. ft.
Basement — 576 sq. ft.
Garage — 620 sq. ft.

# Style and Much More

■ *Total living area 1,800 sq. ft.* ■ *Price Code B*

## No. 98446

■ **This plan features:**

— Three bedrooms

— Two full and one half baths

■ The Foyer is accented by arched openings into the Dining and Living rooms

■ The Dining Room has direct access to the Kitchen for ease in serving

■ The Kitchen includes a serving bar to the family room and an easy flow into the Breakfast Bay

■ The Family Room is accented by fireplace and French door to the rear yard

■ A tray ceiling decorates the Master Suite while a vaulted ceiling highlights the master bath

■ Two additional bedrooms share the full hall bath

■ An optional basement or crawl space foundation — please specify when ordering

■ No materials list is available for this plan

First floor — 1,039 sq. ft.
Second floor — 761 sq. ft.
Bonus — 424 sq. ft.
Basement — 1,039 sq. ft.
Garage — 465 sq. ft.

# Enhanced by a Columned Porch

■ *Total living area  1,754 sq. ft.* ■ *Price Code  C* ■

# No. 92531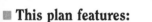

## ■ This plan features:

— Three bedrooms

— Two full baths

■ A Great Room with a fireplace and decorative ceiling

■ A large efficient Kitchen with Breakfast Area

■ A Master Bedroom with a private master bath and walk-in closet

■ A formal Dining Room conveniently located near the Kitchen

■ Two additional bedrooms with walk-in closets and use of full hall bath

■ An optional crawl space or slab foundation available — please specify when ordering

Main floor — 1,754 sq. ft.
Garage — 552 sq. ft.

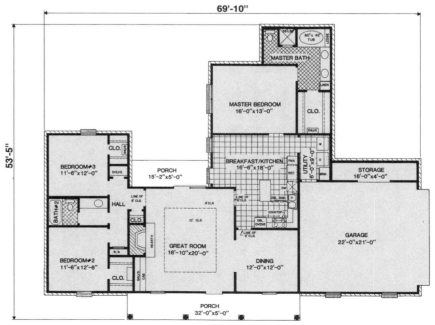

**MAIN FLOOR**

# Regal Residence

■ *Total living area  3,039 sq. ft.* ■ *Price Code  F* ■

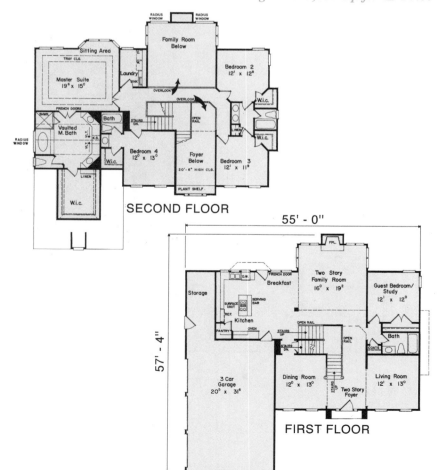

SECOND FLOOR

FIRST FLOOR

## No. 98405

■ **This plan features:**

— Five bedrooms

— Four full baths

■ Keystone, arched windows accent entrance into two-story Foyer

■ Spacious two-story Family Room enhanced by a fireplace

■ Kitchen with a cooktop island/ serving bar and a walk-in Pantry

■ First floor Guest Room/Study with roomy closet and adjoining full bath

■ Luxurious Master Suite offers a tray ceiling, Sitting Area, a huge walk-in closet and a vaulted bath

■ An optional basement or crawl space foundation — please specify when ordering

First floor — 1,488 sq. ft.
Second floor — 1,551 sq. ft.
Basement — 1,488 sq. ft.
Garage — 667 sq. ft.

# Attractive Ranch

## No. 93235

**This plan features:**

– Three bedrooms

– One full and one three-quarter baths

– The large Living Room has a rear wall fireplace and access to the rear Sundeck

– The Kitchen straddles the formal Dining Room and the Breakfast Nook

– Included in the Kitchen are a cooktop, angled counter and a pantry

– The Master Bedroom and the second bedroom both have bay windows on their rear walls

– This home has been designed with plenty of closet space and a large Laundry Room

– In the rear there is a screen Porch and a Sundeck for outdoor entertaining

– No materials list is available for this plan

Main floor — 2,005 sq. ft.
Basement — 1,947 sq. ft.
Garage — 484 sq. ft.

*An*
**EXCLUSIVE DESIGN**
*By Jannis Vann & Associates, Inc.*

■ *Total living area  2,005 sq. ft.*  ■  *Price Code  C*  ■

**FLOOR PLAN**

# Simple Style with Classic Accents

## No. 92286

**This plan features:**

– Three bedrooms

– Two full baths

– Sheltered entry leads into busy living areas

– Spacious Living Room with cozy fireplace and access to rear yard

– An efficient Kitchen with a bright Dining Area next to Utilities and Garage entry

– Two walk-in closets and a plush private bath offered in Master Bedroom

– Two additional bedrooms with ample closets share a double vanity

– No materials list is available for this plan

Main floor — 1,415 sq. ft.
Garage — 440 sq. ft.

■ *Total living area  1,415 sq. ft.*  ■  *Price Code  A*  ■

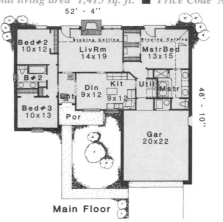

**Main Floor**

# Stately Columns and Keystones

■ Total living area 3,029 sq. ft. ■ Price Code E ■

**An EXCLUSIVE DESIGN By Garrell Associates Inc.**

## No. 93603

■ **This plan features:**

— Four bedrooms

— Three full and one half baths

■ Gracious two-story Foyer opens to vaulted Living Room and arched Dining Room

■ Expansive, two-story Grand Room with impressive fireplace between outdoor views

■ Spacious and efficient Kitchen with a work island, Breakfast area with backyard access, and nearby Laundry/Garage entry

■ Private Master Bedroom offers a decorative ceiling, two walk-in closets and vanities, and a garden window tub

■ Three second floor bedrooms with great closets, share two full baths

■ No materials list is available for this plan

First floor — 2,115 sq. ft.
Second floor — 914 sq. ft.
Basement — 2,115 sq. ft.
Garage — 448 sq. ft.

---

# Sensational Entry

■ Total living area 4,362 sq. ft. ■ Price Code F ■

## No. 98404

■ **This plan features:**

— Four bedrooms

— Three full and one half baths

■ Grand columns frame two-story Portico

■ Two-story Living Room accented by columns and a massive fireplace

■ Vaulted Family Room highlighted by outdoor views and a cozy fireplace

■ Ideal Kitchen with a cooktop island/serving bar

■ Secluded Master Suite offers a vaulted Sitting Area with radius windows

■ Three second floor bedrooms with walk-in closets and private access to full baths

■ An optional basement or crawl space foundation — please specify when ordering

First floor — 2,764 sq. ft.
Second floor — 1,598 sq. ft.
Basement — 2,764 sq. ft.
Garage — 743 sq. ft.

# Executive Home

© 1994 Donald A. Gardner Architects, Inc.

■ *Total living area  2,211 sq. ft.* ■ *Price Code  D* ■

## No. 96449

### ■ This home features:

- Three bedrooms

- Two full baths

■ Exciting roof lines and brick detailing fit in the finest neighborhood

■ Open Kitchen assures great cooks lots of company

■ Large Deck easily accessible from Breakfast area, Great Room and Master Bedroom

■ Great Room also offers cathedral ceiling above arched windows and fireplace nestled between built-ins

■ Private Master Suite features walk-in closet and plush bath with twin vanities, shower and corner window tub

Main floor — 2,211 sq. ft.
Bonus room — 408 sq. ft.
Garage & storage — 700 sq. ft.

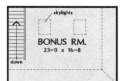

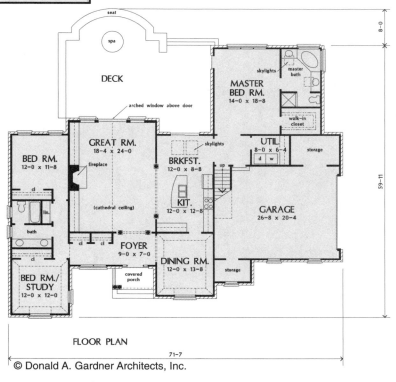

FLOOR PLAN

© Donald A. Gardner Architects, Inc.

# Great Room is Heart of Home

■ *Total living area 1,087 sq. ft.* ■ *Price Code A* ■

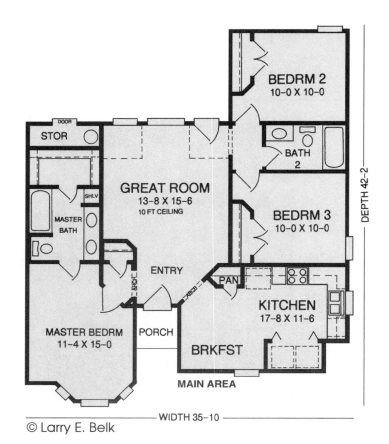

STOR

GREAT ROOM
13-8 X 15-6
10 FT CEILING

MASTER
BATH

SHLV

BEDRM 2
10-0 X 10-0

BATH
2

BEDRM 3
10-0 X 10-0

ENTRY

PAN

KITCHEN
17-8 X 11-6

MASTER BEDRM
11-4 X 15-0

PORCH

BRKFST

DEPTH 42-2

**MAIN AREA**

WIDTH 35-10

© Larry E. Belk

## No. 93015

■ **This plan features:**

— Three bedrooms

— Two full baths

■ Sheltered Porch leads into the entry with arches and a Great Room

■ Spacious Great Room with a ten foot ceiling above a wall of windows and rear yard access

■ Efficient Kitchen with a built-in pantry, a laundry closet and a Breakfast Area accented by a decorative window

■ Bay of windows enhances the Master Bedroom which contains a double vanity bath and a walk-in closet

■ Two additional bedrooms with ample closets share a full bath

■ No materials list is available for this plan

Main area — 1,087 sq. ft.

# Lasting Elegance

## No. 92508

**This plan features:**

- Four bedrooms
- Three full and one half baths
- Rich lines, bays and detailed window treatments add lasting elegance to this home
- Large Foyer leads directly into huge den with hearth fireplace and built-ins
- Both the Living and Dining Rooms have bays which add style and character
- The convenient U-shaped Kitchen is fully complimented and opens into a Nook
- The large first floor Master Suite is second to none and features a private bath
- Upstairs find three bedrooms and two full baths
- An optional crawl space or slab foundation — please specify when ordering

First floor — 2,008 sq. ft.
Second floor — 943 sq. ft.
Garage — 556 sq. ft.

■ *Total living area 2,951 sq. ft.* ■ *Price Code F* ■

FIRST FLOOR PLAN

SECOND FLOOR PLAN

# Two-Story Glass Entry

## No. 93013

**This plan features:**

- Three bedrooms
- Two full and one half baths
- A Living Room and Dining Room with openings defined by traditional square columns
- A large fireplace to add warmth and interest to the Living Room
- An ample Kitchen with cook top island, built-in pantry, angled double sink, and eating bar
- A Master Suite with a lavish Master Bath equipped with oval tub, step-in shower, and double vanity
- Two additional bedrooms with walk-in closets that share a full hall bath
- No materials list is available for this plan

First floor — 1,831 sq. ft.
Second floor — 632 sq. ft.
Garage — 525 sq. ft.
Width 50'-7"
Depth 66'-2"

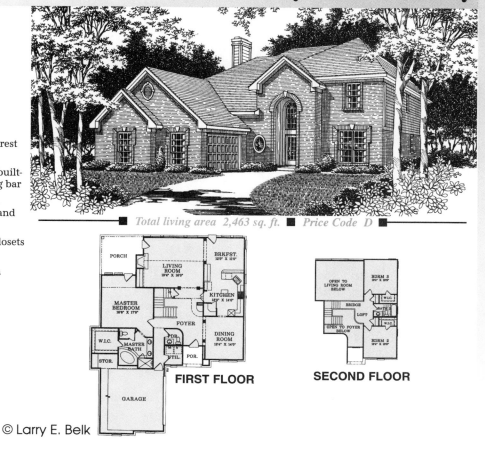

■ *Total living area 2,463 sq. ft.* ■ *Price Code D* ■

FIRST FLOOR

SECOND FLOOR

© Larry E. Belk

# Charming Style

*Total living area 1,372 sq. ft.* ■ *Price Code A* ■

**MAIN FLOOR**

## No. 96510

■ **This plan features:**

— Three bedrooms

— Two full baths

■ Tiled Foyer giving way to a welcoming Living Room highlighted by cozy fireplace

■ Living Room and Dining Area adjoin creating the feeling of more space

■ An efficient galley-styled Kitchen with direct access to the Utility Room and the dining area

■ Private Master Suite containing a walk-in closet and a private double vanity bath

■ Two additional bedrooms located in close proximity to the full bath in the hall

Main floor — 1,372 sq. ft.
Garage — 465 sq. ft.

# Casual Family Living

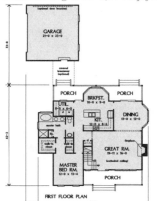

© 1997 Donald A. Gardner Architects, Inc.

*Total living area 1,794 sq. ft.* ■ *Price Code C* ■

SECOND FLOOR PLAN

FIRST FLOOR PLAN
© 1997 Donald A. Gardner Architects, Inc.

## No. 96427

■ **This plan features:**

— Three bedrooms

— Two full baths

■ Country style front Porch offering attractiv curb appeal

■ Spacious Great Room sporting a cathedral ceiling and a fireplace

■ Dining Room with a bay window and open layout with the great room accessing the back Porch directly

■ Sunny and efficient Kitchen including a snack bar and bright Breakfast Bay

■ First floor Master Suite with his and her walk-in closets and private access to a full bath

■ Two additional bedrooms and a full bath o the second floor

First floor — 1,329 sq. ft.
Second floor — 465 sq. ft.
Garage — 513 sq. ft.

© 1995 Donald A Gardner Architects, Inc.

■ *Total living area  1,246 sq. ft.* ■ *Price Code  B* ■

# No. 99806 ⚒

## ■ This plan features:

- Three bedrooms
- Two full baths
- ■ Great Room topped by a cathedral ceiling and enhanced by a fireplace
- ■ Great Room, Dining Room and Kitchen open to each other for a feeling of spaciousness
- ■ Pantry, skylight and peninsula counter add to the comfort and efficiency of the Kitchen
- ■ Cathedral ceiling crowns the Master Suite and has these amenities; walk-in and linen closet, a luxurious private bath
- ■ Swing Room, Bedroom or Study, topped by a cathedral ceiling
- ■ Skylight over full hall bath naturally illuminates the room

Main floor — 1,246 sq. ft.
Garage — 420 sq. ft.

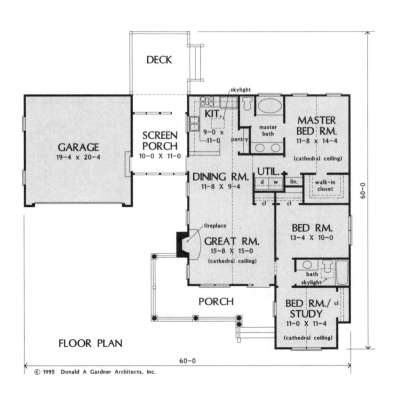

DECK

GARAGE
19-4 x 20-4

SCREEN PORCH
10-0 X 11-0

KIT.
9-0 x
11-0

skylight

pantry

master bath

MASTER BED RM.
11-8 x 14-4
(cathedral ceiling)

DINING RM.
11-8 X 9-4

UTIL.
d  w
lin.

walk-in closet

cl   cl

fireplace

GREAT RM.
15-8 X 15-0
(cathedral ceiling)

BED RM.
13-4 X 10-0

bath
skylight

PORCH

BED RM./ STUDY
11-0 X 11-4
(cathedral ceiling)

cl

FLOOR PLAN

60-0

60-0

© 1995  Donald A Gardner Architects, Inc.

# Grand Country Porch

**Total living area  2,665 sq. ft.** ■ *Price Code E* ■

## No. 94615

### ■ This plan features:

— Four bedrooms

— Three full baths

■ Large front Porch provides shade and Southern hospitality

■ Spacious Living Room with access to Covered Porch and Patio, and a cozy fireplace between built-in shelves

■ Country Kitchen with a cooktop island, bright Breakfast bay, Utility Room and Garage entry

■ Corner Master Bedroom with a walk-in closet and private bath

■ First floor bedroom with private access to a full bath

■ Two second floor bedrooms with dormers, walk-in closets and separate vanities, share a full bath

■ An optional crawl space or slab foundation — please specify when ordering

■ No materials list is available for this plan

First floor — 1,916 sq. ft.
Second floor — 749 sq. ft.
Garage — 479 sq. ft.

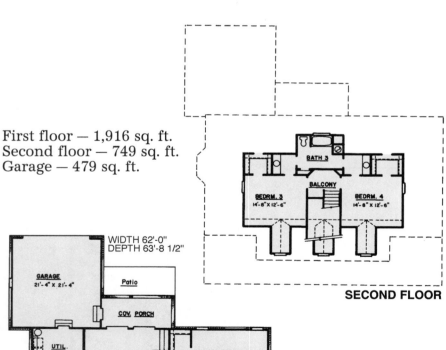

**SECOND FLOOR**

**FIRST FLOOR**

# Classic Colonial

## No. 90469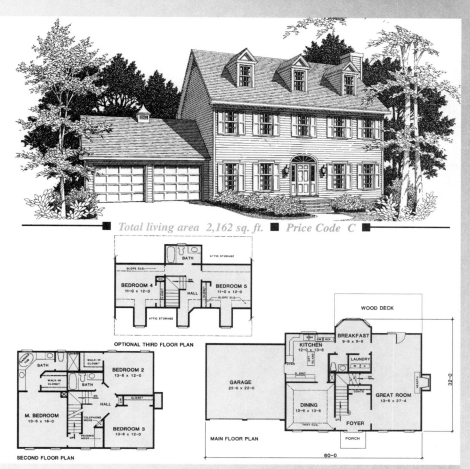

**This plan features:**

- Three bedrooms
- Two full and one half baths
- Colonial with room for expansion comes with an optional five bedrooms plan
- Great Room features fireplace and access to the rear Deck
- Dining Room with a tray ceiling is convenient to the Kitchen
- Breakfast bay adjoins L-shaped Kitchen which includes a center island
- Second floor Master Suite has a luxurious bath with a garden tub
- Two secondary bedrooms share a full bath
- An optional basement or crawl space foundation — please specify when ordering

First floor — 1,098 sq. ft.
Second floor — 1,064 sq. ft.
Basement — 1,098 sq. ft.
Garage — 484 sq. ft.

■ *Total living area  2,162 sq. ft.* ■ *Price Code  C* ■

# Not Your Typical Ranch

## No. 99855

**This plan features:**

- Three bedrooms
- Two full baths
- The covered front entry reveals a door with sidelights
- Past the Foyer is the Great Room which is highlighted by a cathedral ceiling, skylights and a fireplace
- The Dining Room has windows that overlook the rear Deck
- The Kitchen has a center island with a cooktop and is open to the Breakfast Bay
- The Master Bedroom has a walk-in closet, a whirlpool bath, and a private covered Deck
- Two more bedrooms in the front of the home have access to a full bath in the hall
- This home has a two-car Garage

Main floor — 1,817 sq. ft.
Garage — 413 sq. ft.

■ *Total living area  1,817 sq. ft.* ■ *Price Code  C* ■

163

# Exceptional Family Living

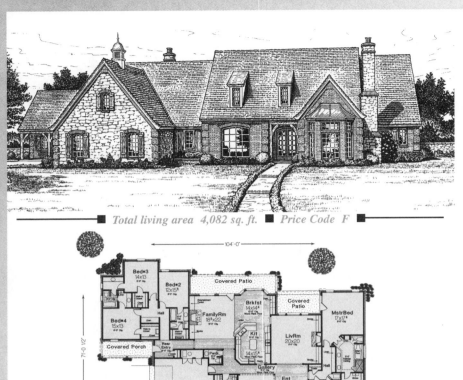

■ *Total living area  4,082 sq. ft.* ■ *Price Code  F* ■

Floor Plan

## No. 98538

■ **This plan features:**

— Four bedrooms

— Three full and one half baths

■ A decorative dormer, a bay window and an eyebrow arched window provide for a pleasing country farmhouse facade

■ The cozy Study has its own fireplace and a bay window

■ The large formal Living Room has a fireplace and built-in bookcases

■ The huge island Kitchen is open to the Breakfast Bay and the Family Room

■ The Master Suite includes a large bath with a unique closet

■ Three more bedrooms located at the other end of the home each have private access to a full bath

■ No materials list is available for this plan

Main floor — 4,082 sq. ft.
Garage — 720 sq. ft.

# Stucco and Brick

■ *Total living area  3,504 sq. ft.* ■ *Price Code  F* ■

FIRST FLOOR PLAN

SECOND FLOOR PLAN

## No. 92505

■ **This plan features:**

— Four bedrooms

— Three full and one half baths

■ A unique facade

■ A grand Foyer with an open staircase, two story ceiling and a magnificent balcony

■ An expansive, two-story Den, with highlights such as a two-story fireplace

■ Kitchen that includes a cooktop snackbar, a built-in pantry, and a separate Breakfast area

■ A private Sitting Area with a vaulted ceiling provides quiet moments in the Master Suite

■ A master bath with his-n-her walk-in closets separate vanities and linen closets

■ An optional crawl space or slab foundation — please specify when ordering

First floor — 2,442 sq. ft.
Second floor — 1,062 sq. ft.
Garage — 565 sq. ft.

# Open Plan is Full of Air & Light

■ *Total living area  1,505 sq. ft.* ■ *Price Code  B* ■

# No. 98463

■ **This plan features:**

– Three bedrooms

– Two full and one half baths

■ Foyer open to the Family Room and highlighted by a fireplace

■ Dining Room with a sliding glass door to rear yard adjoins Family Room

■ Kitchen and Nook in an efficient open layout

■ Second floor Master Suite topped by tray ceiling over the bedroom and a vaulted ceiling over the lavish bath

■ Two additional bedrooms sharing a full bath in the hall

■ An optional basement or crawl space foundation — please specify when ordering

■ No materials list is available for this plan

First floor — 767 sq. ft.
Second floor — 738 sq. ft.
Bonus room — 240 sq. ft.
Basement — 767 sq. ft.
Garage — 480 sq. ft.

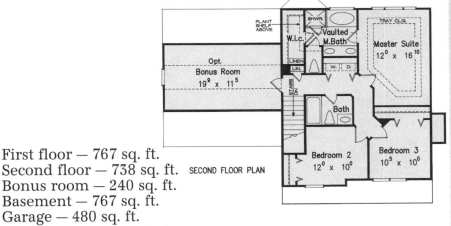

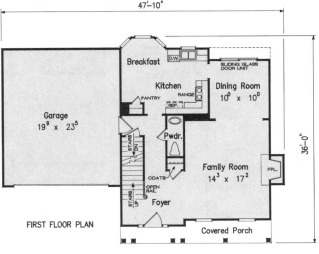

# Rear of Home as Attractive as Front

■ *Total living area 2,440 sq. ft.* ■ *Price Code D* ■

**SECOND FLOOR**

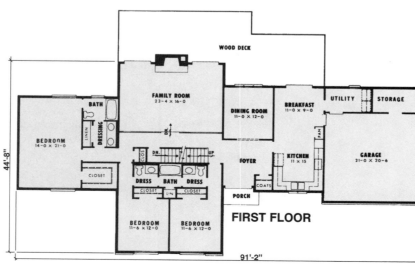

**FIRST FLOOR**

## No. 90413

■ **This plan features:**

— Three bedrooms

— Two full and one half baths

■ A sunken Family Room with a cathedral ceiling and a stone fireplace

■ Two front bedrooms sharing a unique bath-and-a-half arrangement

■ A Master Bedroom with a compartmentalized bath, a double vanity and linen closet

■ A U-shaped Kitchen, serving the Breakfast Nook and the formal Dining Room with ease

■ A second floor with a large Studio

■ An optional basement or crawl space foundation — please specify when ordering

First floor — 2,192 sq. ft.
Second floor — 248 sq. ft.
Basement — 2,192 sq. ft.

# Narrow Lot Home

## No. 99884

**This plan features:**

– Three bedrooms

– Two full and one half baths

■ Double gables and a porch with a hip roof giving this narrow lot home a storybook look

■ Deck at the rear expanding living and entertaining space from the Great Room

■ Great Room opens to the center island Kitchen with pantry

■ Formal Dining Room accented by columns, located directly off the Foyer

■ Second floor Master Suite placed for utmost privacy with separate shower, garden tub and double vanity

■ Two additional bedrooms sharing a full bath

First floor — 875 sq. ft.
Second floor — 814 sq. ft.
Garage & storage — 317 sq. ft.

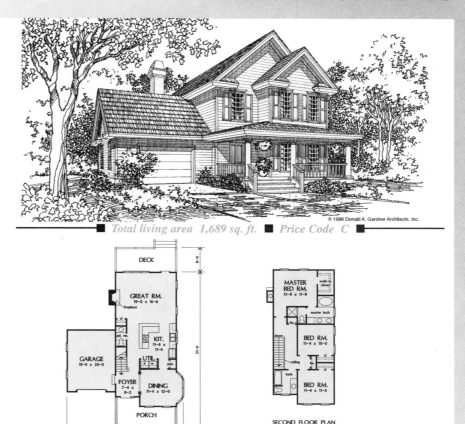

■ *Total living area  1,689 sq. ft.* ■ *Price Code  C* ■

© 1996 Donald A. Gardner Architects, Inc.

FIRST FLOOR PLAN

SECOND FLOOR PLAN

© 1996 Donald A Gardner Architects, Inc.

# Spacious Family Areas

## No. 93220

**This plan features:**

– Three bedrooms

– Two full and one half baths

■ Two-story Foyer with landing staircase leads to formal Living and Dining Rooms

■ Open layout for Kitchen/Breakfast area and Family Room offers a spacious feeling and easy interaction

■ Efficient Kitchen with cooktop peninsula, built-in pantry and a glassed Breakfast area

■ Comfortable Family Room with a focal point fireplace and a wall of windows with access to Sundeck

■ Master Bedroom enhanced by decorative ceiling and French doors into private bath and walk-in closet

■ An optional basement, slab or crawl space foundation — please specify when ordering

First floor — 902 sq. ft.
Second floor — 819 sq. ft.
Bonus room — 210 sq. ft.
Finished staircase — 28 sq. ft.
Basement — 874 sq. ft.
Garage — 400 sq. ft.

■ *Total living area  1,749 sq. ft.* ■ *Price Code  B* ■

FIRST FLOOR

SECOND FLOOR

*An*
EXCLUSIVE DESIGN
*By Jannis Vann & Associates, Inc.*

# Unique Keeping Room

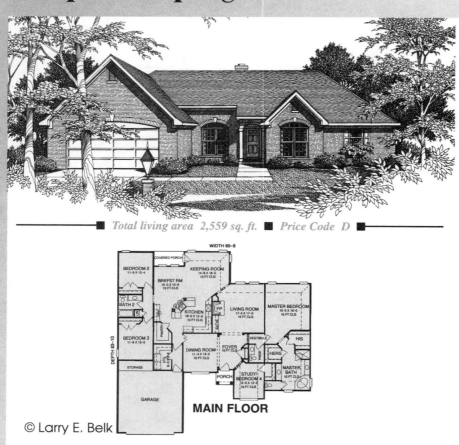

■ *Total living area  2,559 sq. ft.* ■ *Price Code  D* ■

© Larry E. Belk

**MAIN FLOOR**

## No. 93059

■ **This plan features:**

— Four bedrooms

— Two full and one half baths

■ Sheltered Porch and an open Foyer lead into the Dining and Living Rooms with 10' ceilings

■ Huge fireplace, built-ins and windows overlooking the rear yard highlight the Living Room

■ Open, efficient Kitchen with an island counter/serving bar, a walk-in pantry, a built-in desk, a Utility Room and a Garage

■ Spacious Keeping/Breakfast rooms adjoin the Kitchen and access the Covered Porch

■ Private Master Bedroom with his-n-her closets and a master bath with two vanities and a corner whirlpool tub

■ Two additional bedrooms with large closets, share a full bath

■ Walk-in closet in the Study/Bedroom, which offers many options

■ An optional slab or crawl space foundation available — please specify when ordering

■ No materials list is available for this plan

Main floor — 2,559 sq. ft.
Garage — 544 sq. ft.

# Distinguished Styling

■ *Total living area 2,354  sq. ft.* ■ *Price Code  D* ■

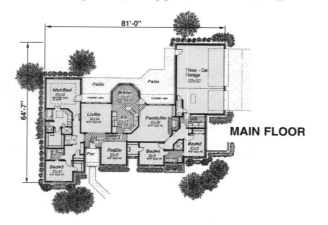

**MAIN FLOOR**

## No. 92289

■ **This plan features:**

— Four bedrooms

— Two full and one three-quarter baths

■ Brick quoins, segmented arches, plus oval and fan shaped windows create a distinguished style

■ The Family Room has a cozy fireplace and flows into the Breakfast Bay

■ The Living Room and the Family Room both access the rear Patio

■ The formal Dining Room is steps away from the gourmet Kitchen

■ The Master Bedroom features a vaulted ceiling, a walk-in closet and a private bath

■ There are three additional bedrooms and a full and a three-quarter bath

■ This plan has a three-car Garage

■ No materials list is available for this plan

Main floor — 2,354 sq. ft.
Garage — 704 sq. ft.

■ *Total living area  1,884 sq. ft.* ■ *Price Code  C* ■

# No. 98430

■ **This plan features:**

– Three bedrooms

– Two full and one half baths

■ Arched openings highlight the hallway accessing the Great Room

■ A French door to the rear yard and decorative columns at its arched entrance

■ Another vaulted ceiling topping the Dining Room

■ An expansive Kitchen features a center work island, a built-in pantry and a Breakfast Area

■ A Master Suite also has a tray ceiling treatment and has a lavish private bath

■ An optional basement, slab or crawl space foundation — please specify when ordering

Main floor — 1,884 sq. ft.
Basement — 1,908 sq. ft.
Garage — 495 sq. ft.

# Exterior Shows Attention to Detail

■ *Total living area  2,165 sq. ft.* ■ *Price Code D* ■

## No. 94811

■ **This plan features:**

—Three bedrooms

—Two full and one half baths

■ Privately located Master Suite is complimented by a luxurious bath with two walk-in closets

■ Two additional bedrooms have ample closet space and share a full bath

■ The Activity Room has a sloped ceiling, large fireplace and is accented with columns

■ Access to Sundeck from the Dining Room

■ The island Kitchen and Breakfast Area have access to Garage for ease when bringing in groceries

Main floor — 2,165 sq. ft.
Garage — 484 sq. ft.
Basement — 2,165 sq. ft.

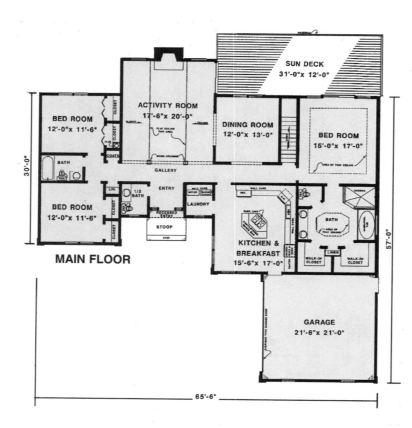

**MAIN FLOOR**

# Elegantly Styled

## No. 98449 

**This plan features:**

- Three bedrooms
- Two full and one half baths
- Architectural details create eye-catching appeal to this home's facade
- The two-story Foyer is flanked by the formal Living and Dining rooms
- A convenient Kitchen with angled snack bar has easy access to the Dining Room, Breakfast Area, backyard and the Laundry/ Garage
- Open and comfortable, the Family Room is highlighted by a fireplace and windows
- The Master Bedroom suite is enhanced by a tray ceiling and a plush bath with a vaulted ceiling
- The second floor offers an optional Bonus Room for future expansion
- An optional basement or crawl space foundation — please specify when ordering

First floor — 922 sq. ft.
Second floor — 778 sq. ft.
Bonus Room — 369 sq. ft.
Basement — 922 sq. ft.
Garage & storage — 530 sq. ft.

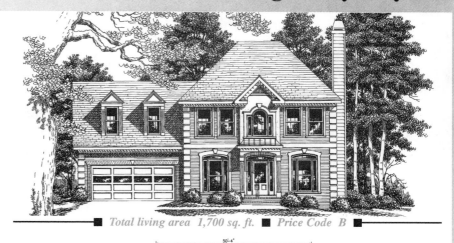

■ *Total living area  1,700 sq. ft.* ■ *Price Code  B* ■

# Uncommon Brickwork Enhances Facade

## No. 92207

**This plan features:**

- Four bedrooms
- Three full and one half baths
- Sheltered Porch leads into Entry and spacious Living Room with pool access
- Quiet Study with focal point fireplace and open formal Dining Room
- Expansive Kitchen with cooktop work island, efficiently serves Breakfast Nook, Patio and Dining Room
- Master Bedroom wing offers a vaulted ceiling, two walk-in closets and a corner window tub
- Three second floor bedrooms share two full baths
- No materials list is available for this plan

First floor — 2,304 sq. ft.
Second floor — 852 sq. ft.
Garage — 690 sq. ft.

■ *Total living area  3,156 sq. ft.* ■ *Price Code  E* ■

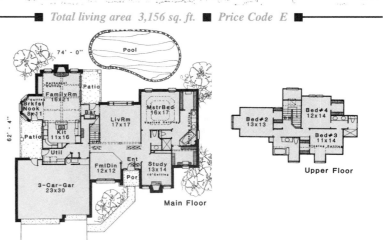

# Reminiscent of the Deep South

■ *Total living area  1,939 sq. ft.* ■ *Price Code  C* ■

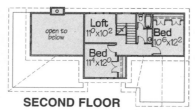

**SECOND FLOOR**

Loft 11⁰x10²
Bed 10⁶x12²
Bed 11⁴x12⁰
open to below

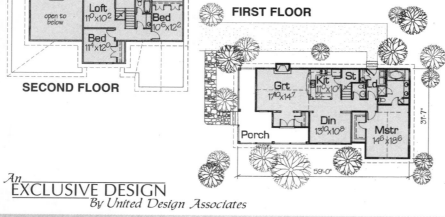

**FIRST FLOOR**

Grt 17¹⁰x14⁷
Kit 11⁰x10⁰
St
Porch
Din 13¹⁰x10⁸
Mstr 14⁶x18⁶
31'-7"
59'-0"

*An* EXCLUSIVE DESIGN
*By United Design Associates*

## No. 94713

■ **This plan features:**

— Three bedrooms

— Two full and one half baths

■ Victorian Porch leads into Foyer and two-story Great Room with a focal point fireplace

■ Efficient, U-shaped Kitchen opens to Great Room and Dining Room

■ Private Master Suite with triple windows, walk-in closet and luxurious bath with a double vanity and garden window tub

■ Two second floor bedrooms with large closets, share a full bath and Loft

First floor — 1,350 sq. ft.
Second floor — 589 sq. ft.

HIGH WIND
LOAD ENGINEERING
AVAILABLE
SEE PAGE 339 FOR DETAILS

# Perfect for Narrow Lot

■ *Total living area  1,858 sq. ft.* ■ *Price Code  C* ■

**WIDTH 51'-0"**
**DEPTH 90'-8"**

GARAGE 20'-4 x 23'-4
DECK
covered breezeway
DECK
BRKFST.
MASTER BED RM.
KIT.
DINING
UTIL.
GREAT RM.
BED RM.
FOYER
PORCH
BED RM./STUDY
FLOOR PLAN

## No. 96437

■ **This plan features:**

— Three bedrooms

— Two full baths

■ Columns open interior for circulation and spaciousness

■ Cathedral ceilings enhance Great Room and Bedroom/Study

■ Tray ceilings dress up Dining Room, Breakfast area and Master Bedroom

■ Open Kitchen and Dining Room access Porch and Deck areas

■ Master Suite features walk-in closet, dual vanity, shower and whirlpool tub

Main floor — 1,858 sq. ft.
Garage & storage — 504 sq. ft.

■ *Total living area  3,783 sq. ft.* ■ *Price Code  F* ■

# No. 92237

## This plan features:

- Four bedrooms

- Three full and one half baths

■ A stone hearth fireplace and built-in book shelves enhance the Living Room

■ Family Room with a huge fireplace, cathedral ceiling and access to Covered Veranda

■ Spacious Kitchen with cooktop island/snackbar, built-in pantry and Breakfast Room

■ Master Bedroom with a pullman ceiling, sitting area, private Covered Patio, two walk-in closets and a whirlpool tub

■ No materials list is available for this plan

Lower level — 2,804 sq. ft.
Upper level — 979 sq. ft.
Basement — 2,804 sq. ft.
Garage — 802 sq. ft.

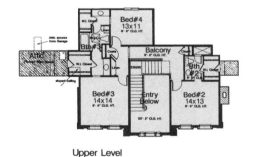

Upper Level

Lower Level

# Home Builders on a Budget

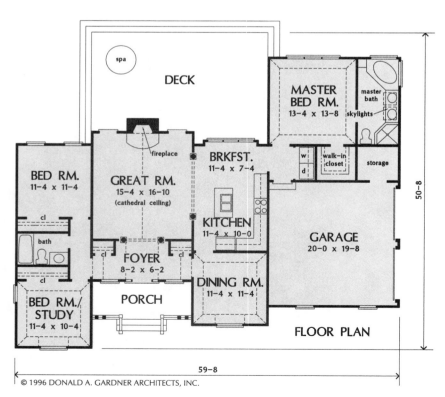

© 1996 Donald A. Gardner Architects, Inc.

■ *Total living area  1,498 sq. ft.* ■ *Price Code B* ■

## No. 99860

### ■ This plan features:

— Three bedrooms

— Two full baths

■ Down-sized Country style plan for a home builder on a budget

■ Columns punctuate open, one-level floor plan and connect Foyer with clerestory window dormers

■ Front Porch and large, rear Deck extend living space outdoors

■ Tray ceilings decorate Master Bedroom, Dining Room and Bedroom/Study

■ Private master bath features garden tub, dual vanity, separate shower and skylights

Main floor — 1,498 sq. ft.
Garage & storage — 427 sq. ft.

**FLOOR PLAN**

© 1996 DONALD A. GARDNER ARCHITECTS, INC.

174

# Splendid Front Window Adds Style and Appeal

## No. 93006

**This plan features:**

- Three bedrooms
- Two full baths
- A Great Room with a fireplace and easy access to patio area
- A Master Bedroom with a walk-in closet and double vanitied, private Master Bath
- Ample closet space in the two additional bedrooms
- A two-car Garage with added storage space
- No materials list is available for this plan

Main floor — 1,163 sq. ft.
Garage — 449 sq. ft.
Porch — 19 sq. ft.

Total living area 1,163 sq. ft. ■ Price Code A

© Larry E. Belk

MAIN AREA
WIDTH — 39'-2"
DEPTH — 55'-10"

---

# Stupendous Vaulted Family Room

## No. 98451

**This plan features:**

- Four bedrooms
- Three full baths
- A two-story Foyer is flanked by the Living Room that is topped by a high ceiling
- There is direct access to the Dining Room from the Kitchen
- The efficient Kitchen is highlighted by a peninsula counter/serving bar that separates it from the breakfast room and the Family Room
- A walk-in closet and private access to a full bath can be found in the first floor secondary bedroom/Study
- The Master Suite is topped by a tray ceiling in the bedroom and a vaulted ceiling in the private bath
- Two additional bedrooms, on the second floor, share a full bath
- An optional basement or crawl space foundation — please specify when ordering
- No material list is available for this plan

First floor — 1,226 sq. ft.
Second floor — 1,041 sq. ft.
Basement — 1,226 sq. ft.
Garage — 440 sq. ft.

Total living area 2,267 sq. ft. ■ Price Code E

175

# Fieldstone Facade

Total living area 2,261 sq. ft. ■ Price Code D

MAIN FLOOR

## No. 92284

**■ This plan features:**

— Four bedrooms

— Two full and one half baths

■ Covered porch shelters entrance into Gallery and Great Room with a focal point fireplace and Patio access

■ Formal Dining Room conveniently located for entertaining

■ Cooktop island, built-in pantry and a bright Breakfast Area highlight Kitchen

■ Secluded Master Bedroom with Patio access, large walk-in closet and corner spa tub

■ Three additional bedrooms with ample closets, share a double vanity bath

■ No materials list is available for this plan

Main floor — 2,261 sq. ft.
Garage — 640 sq. ft.

# Coastal Delight

## No. 94202

Total living area 3,216 sq. ft. ■ Price Code F

LOWER FLOOR

SECOND FLOOR

FIRST FLOOR

**■ This plan features:**

— Three bedrooms

— Two full baths

■ Living area above the Garage and Storage/Bonus areas offering a "piling" design for coastal, waterfront or low-lying terrain

■ Double-door Entry into an open Foyer with landing staircase leads into the Great Room

■ Three sets of double doors below a vaulted ceiling in the Great Room offer lots of air, light and easy access to both the Sun Deck and Veranda

■ A Dining Room convenient to the Great Room and Kitchen featuring vaulted ceilings and decorative windows

■ A glassed-in Nook adjacent to the efficient Kitchen with an island work center

■ Two secondary bedrooms, a full bath and a Utility room on the first floor

■ A second floor Master Suite with a vaulted ceiling, double door to a private Deck, his-her closets and a plush bath

First floor — 1,736 sq. ft.
Second floor — 640 sq. ft.
Lower floor — 840 sq. ft.
Bonus room — 253 sq. ft.
Garage — 840 sq. ft.

HIGH WIND LOAD ENGINEERING AVAILABLE
SEE PAGE 339 FOR DETAILS

# Lavish Accommodations

■ *Total living area 2,733 sq. ft.* ■ *Price Code F* ■

## No. 92538

**■ This plan features:**

- Four bedrooms

- Three full baths

■ A central Den with a large fireplace, built-in shelves and cabinets and a decorative ceiling

■ Columns defining the entrance to the formal Dining Room, adding a touch of elegance

■ An island Kitchen that has been well thought out and includes a walk-in Pantry

■ An informal Eating area

■ A Master Bedroom with a decorative ceiling, a walk-in closet, and a luxurious master bath

■ Four additional bedrooms, each with private access to a full bath, two of which have walk-in closets

■ An optional crawl space or slab foundation — please specify when ordering

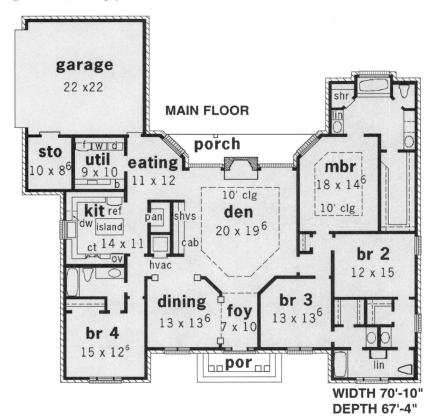

MAIN FLOOR

garage
22 x22

sto
10 x 8⁶

util
9 x 10

eating
11 x 12

porch

mbr
18 x 14⁶
10' clg

kit
14 x 11

pan

shvs

cab

10' clg

den
20 x 19⁶

br 2
12 x 15

hvac

dining
13 x 13⁶

foy
7 x 10

br 3
13 x 13⁶

lin

br 4
15 x 12⁶

por

WIDTH 70'-10"
DEPTH 67'-4"

shr
lin

Main floor — 2,733 sq. ft.
Garage and storage — 569 sq. ft.

# French Country Styling

*Total living area  2,567 sq. ft.* ■ *Price Code D*

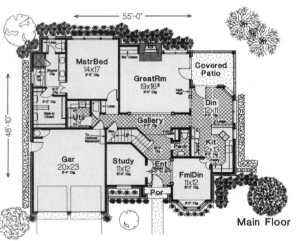

**Main Floor**

*Optional 3-Car Garage – 55'-0" Wide*

Main floor — 1,765 sq. ft.
Upper floor — 802 sq. ft.
Bonus room — 275 sq. ft.
Garage — 462 sq. ft.

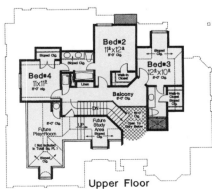

**Upper Floor**

# No. 98533

■ **This plan features:**

— Four bedrooms

— Two full, one half and one three-quarter baths

■ A bay window with a copper roof, a large eyebrow dormer and an arched covered entry

■ The Great Room includes a brick fireplace and a built-in entertainment center

■ An elegant formal Dining Room and angled Study are located to each side of the entry

■ Convenient Kitchen with an informal Dining Area

■ The Master Suite is located on the first floor and has a large bath

■ An optional basement or slab foundation — please specify when ordering

■ No materials list is available for this plan

# Grace and Style

## No. 96483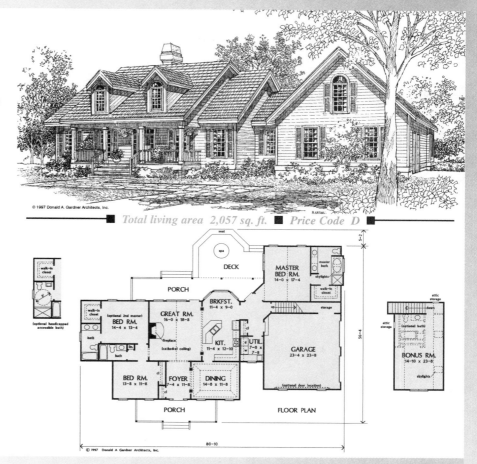

**This plan features:**

- Three bedrooms
- Three full baths
- Foyer accented by columns gives entry into the formal Dining Room
- Angled island Kitchen is open to the Breakfast Bay
- Great Room topped by a cathedral ceiling and enhanced by a fireplace and access to the rear porch
- Secluded Master Suite with a skylit bath
- Two secondary bedrooms, one with a private bath, an alternate bath design creates a wheel chair accessibility option for the disabled
- Bonus Room may create a terrific fourth bedroom and bath

Main floor — 2,057 sq. ft.
Garage & storage — 622 sq. ft.
Bonus room — 444 sq. ft.

*Total living area  2,057 sq. ft.* ■ *Price Code  D*

© 1997 Donald A. Gardner Architects, Inc.

# Eye-Appealing Balance

## No. 92257

**This plan features:**

- Three bedrooms
- Two full and one half baths
- Arched Portico enhances entry into Gallery and spacious Living Room, with focal point fireplace surrounded by glass
- Cathedral ceilings top Family Room and formal Dining Room
- An efficient Kitchen with breakfast area opens to Family Room, and has a connecting Utility Room with convenient Garage entry
- Corner Master Suite with access to covered Patio and private bath with a double vanity and garden window tub
- Two additional bedrooms with walk-in closets share a full bath
- No materials list is available for this plan

Main floor — 2,470 sq. ft.
Garage — 483 sq. ft.

*Total living area  2,470 sq. ft.* ■ *Price Code  D*

Main Floor

# Welcoming Front Porch Accented by Columns

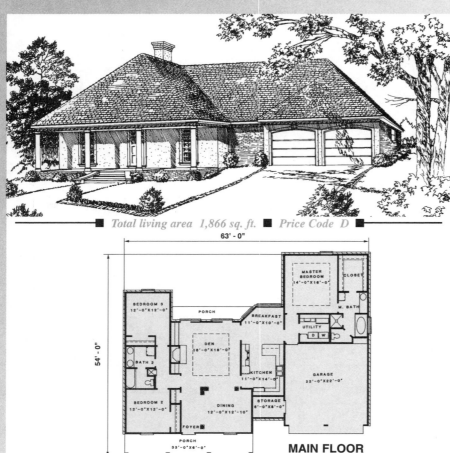

*Total living area 1,866 sq. ft.* ■ *Price Code D*

**MAIN FLOOR**

## No. 92542

■ **This plan features:**

— Three bedrooms

— Two full baths

■ Open Foyer leads into the Dining Room defined by columns and a spacious Den

■ Cozy fireplace in the Den with built-in shelves and sliding glass doors to the rear Porch below a decorative ceiling

■ Efficient U-shaped Kitchen with a peninsula snackbar and a glass Breakfast Area

■ Secluded Master Suite with a decorative ceiling, a huge walk-in closet and a private bath

■ Two additional bedrooms with ample closets, share the double vanity bath

■ An optional crawl space or slab foundation — please specify when ordering

Main floor — 1,866 sq. ft.
Garage/Storage — 538 sq. ft.

# Luxurious Bedrooms Abound

*Total living area 3,302 sq. ft.* ■ *Price Code F*

**FIRST FLOOR**

**SECOND FLOOR**

## No. 93243

■ **This plan features:**

— Five bedrooms

— Three full and one half baths

■ The formal Living Room and Dining Room have special window treatments

■ The Family Room has a focal point fireplace

■ The Kitchen, Family Room and Breakfast Nook open to each other

■ The Screen Porch adds to the living space

■ Sleeping quarters are located on the second floor

■ The Master Suite has a decorative ceiling, a fireplace, a private master bath and a screen Porch

■ No materials list is available for this plan

First floor — 1,491 sq. ft.
Second floor — 1,811 sq. ft.
Basement — 1,164 sq. ft.
Garage — 564 sq. ft.
Deck — 573 sq. ft.

*An* EXCLUSIVE DESIGN
*By Jannis Vann & Associates, Inc*

# Four Bedroom with One Floor Convenience

■ *Total living area 2,675 sq. ft.* ■ *Price Code E* ■

## No. 92275

■ **This plan features:**

– Four bedrooms

– Three full baths

■ A distinguished brick exterior adds curb appeal

■ Formal Entry/Gallery opens to large Living Room with hearth fireplace set between windows overlooking Patio and rear yard

■ Efficient Kitchen with angled counters and serving bar easily serves Breakfast Room, Patio and formal Dining Room

■ Corner Master Bedroom enhanced by a vaulted ceiling and pampering bath with a large walk-in closet

■ Three additional bedrooms with walk-in closets have access to full baths

■ No materials list is available for this plan

Main floor — 2,675 sq. ft.
Garage — 638 sq. ft.

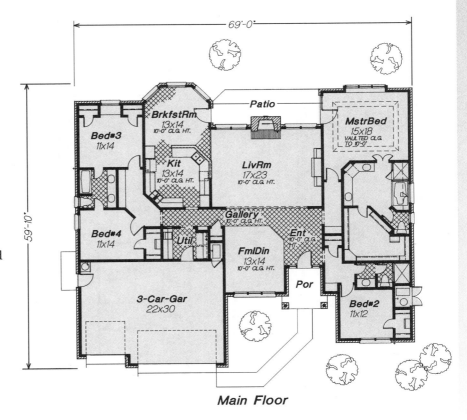

**Main Floor**

# Modernized Traditional Ranch

■ *Total living area  2,301 sq. ft.* ■ *Price Code D* ■

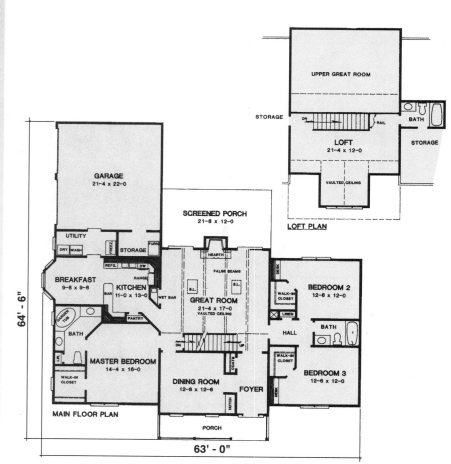

**MAIN FLOOR PLAN**

**LOFT PLAN**

# No. 90444

## ■ This plan features:

— Three bedrooms

— Three full baths

■ A vaulted-ceiling Great Room with skylights and a fireplace

■ A double L-shaped Kitchen with an eating bar opening to a bayed Breakfast Room

■ A Master Suite with a walk-in closet, corner garden tub, separate vanities and a linen closet

■ Two additional bedrooms each with a walk-in closet and built-in desk, sharing a full hall bath

■ A loft that overlooks the Great Room which includes a vaulted ceiling and open rail balcony

■ An optional basement or crawl space foundation — please specify when ordering

Main floor — 1,996 sq. ft.
Loft — 305 sq. ft.

# Porches Expands Living Space

## No. 96529

■ **This plan features:**

— Three bedrooms

— Two full and one half baths

■ Porches on the front and the rear of this home expand the living space to the outdoors

■ The rear Porch is accessed directly from the Great Room

■ The spacious Great Room is enhanced by a 12-foot ceiling and a fireplace

■ The well-appointed kitchen has an extended counter/eating bar and easy access to the Dining Room

■ Secondary bedrooms have a full bath located between the rooms

■ The Master Suite is enhanced by his and her walk-in closets, a whirlpool tub, and a separate shower

■ Bonus Room for future expansion

Main floor — 2,089 sq. ft.
Bonus room — 497 sq. ft.
Garage — 541 sq. ft.

■ Total living area 2,089 sq. ft. ■ Price Code C ■

MAIN FLOOR

# Rustic Simplicity

## No. 99864

■ **This plan features:**

— Three bedrooms

— Two full and one half baths

■ The central living area is large and boasts a cathedral ceiling, exposed wood beams and a clerestory

■ A long screened Porch has a bank of skylights

■ The open Kitchen contains a convenient serving and eating counter

■ The generous Master Suite opens to the screened porch, and is enhanced by a walk-in closet and a whirlpool tub

■ Two more bedrooms share a second full bath

Main floor — 1,426 sq. ft.

■ Total living area 1,426 sq. ft. ■ Price Code C ■

© 1987 Donald A. Gardner Architects, Inc.

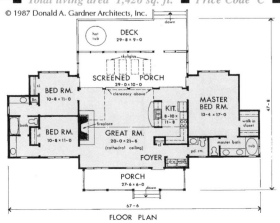

FLOOR PLAN

# Accented by Vaulted Ceilings & Columns

■ *Total living area  2,094 sq. ft.* ■ *Price Code  C* ■

**MAIN FLOOR**

## No. 98421

■ **This plan features:**

— Three bedrooms

— Two full and one half baths

■ Corner quoins, arched windows and keystones accent the exterior

■ Columns define the entrances of the Dining Room, Family Room and the Breakfast Room

■ Vaulted ceilings add volume to the Foyer, Dining Room, Living Room, Family Room, Breakfast Room and the Master Bath

■ An efficient and well-appointed Kitchen highlighted by serving bar to the Family Room

■ A large focal point fireplace enhances the Family Room

■ Private Master Suite topped by a tray ceiling and enhanced by a walk-in closet and lavish bath

■ Two additional bedrooms share the full hall bath

■ An optional basement, crawl space or slab foundation — please specify when ordering

Main floor — 2,094 sq. ft.
Basement — 2,108 sq. ft.
Garage — 453 sq. ft.

# Thoughtfully Designed

■ *Total living area  2,411 sq. ft.* ■ *Price Code  D* ■

**FIRST FLOOR**

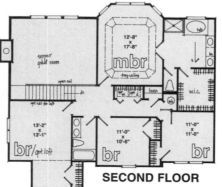

**SECOND FLOOR**

## No. 93602

■ **This plan features:**

— Four bedrooms

— Two full and one half baths

■ Foyer opens to formal Living and Dining rooms defined with columns for gracious entertaining

■ Two-story Great Room with an impressive fireplace and a wall of windows

■ Hub Kitchen with cooktop work island, built-in pantry and desk, and breakfast alcove with backyard access

■ Elegant Master Bedroom with a tray ceiling, window alcove, a huge walk-in closet and plush bath

■ Three additional bedrooms with ample closets share a full bath and laundry

■ No materials list is available for this plan

First floor — 1,209 sq. ft.
Second floor — 1,202 sq. ft.
Basement — 1,209 sq. ft.
Garage — 370 sq. ft.

*An*
**EXCLUSIVE DESIGN**
*By Garrell Associates Inc.*

# Multiple Roof Lines Add to Charm

■ *Total living area  3,292 sq. ft.* ■ *Price Code  F* ■

# No. 92209

■ **This plan features:**

- Four bedrooms

- Three full baths

■ Entry opens to Gallery, and formal Dining and Living rooms with decorative ceilings

■ Spacious Kitchen with a work island opens to dining alcove, Family Room and Patio beyond

■ Comfortable Family Room offers vaulted ceiling above fireplace, and a wetbar

■ Corner Master Suite enhanced by a vaulted ceiling, double vanity bath and huge walk-in closet

■ Three additional bedrooms with walk-in closets have access to full baths

■ No materials list is available for this plan

Main floor — 3,292 sq. ft.
Garage — 670 sq. ft.

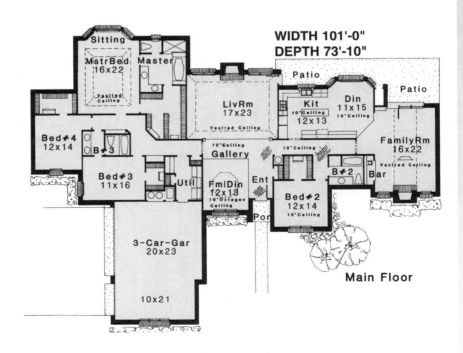

Main Floor

# Split Bedroom Plan

■ *Total living area  1,429 sq. ft.*  ■  *Price Code A*  ■

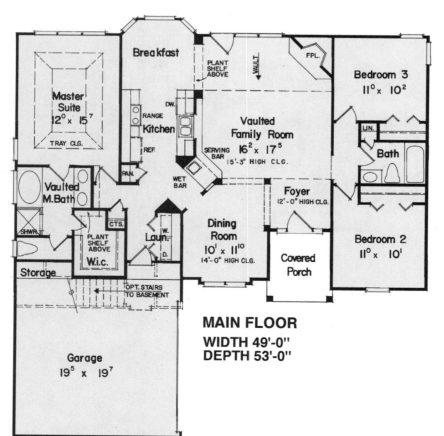

**MAIN FLOOR**
**WIDTH 49'-0"**
**DEPTH 53'-0"**

# No. 98415

**■ This plan features:**

— Three bedrooms

— Two full baths

■ A tray ceiling adds a decorative touch to the Master Bedroom

■ A full bath is located between the secondary bedrooms

■ A corner fireplace and a vaulted ceiling highlight the Family Room

■ A wetbar/serving bar in the Family Room and a built-in Pantry add to the convenience of the Kitchen

■ The Dining Room is crowned by an elegant high ceiling

■ An optional basement, crawl space or slab foundation — please specify when ordering

Main floor — 1,429 sq. ft.
Basement — 1,472 sq. ft.
Garage — 438 sq. ft.

# A Compact Home

## No. 93018

**This plan features:**

— Three bedrooms

— Two full baths

■ Siding with brick wainscoting distinguishing the elevation

■ A large Family Room with a corner fireplace and direct access to the outside

■ An arched opening leading to the Breakfast Area

■ A bay window illuminating the Breakfast Area with natural light

■ An efficiently designed, U-shaped Kitchen with ample cabinet and counter space

■ A Master Suite with a private Master Bath

■ Two additional bedrooms that share a full hall bath

■ No materials list is available for this plan

Main floor — 1,142 sq. ft.
Garage — 428 sq. ft.

■ *Total living area  1,142 sq. ft.* ■ *Price Code  A* ■

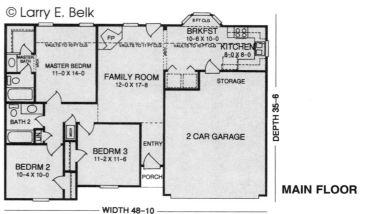

© Larry E. Belk

**MAIN FLOOR**

---

# Superbly Styled

## No. 92268

**This plan features:**

— Four bedrooms

— Two full baths

■ A covered Porch and an Entry with a 9' ceiling greet you

■ The Living Room has a rear wall fireplace and access to the covered Patio

■ The L-shaped Kitchen which features a center island opens into the Dining Room

■ The Master Bedroom has a 10-foot vaulted ceiling, plus a private bath with a cathedral ceiling

■ Two secondary bedrooms share a hall bath, while a fourth bedroom can be used as a Study

■ This plan has a two-car Garage

■ No materials list available for this plan

Main floor — 1,706 sq. ft.
Garage — 399 sq. ft.

■ *Total living area  1,706 sq. ft.* ■ *Price Code  B* ■

Floor Plan

# Romance Personified

■ Total living area 2,562 sq. ft. ■ Price Code D ■

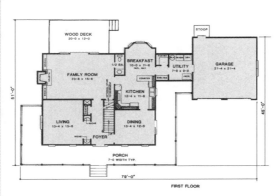

FIRST FLOOR

SECOND FLOOR

## No. 90439

■ **This plan features:**

— Three bedrooms

— Two full and one half baths

■ A spacious Family Room including a fireplace flanked by bookshelves

■ A sunny Breakfast Bay and adjoining country Kitchen with a peninsula counter

■ An expansive Master Suite spanning the width of the house including built-in shelves, walk-in closet, and a private bath with every amenity

■ A full bath that serves the two other bedrooms tucked into the gables at the front of the house

■ An optional basement or crawl space foundation — please specify when ordering

First floor — 1,366 sq. ft.
Second floor — 1,196 sq. ft.
Basement — 1,250 sq. ft.
Garage — 484 sq. ft.

# Convenience with a Touch of Class

■ Total living area 1,918 sq. ft. ■ Price Code C ■

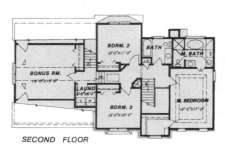

SECOND FLOOR

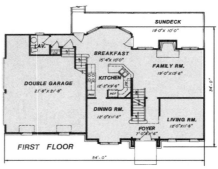

FIRST FLOOR

## No. 93216

■ **This plan features:**

— Three bedrooms

— Two full and one half baths

■ Formal Living Room and Dining Room flanking the Foyer in a traditional layout

■ An open layout between the Family Room, Breakfast Room and Kitchen making this active area seem more spacious

■ A large Family Room with a fireplace flanked by windows overlooking the Deck

■ A bright Breakfast Room with direct access to the Sun Deck

■ An efficient, well-appointed Kitchen equipped with a peninsula counter/eating bar and a built-in pantry

■ A Master Suite graced by a decorative ceiling and a private Bath equipped with an oval tub, separate shower and two vanities

■ A Bonus Room for future expansion

■ An optional basement, crawl space or slab foundation — please specify when ordering

First floor — 986 sq. ft.
Second floor — 932 sq. ft.
Bonus room — 274 sq. ft.
Basement — 882 sq. ft.
Garage — 532 sq. ft.

*An* EXCLUSIVE DESIGN
*By Jannis Vann & Associates, Inc.*

# Classic Blend of Brick and Stucco

■ *Total living area  1,668 sq. ft.* ■ *Price Code  C* ■

## No. 92555

**This plan features:**

- Three bedrooms

- Two full baths

■ Arched windows on the front of this home combining with brick and stucco, brick quoins and dentil molding

■ Foyer giving access to the formal Dining Room accented by columns

■ Den includes a raised ceiling and a focal point fireplace

■ Kitchen and Breakfast Nook open into the Den creating a feeling of spaciousness

■ Master Suite is situated to the left, rear corner and features a five-piece bath and walk-in closet

■ An optional crawl space or slab foundation — please specify when ordering

Main floor — 1,668 sq. ft.
Garage — 537 sq. ft.

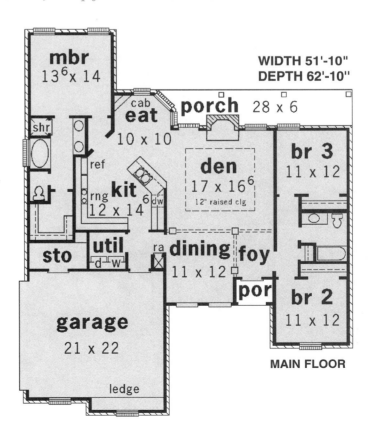

WIDTH 51'-10"
DEPTH 62'-10"

mbr
13⁶ x 14

cab

eat
10 x 10

porch  28 x 6

shr

ref

den
17 x 16⁶
12" raised clg

br 3
11 x 12

rng

kit
12 x 14

dw

sto

util
d | w

ra

dining
11 x 12

foy

br 2
11 x 12

por

garage
21 x 22

ledge

**MAIN FLOOR**

# Exciting Ceilings Add Appeal

©1994 Donald A. Gardner Architects, Inc.

■ *Total living area 1,475 sq. ft.* ■ *Price Code B* ■

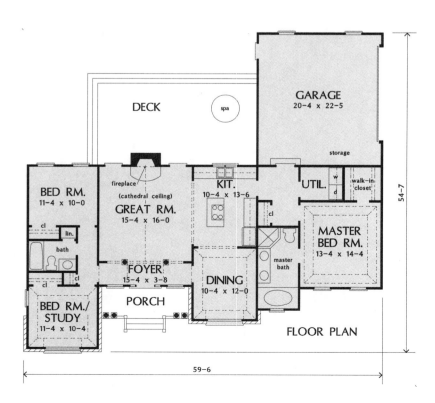

FLOOR PLAN

## No. 96452

### ■ This plan features:

— Three bedrooms

— Two full baths

■ Open design enhanced by cathedral and tray ceilings above arched windows

■ Foyer with columns defining Great Room with central fireplace and Deck access

■ Cooktop island in Kitchen provides great cooks with convenience and company

■ Ultimate Master Bedroom Suite offers walk-in closet, tray ceiling, and whirlpool bath

■ Front Bedroom/Study offers multiple uses with tray ceiling and arched window

Main floor — 1,475 sq. ft.
Garage & storage — 478 sq. ft.

# Varied Roof Lines Add Interest

## No. 93255

**This plan features:**

- Three bedrooms
- Two full and one half baths
- A modern, convenient floor plan
- Formal areas located at the front of the home
- A decorative ceiling in the Dining Room
- Columns accenting the Living Room
- A large Family Room with a cozy fireplace and direct access to the Deck
- An efficient Kitchen located between the formal Dining Room and the informal Breakfast Room
- A private Master Suite that includes a master bath and walk-in closet
- Two additional bedrooms that share a full hall bath

Main area — 2,192 sq. ft.
Basement — 2,192 sq. ft.
Garage — 564 sq. ft.

*An* EXCLUSIVE DESIGN
*By Jannis Vann & Associates, Inc.*

■ *Total living area  2,192 sq. ft.* ■ *Price Code  C* ■

# Quoins and Arch Window Accents

## No. 94602

**This plan features:**

Three bedrooms

Two full baths

Sheltered entry leads into pillared Foyer defining Living and Dining Room areas

A cozy fireplace and access to covered Porch featured in Living Room

Efficient Kitchen offers a work island, Utility and bright Breakfast Area

Master Bedroom wing enhanced by a luxurious bath with a walk-in closet, double vanity and spa tub

Two additional bedrooms with over-sized closet share a double vanity bath

An optional crawl space or slab foundation — please specify when ordering

No materials list is available for this plan

Main floor — 1,704 sq. ft.

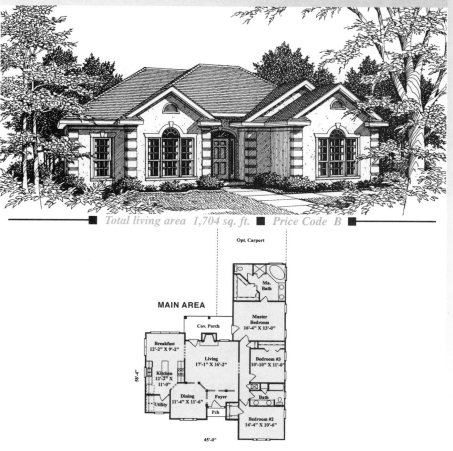

■ *Total living area  1,704 sq. ft.* ■ *Price Code  B* ■

# Impressive Exterior

■ *Total living area  1,858 sq. ft.* ■ *Price Code  D* ■

**WIDTH 62'-4"**
**DEPTH 34'-0"**

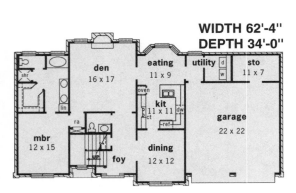

first floor

## No. 92543

■ **This plan features:**

— Three bedrooms

— Two full and one half baths

■ Two-story Foyer with a lovely, landing staircase and balcony

■ Spacious Den with an inviting fireplace between windows

■ Convenient Kitchen with an open serving counter for Eating bay, and nearby Dining Area, Utility and Garage entry

■ Elegant Master Bedroom wing with a plush dressing area

■ Two second floor bedrooms with large closets and separate vanities share a full bath

■ An optional crawl space or slab foundation — please specify when ordering

First floor — 1,322 sq. ft.
Second floor — 536 sq. ft.
Garage & Storage — 565 sq. ft.

# Year Round Indoor/Outdoor Living

■ *Total living area 1,764 sq. ft.* ■ *Price Code  B* ■

**HIGH WIND LOAD ENGINEERING AVAILABLE**
SEE PAGE 339 FOR DETAILS

**SECOND FLOOR**

**FIRST FLOOR**

**LOWER FLOOR**

## No. 94204

■ **This plan features:**

— Three bedrooms

— Two full baths

■ A "piling" design with a Garage and Storage/Bonus area below the living area for coastal, waterfront or low-lying terrain

■ An entry Porch into an expansive Great Room with a hearth fireplace, a vaulted ceiling and double door to a Sundeck

■ An inviting Dining Area with a vaulted ceiling and double doors leading to the screened Veranda and Sundeck

■ An efficient Kitchen with a peninsula counter and adjacent Laundry

■ An airy Master Suite with a walk-in closet, double vanity and direct access to the outdoors

■ Another bedroom and a bedroom/loft area on the second floor sharing a full bath

■ No materials list is available for this plan

First floor — 1,189 sq. ft.
Second floor — 575 sq. ft.
Bonus room — 581 sq. ft.
Garage — 658 sq. ft.

# Sense of Spaciousness

©1994 Donald A. Gardner Architects, Inc.

■ *Total living area 1,639 sq. ft.* ■ *Price Code C* ■

## No. 96456

### This plan features:

- Three bedrooms
- Two full and one half baths
- Creative use of natural lighting gives a feeling of spaciousness to this country home
- Traffic flows easily from the bright Foyer into the Great Room which has a vaulted ceiling and skylights
- The open floor plan is efficient for Kitchen/Breakfast Area and the Dining Room
- Master Bedroom features a walk-in closet and a private bath with whirlpool tub
- Two second floor bedrooms with storage access share a full bath

First floor — 1,180 sq. ft.
Second floor — 459 sq. ft.
Bonus room — 385 sq. ft.
Garage & storage — 533 sq. ft.

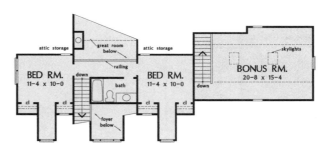

SECOND FLOOR PLAN

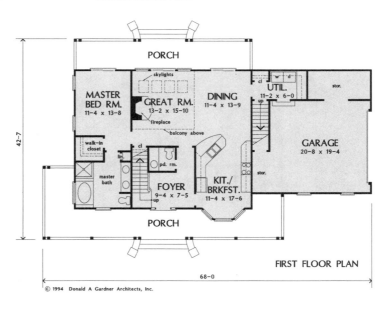

FIRST FLOOR PLAN

© 1994 Donald A Gardner Architects, Inc.

# Arches Add Ambiance

**Total living area  2,033 sq. ft.**  ■  **Price Code D**  ■

## No. 92539

■ **This plan features:**

— Four bedrooms

— Two full and one half baths

■ Arched two-story entrance with a lovely arched window

■ Den offers hearth fireplace between bookshelves, raised ceiling and access to rear yard

■ Kitchen with peninsula counter, built-in pantry, breakfast bay, Garage entry, and laundry access

■ Private Master Bedroom with a walk-in closet and plush bath

■ Three bedrooms with walk-in closets share a double vanity bath

■ An optional slab or crawl space foundation — please specify when ordering

First floor — 1,250 sq. ft.
Second floor — 783 sq. ft
Garage and Storage —
555 sq. ft.

33'-0"

OPEN TO DEN

BEDROOM 2
11'-0" x 13'-0"

DOWN

40'-0"

LIN. LIN.

HVAC

BEDROOM 3
11'-0" x 13'-0"

OPEN TO FOYER

BEDROOM 4
14'-0" x 12'-0"

**SECOND FLOOR**

57'-0"

BOOKS

DEN
18'-0" x 16'-0"

BREAKFAST
11'-0" x 10'-0"

STORAGE
12'-0" x 6'-0"

WASH DRY

BOOKS

UP

PANT

HVAC

SINK

KITCHEN

RANGE

DW

REF.

40'-0"

M. BATH

LIN

GARAGE
22'-0" x 22'-0"

DINING
11'-0" x 14'-0"

MASTER BED
14'-0" x 12'-0"

FOYER

PORCH

**FIRST FLOOR**

# European Flair in Tune with Today

## No. 94804 ✕

**This plan features:**

- Three bedrooms
- Two full baths
- European flavor with decorative windows, gable roof lines and a stucco finish
- Formal Dining Room with floor to ceiling window treatment
- Expansive Activity Room with decorative ceiling, hearth fireplace and Deck access
- Open, efficient Kitchen with snack bar, Laundry, Breakfast Area and Screened Porch beyond
- Private Master Bedroom Suite with a decorative ceiling, large walk-in closet and luxurious bath
- Two additional bedroom, one with a bay window share a full bath

Main floor — 1,855 sq. ft.
Basement — 1,855 sq. ft.
Garage — 439 sq. ft.

Total living area 1,855 sq. ft. ■ Price Code C

**MAIN FLOOR**

# Quoins and Keystones Accent Stucco

## No. 93247

**This plan features:**

- Three bedrooms
- Two full and four half baths
- Impressive entrance with two-story window
- Spacious Living Room with a vaulted ceiling
- Elegant Dining Room with decorative ceiling and corner built-ins
- Ideal Kitchen with extended cooktop serving counter
- Palatial Master Bedroom Suite with a fireplace
- Second floor offers three additional bedrooms
- No materials list is available for this plan

First floor — 2,656 sq. ft.
Second floor — 1,184 sq. ft.
Bonus — 508 sq. ft.
Basement — 2,642 sq. ft.
Garage — 528 sq. ft.

Total living area 3,840 sq. ft. ■ Price Code F

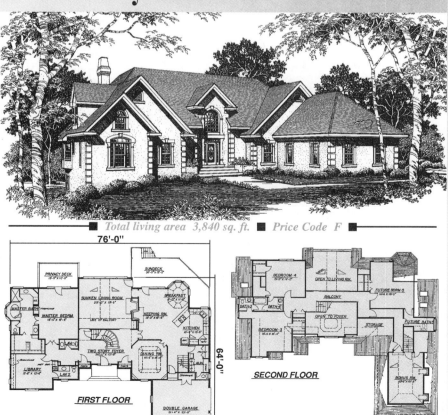

*An* EXCLUSIVE DESIGN *By Jannis Vann & Associates, Inc.*

# Two-Story Entry Adds Grace

© Larry E. Belk

■ *Total living area 3,034 sq. ft.* ■ *Price Code E* ■

## No. 93041

■ **This plan features:**

— Five bedrooms

— Two full and one half baths

■ A stucco designed facade accented by an arched two-story Entry

■ All major living areas are located with views to the rear grounds

■ The Kitchen, Breakfast Room and Family Room are adjacent and open to one another

■ An island cooktop and double sinks, along with an abundance of storage space making the Kitchen even more convenient

■ The Master Suite with an angled whirlpool tub, separate shower and his-n-her vanities

■ Three additional bedrooms located on the second floor

■ No materials list is available for this plan

First floor — 1,974 sq. ft.
Second floor — 1,060 sq. ft.
Garage — 531 sq. ft.

**WIDTH 64'-4"**
**DEPTH 53'-4"**

**FIRST FLOOR**

**SECOND FLOOR**

# Grand Impression

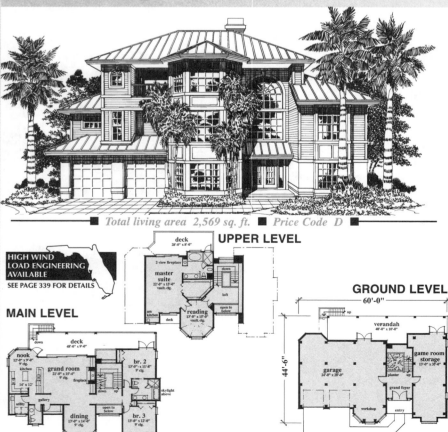

■ *Total living area 2,569 sq. ft.* ■ *Price Code D* ■

**HIGH WIND LOAD ENGINEERING AVAILABLE**
**SEE PAGE 339 FOR DETAILS**

**MAIN LEVEL**

**UPPER LEVEL**

**GROUND LEVEL**

## No. 94214

■ **This plan features:**

— Three bedrooms

— Two full and one half baths

■ A three-story turret creates a tremendous first impression

■ The Dining Room with a bay window flows easily into the Grand Room

■ The Grand Room has a fireplace entertainment center and rear access to the Deck

■ The third floor is devoted to the Master Suite with a Loft area and reading room, plus fireplace and a bath

■ On ground level find the grand Foyer, Game Room and Garage with Workshop

Main level — 1,642 sq. ft.
Upper level — 927 sq. ft.
Ground level — 1,642 sq. ft.

196

**Total living area 1,808 sq. ft. ■ Price Code C**

## No. 93413

**This plan features:**

- Three bedrooms

- Two full and one half baths

- The Foyer is naturally lit by a dormer window above

- Family Room is highlighted by two front windows and a fireplace

- Kitchen includes an angled extended counter/snack bar and an abundance of counter/cabinet space

- Dining Area opens to the Kitchen, for a more spacious feeling

- The roomy Master Suite is located on the first floor and has a private five-piece bath plus a walk-in closet

- Laundry Room doubles as a mudroom from the side entrance

- No materials list is available for this plan

*An* EXCLUSIVE DESIGN *By Greg Marquis*

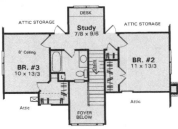

**SECOND FLOOR**

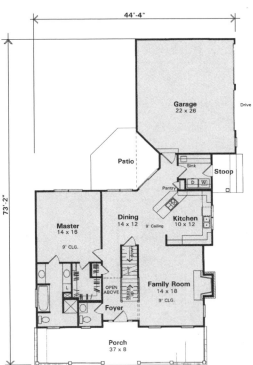

**FIRST FLOOR**

First floor — 1,271 sq. ft.
Second floor — 537 sq. ft.
Basement — 1,271 sq. ft.
Garage — 555 sq. ft.

# Charming, Compact and Convenient

■ *Total living area 1,752 sq. ft.* ■ *Price Code B* ■

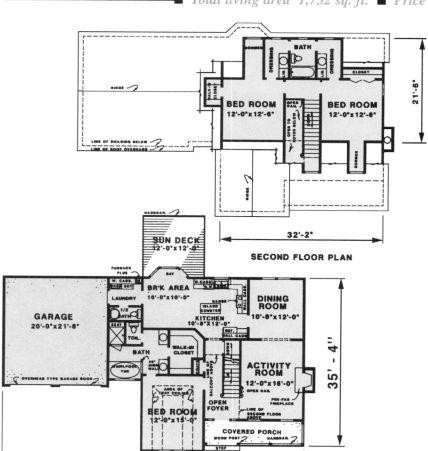

SECOND FLOOR PLAN

## No. 94803

■ **This plan features:**

— Three bedrooms

— Two full and one half bath

■ Spacious Activity Room with a pre-fab fireplace opens to formal Dining Room

■ Country-size Kitchen/ Breakfast Area with island counter and access to Sun Deck and Laundry/Garage entry

■ First floor bedroom highlighted by lovely arched window below a tray ceiling and a pampering bath

■ Two upstairs bedrooms share a twin vanity bath

■ An optional basement or crawl space foundation — please specify when ordering

First floor — 1,165 sq. ft.
Second floor — 587 sq. ft.
Garage — 455 sq. ft.
Basement — 1,165 sq. ft.

# Balcony Offers Sweeping Views

## No. 10778

**This plan features:**

– Three bedrooms

– Three and one half baths

■ A Living Room and a formal Dining Room located off the Foyer

■ A convenient island Kitchen steps away from both the Dining Room and the Three Season Porch

■ A cozy Master Suite including a fireplace and large a bath area

First floor — 1,978 sq. ft
Second floor — 1,768 sq. ft.
Basement — 1,978 sq. ft.

■ Total living area 3,746 sq. ft. ■ Price Code F ■

**SECOND FLOOR**

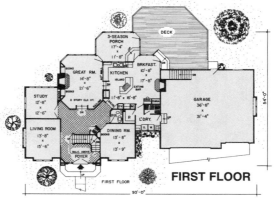

**FIRST FLOOR**

# Keystones and Arched Windows

## No. 98432

**This plan features:**

– Three bedrooms

– Two full baths

■ A large arched window in the Dining Room offers eye-catching appeal

■ A decorative column helps to define the Dining Room from the Great Room

■ A fireplace and French door to the rear yard can be found in the Great Room

■ An efficient Kitchen includes a serving bar, pantry and pass through to the Great Room

■ A vaulted ceiling over the Breakfast Room

■ A plush Master Suite includes a private bath and a walk-in closet

■ Two additional bedrooms share a full bath in the hall

■ An optional basement, slab or crawl space foundation — please specify when ordering

Main floor — 1,670 sq. ft.
Garage — 240 sq. ft.

■ Total living area 1,670 sq. ft. ■ Price Code B ■

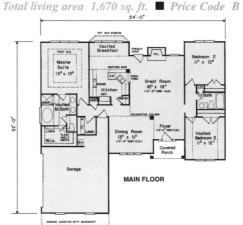

**MAIN FLOOR**

199

# Great Room is Center of Activity

■ Total living area 1,208 sq. ft. ■ Price Code B ■

**FLOOR PLAN**

## No. 92520

■ **This plan features:**

— Three bedrooms

— Two full baths

■ Sheltered entry leads into open Foyer and Great Room beyond

■ Raised, brick hearth and wood bin enhance fireplace in spacious Great Room with access to back Porch

■ Formal Dining Room adjoins Great Room and Kitchen for easy entertaining

■ Efficient Kitchen with laundry alcove and Garage entrance

■ Vaulted ceiling tops arched transom window in the Master Bedroom with private bath and walk-in closet

■ Two additional bedrooms with ample closet space, share a full bath

■ An optional crawl space or slab foundation — please specify when ordering

Main floor — 1,208 sq. ft.

# Beautiful From Front to Back

■ Total living area 1,632 sq. ft. ■ Price Code C ■

**FLOOR PLAN**

## No. 99840

■ **This plan features:**

— Three bedrooms

— Two full baths

■ Porches, front and back, gables and dormers providing special charm

■ Central Great Room with a cathedral ceiling, fireplace, and a clerestory window which brings in natural light

■ Columns dividing the open Great Room from the Kitchen and the Breakfast Bay

■ A tray ceiling and columns dress up the formal Dining Room

■ Skylit master bath with shower, whirlpool tub, dual vanity and spacious walk-in closet

Main floor — 1,632 sq. ft.
Garage & Storage — 561 sq. ft.

■ *Total living area  1,454 sq. ft.* ■ *Price Code  A* ■

# No. 90412

## This plan features:

- Three bedrooms

- Two full baths

■ A centrally located Great Room with a cathedral ceiling, exposed wood beams, and large areas of fixed glass

■ The Living and Dining areas separated by a massive stone fireplace

■ A secluded Master Suite with a walk-in closet and private master bath

■ An efficient Kitchen with a convenient laundry area

■ An optional basement, slab or crawl space foundation — please specify when ordering

Main area — 1,454 sq. ft.

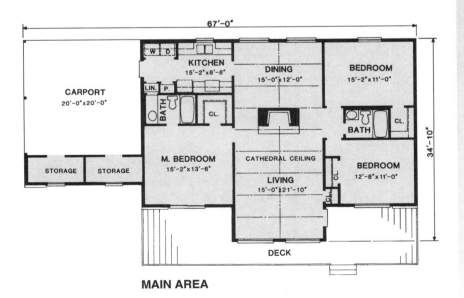

**MAIN AREA**

# Perfect for Entertaining

© 1997 Donald A. Gardner Architects, Inc.

■ *Total living area  2,772 sq. ft.* ■ *Price Code E* ■

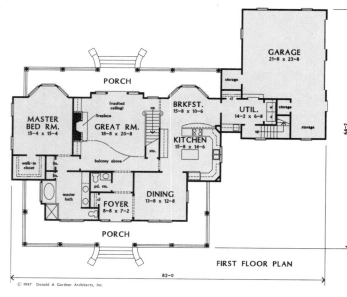

BED RM.
12-4 x 13-0

great room
below

BED RM.
12-8 x 13-0

attic storage

BED RM.
11-4 x 11-6

down

railing

bath

bath

foyer
below

attic storage

BONUS RM.
14-2 x 23-8

attic storage

down

SECOND FLOOR PLAN

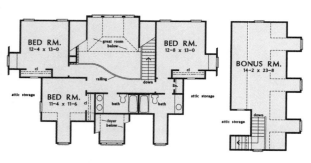

PORCH

MASTER
BED RM.
15-4 x 15-4

(vaulted
ceiling)

fireplace

GREAT RM.
18-8 x 20-8

walk-in
closet

balcony above

master
bath

pd. rm.

FOYER
8-8 x 7-2

BRKFST.
15-8 x 10-6

KITCHEN
15-8 x 14-6

sto.

up

DINING
13-8 x 12-8

UTIL.
14-2 x 6-8

storage

GARAGE
21-8 x 23-8

storage

up

64-2

PORCH

82-0

FIRST FLOOR PLAN

© 1997  Donald A Gardner Architects, Inc.

# No. 96407

■ **This plan features:**

— Four bedrooms

— Three full and one half baths

■ With front dormers and wrap-around Porch, the home offers formal entertaining and casual living

■ Dramatic Great Room boasts cathedral ceiling and fireplace nestled between built-in shelves

■ French doors expand living space to full length rear Porch

■ Center island and peninsula counter create an efficient Kitchen/Breakfast Area

■ First floor Master Suite features a walk-in closet and spacious master bath

First floor — 1,831 sq. ft.
Second floor — 941 sq. ft.
Bonus room — 539 sq. ft.
Garage & storage — 684 sq. ft.

# Especially Unique

## No. 98528

### This plan features:

- Four bedrooms
- Three full and one half baths
- An arch covered entry and arched windows add a unique flair to this home
- From the 11-foot entry turn left into the Study/Media room
- The formal Dining Room is open to the Gallery, and the Living Room beyond
- The Family Room has a built in entertainment center, a fireplace, and access to the rear patio
- The Master Bedroom is isolated, and has a fireplace, a private bath and walk-in closet
- Three additional bedrooms are on the opposite side of the home share two full baths
- A three-car Garage
- No materials list is available for this plan

Main floor — 2,748 sq. ft.
Garage — 660 sq. ft.
Width — 75'-0"
Depth — 64'-5"

■ *Total living area 2,748 sq. ft.* ■ *Price Code E* ■

**MAIN FLOOR**

# Covered Porch Shelters Entry

## No. 98422

### This plan features:

- Three bedrooms
- Two full and one half baths
- There is a convenient pass-through from the Kitchen into the Family Room
- An easy flow into the Dining Room enhances the interaction of the living spaces on the first floor
- A fireplace highlights the spacious Family Room
- The Kitchen opens to the Breakfast Room which has French door access to the rear yard
- Decorative ceiling treatment highlights the Master Bedroom while a vaulted ceiling tops the master bath
- Two additional bedrooms share the use of the full bath in the hall
- An optional basement or crawl space foundation — please specify when ordering

First floor — 719 sq. ft.
Second floor — 717 sq. ft.
Bonus — 290 sq. ft.
Basement — 719 sq. ft.
Garage — 480 sq. ft.

■ *Total living area 1,436 sq. ft.* ■ *Price Code A* ■

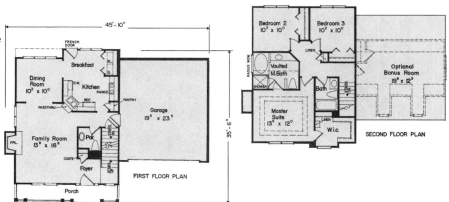

# A Country Estate

*Total living area  5,730 sq. ft.  ■  Price Code  F*

*An* EXCLUSIVE DESIGN
*By Jannis Vann & Associates, Inc.*

## No. 93200

■ **This plan features:**

— Four bedrooms

— Four full and one half baths

■ A gorgeous two-story Foyer, naturally illuminated by a transom above the door and a large second story window

■ A first floor Guest Room with two closets and a private entry to a full bath

■ A Library tucked into a corner of the house for quiet study

■ A sunken Family Room highlighted by a fireplace and built-in shelves

■ A Breakfast Room warmed by a see-through fireplace that is shared with the Sun Room

■ A gourmet Kitchen with two built-in pantries, generous counter and storage space and an island with a vegetable sink

■ A second floor Master Suite, enhanced by a decorative ceiling, two walk-in closets, a splendid bath and a private balcony

■ A future Sitting Room option for the Master Suite, and an optional Bonus Room

■ No materials list is available for this plan

First floor — 3,199 sq. ft.
Second floor — 2,531 sq. ft.
Bonus — 440 sq. ft.
Basement — 3,199 sq. ft.
Garage — 748 sq. ft.

# Brick Traditional

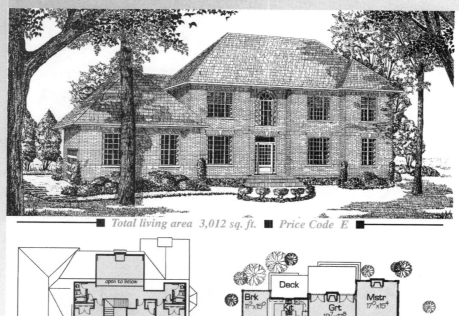

*Total living area  3,012 sq. ft.  ■  Price Code  E*

*An* EXCLUSIVE DESIGN
*By United Design Associates*

## No. 94715

■ **This plan features:**

— Four bedrooms

— Three full and one half baths

■ Old southern architecture incorporates today's open floor plan

■ Gracious two-story Foyer between formal Living and Dining rooms

■ Comfortable Great Room with a fireplace is nestled between French doors to the rear Decks

■ Hub Kitchen offers a cooktop island, an eating bar and a Breakfast Area

■ Master Suite is enhanced by a fireplace and a plush bath

First floor — 2,094 sq. ft.
Second floor — 918 sq. ft.
Garage — 537 sq. ft.
Width — 71'-10"
Depth — 46'-0"

HIGH WIND LOAD ENGINEERING AVAILABLE
SEE PAGE 339 FOR DETAILS

# An Old-Fashioned Country Feel

■ *Total living area  2,091 sq. ft.* ■ *Price Code  C* ■

## No. 93212

■ **This plan features:**

– Three bedrooms

– Two full and one half baths

■ Living Room with a cozy fireplace

■ A formal Dining Room with a bay window and direct access to the Sun Deck

■ U-shaped Kitchen efficiently arranged with ample work space

■ Master Suite with an elegant private bath complete with jacuzzi and a step-in shower

■ A future Bonus Room to finish, tailored to your needs

■ An optional basement, crawl space or slab foundation — please specify when ordering

■ No materials list is available for this plan

First floor — 1,362 sq. ft.
Second floor —  729 sq. ft.
Bonus room —  384 sq. ft.
Basement —  988 sq. ft.
Garage —  559 sq. ft.

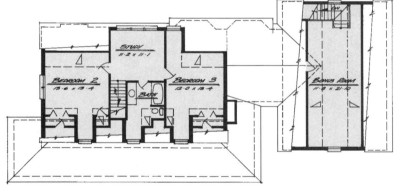

**SECOND  FLOOR**

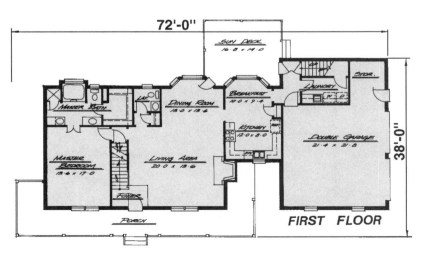

**FIRST  FLOOR**

*An*
EXCLUSIVE DESIGN
*By Jannis Vann & Associates, Inc.*

# Charm and Personality

© 1996 Donald A. Gardner Architects, Inc.

■ *Total living area  1,655 sq. ft.* ■ *Price Code C* ■

Main floor — 1,655 sq. ft.
Garage — 434 sq. ft.

# No. 99871

■ **This plan features:**

— Three bedrooms

— Two full baths

■ Charm and personality radiate through this country home

■ Interior columns dramatically open the Foyer and Kitchen to the spacious Great Room

■ Drama is heightened by the Great Room cathedral ceiling and fireplace

■ Master Suite with a tray ceiling combines privacy with access to the rear Deck with spa, while the skylit bath has all the amenities expected in a quality home

■ Tray ceilings with arched picture windows bring a special elegance to the Dining Room and the front Swing Room

■ An optional basement or crawl space foundation — please specify when ordering

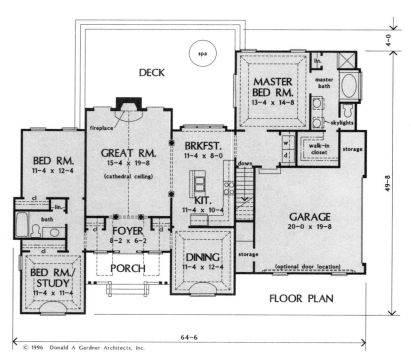

FLOOR PLAN

© 1996  Donald A Gardner Architects, Inc.

# Traditional Elegance

## No. 93042

**This plan features:**

- Four bedrooms

- Two full and one half baths

- Twin bay windows and an angled Garage

- A tiled Foyer that opens to a two-story Living Room

- A formal Dining Room that includes one of the lovely bay windows

- An island Kitchen, with a peninsula counter and eating bar, connecting with the Breakfast Room that flows easily into the Family Room

- A spacious Family Room that includes a focal point fireplace

- A Master Suite with an intimate sitting area and a master bath

- Three bedrooms that share a full double vanity hall bath

- No materials list is available for this plan

First floor — 1,832 sq. ft.
Second floor — 1,163 sq. ft.
Garage — 591 sq. ft.

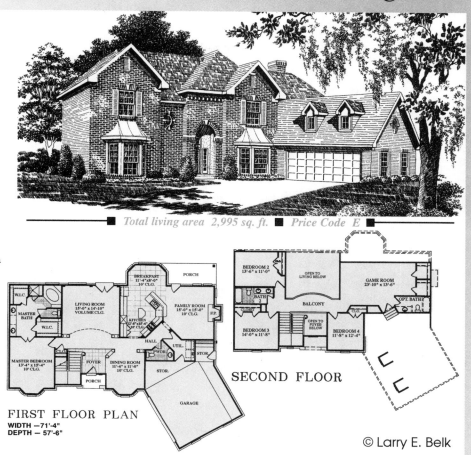

■ *Total living area  2,995 sq. ft.* ■ *Price Code  E* ■

FIRST FLOOR PLAN
WIDTH —71'-4"
DEPTH — 57'-6"

SECOND FLOOR

© Larry E. Belk

# For a Narrow Lot

## No. 99868

**This plan features:**

- Three bedrooms

- Two full baths

- A Great Room topped by a cathedral ceiling and accented by a fireplace

- A convenient pass-through opening from the Kitchen

- The Master Suite is loaded with luxuries, including a walk-in closet and a private bath with a separate shower and garden tub

- Two additional bedrooms share a full bath

Main floor — 1,350 sq. ft.
Garage & storage — 309 sq. ft.

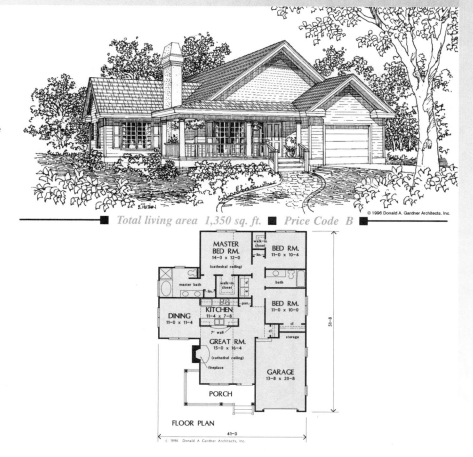

■ *Total living area  1,350 sq. ft.* ■ *Price Code  B* ■

© 1996 Donald A. Gardner Architects, Inc.

FLOOR PLAN

© 1996 Donald A Gardner Architects, Inc.

# Country Charm and Modern Convenience

©1995 Donald A. Gardner Architects, Inc.

■ *Total living area 2,370 sq. ft.* ■ *Price Code D* ■

**SECOND FLOOR**

**FIRST FLOOR**

© 1995 Donald A Gardner Architects, Inc.

## No. 96459

■ **This plan features:**

— Three bedrooms

— Two full and one half baths

■ Great Room crowned in a cathedral ceiling and accented by a cozy fireplace with built-ins

■ Centrally located Kitchen with nearby pantry serving Breakfast Area and Dining Room with ease

■ Master Suite elegantly appointed by a walk-in closet and a lavish bath

■ A Sitting Room with bay window off the Master Suite

■ Two secondary bedrooms sharing a full bath

First floor — 1,778 sq. ft.
Second floor — 592 sq. ft.
Garage & storage — 622 sq. ft.
Bonus room — 404 sq. ft.

# Graceful Arches Accent Elevation

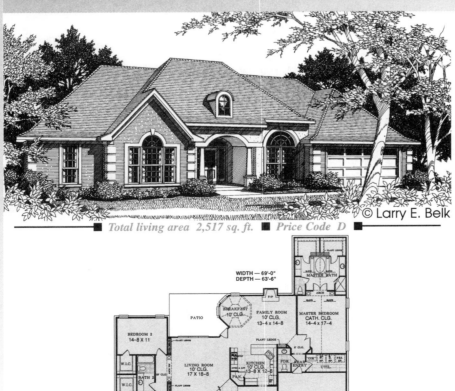

© Larry E. Belk

■ *Total living area 2,517 sq. ft.* ■ *Price Code D* ■

**MAIN FLOOR**

## No. 93056

■ **This plan features:**

— Four bedrooms

— Two full and one half baths

■ Arched portico entrance leads into the raised Foyer, Dining and Living rooms

■ Expansive Living Room with plant ledges and a wall of windows overlooks the Patio

■ Arched window below a sloped ceiling in the Dining Room

■ Ultimate Kitchen with a walk-in pantry and a peninsula snackbar that services the glass octagon Breakfast Area and the Family Room with a cozy fireplace

■ Double door entrance to the Master Suite with a cathedral ceiling, a lavish master bath with a garden tub and two walk-in closets

■ Versatile Bedroom/Study with a walk-in closet and a coffered ceiling over an arched window

■ Two additional bedrooms, with walk-in closets, share a full bath

■ An optional crawl space or slab foundation — please specify when ordering

Main floor — 2,517 sq. ft.
Garage — 443 sq. ft.

# Quoin Accents Distinguish this Plan

© Larry E. Belk

■ *Total living area 1,142 sq. ft.* ■ *Price Code A* ■

# No. 93017

**This plan features:**

- Three bedrooms

- Two full baths

- A traditional brick elevation with quoin accents

- A large Family Room with a corner fireplace and direct access to the outside

- An arched opening leading to the Breakfast Area

- A bay window illuminating the Breakfast Area with natural light

- An efficiently designed, U-shaped kitchen with ample cabinet and counter space

- A Master Suite with a private master bath

- Two additional bedrooms that share a full hall bath

- No materials list is available for this plan

**MAIN FLOOR**

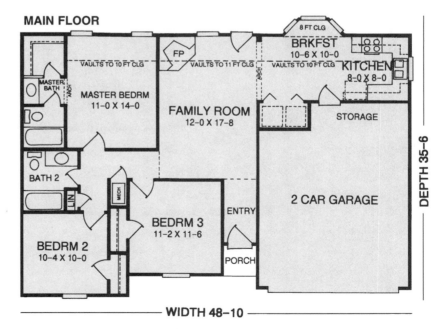

Main floor — 1,142 sq. ft.
Garage — 428 sq. ft.

# Stately Colonial Home

■ *Total living area 2,959 sq. ft.* ■ *Price Code E* ■

**SECOND FLOOR**

BDRM.#2 13X11
BDRM.#3 13X12
BALCONY
STAIRS DOWN
ENTRY BELOW
BDRM.#4 13X12
LOFT AREA 13X14
PLANT LEDGE
PORCH BELOW

**WIDTH 73'-4"**
**DEPTH 44'-0"**

PATIO AREA
COVERED AREA
PATIO
THREE CAR TANDEM GARAGE 22X40
BREAKFAST 13X12
GREAT ROOM 19X16
MSTR. BDRM. 18X14
KITCHEN 13X13
UTLY
HALL
MSTR. BATH
WALK-IN CLOSET
SHOP AREA
FORMAL DINING 13X13
ENT.
FORMAL LIVING 13X13
STAIRS
PORCH

**FIRST FLOOR**

# No. 98534

## ■ This plan features:

— Four bedrooms

— Three full and one half baths

■ Stately columns and lovely arched windows

■ The Entry is highlighted by a palladian window, a plant shelf and an angled staircase

■ The formal Living and Dining Rooms located off the Entry for ease in entertaining

■ Great Room has a fireplace and opens to Kitchen/Breakfast area and the Patio

■ The Master Bedroom wing offers Patio access, a luxurious bath and a walk-in closet

■ No materials list is available for this plan

First floor — 1,848 sq. ft.
Second floor — 1,111 sq. ft.
Garage & shop — 722 sq. ft.

# Functional Floor Plan

## No. 94600

**This plan features:**

Four bedrooms

Three full baths

Columns accent front Porch and entrance into two-story Foyer

Expansive Living Room with hearth fireplace between French doors leading to covered Porch and Patio

Efficient Kitchen with peninsula counter, bright Breakfast Area and adjoining Utility, Dining Room and Garage entry

Private Master Bedroom wing with a large walk-in closet and plush bath with two vanities

First floor bedroom with another walk-in closet and full bath access, offers multiple uses

Two additional bedrooms on second floor with dormers and large closets share a full bath with separate vanities

An optional crawl space or slab foundation — please specify when ordering

No materials list is available for this plan

First floor — 1,685 sq. ft.

Second floor — 648 sq. ft.

Garage — 560 sq. ft.

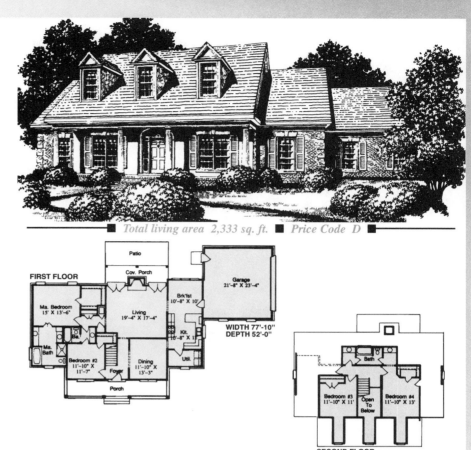

■ *Total living area  2,333 sq. ft.* ■ *Price Code  D* ■

# Outstanding Family Home

## No. 96504

**This plan features:**

Three bedrooms

Two full baths

Split bedroom layout, perfect floor plan for a family with older children

Great Room including a cozy fireplace, access to the rear porch and an open layout with the Nook and Kitchen

Extended counter in the Kitchen providing a snack bar for meals or snacks

Formal Dining Room directly accessing the Kitchen

Bright Nook with a built-in Pantry

Master Suite includes access to rear Porch and a pampering bath and walk-in closet

Main floor — 2,162 sq. ft.

Garage — 498 sq. ft.

■ *Total living area  2,162 sq. ft.* ■ *Price Code  C* ■

**Main floor**

# Dream Home for Contemporary Buyers

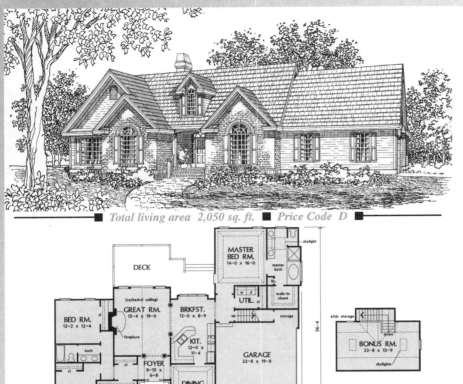

*Total living area 2,050 sq. ft.* ■ *Price Code D* ■

FLOOR PLAN

© 1995 Donald A Gardner Architects, Inc.

## No. 96465

■ **This plan features:**

— Three bedrooms

— Two full baths

■ Gables, a center front dormer, and a touch of brick combine with desirable amenities and an efficient floor plan

■ Dormer floods the Foyer with sunlight and intrigue, while a cathedral ceiling enlarges the Great Room

■ The Kitchen and Breakfast Area, located next to the Great Room, is punctuated by interior columns

■ Tray ceilings and circle top picture windows are featured in the Dining Room and the Living Room

■ Two family Bedrooms share a large full bath with a double vanity in one wing, while the luxurious Master Suite enjoys privacy in the rear

Main floor — 2,050 sq. ft.
Bonus — 377 sq. ft.
Garage — 503 sq. ft.

# Cottage Influence

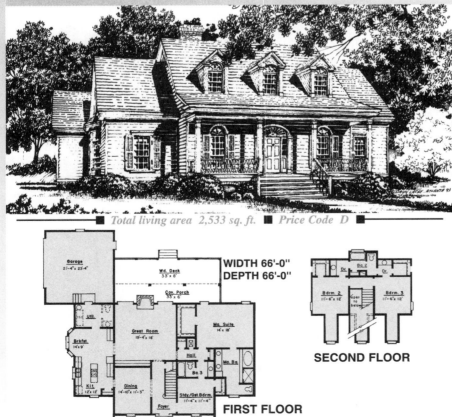

*Total living area 2,533 sq. ft.* ■ *Price Code D* ■

WIDTH 66'-0"
DEPTH 66'-0"

SECOND FLOOR

FIRST FLOOR

## No. 94614

■ **This plan features:**

— Three or four bedrooms

— Three full and one half baths

■ Cozy Porch entrance into Foyer with banister staircase and coat closet

■ Expansive Great Room with focal point fireplace and access to covered Porch and Deck

■ Cooktop island in Kitchen easily serves Breakfast Bay and formal Dining Room

■ Large Master Suite with access to Covered Porch, walk-in closet and double vanity bat

■ Study/Guest Bedroom with private access full bath, offers many uses

■ Two second floor bedrooms with dormers, private vanities and walk-in closets

■ An optional crawl space or slab foundation — please specify when ordering

■ No materials list is available for this plan

First floor — 1,916 sq. ft.
Second floor — 617 sq. ft.
Garage — 516 sq. ft.

# Multiple Porches Provide Added Interest

■ *Total living area  3,149 sq. ft.* ■ *Price Code  E* ■

## No. 94622

■ **This plan features:**

– Four bedrooms

– Three full and one half baths

■ Great Room with large fireplace and French doors to Porch and Deck

■ Country-size Kitchen with cooktop work island, walk-in pantry and Breakfast Area with Porch access

■ Pampering Master Bedroom offers a decorative ceiling, sitting area, Porch and Deck access, a huge walk-in closet and lavish bath

■ Three second floor bedrooms with walk-in closets have private access to a full bath

■ An optional crawl space or slab foundation — please specify when ordering

■ No materials list is available for this plan

First floor — 2,033 sq. ft.
Second floor — 1,116 sq. ft.

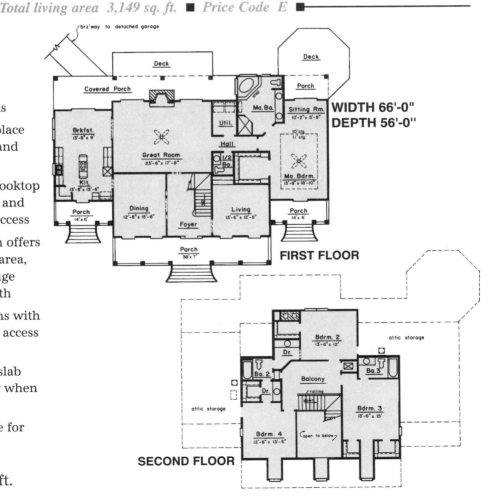

brz'way to detached garage

Deck

Deck

Covered Porch

Porch

Ma. Ba.

Sitting Rm.
10'-2" x 5'-9"

**WIDTH 66'-0"**
**DEPTH 56'-0"**

Brkfst.
13'-8" x 9'

Great Room
23'-6" x 17'-8"

Util.

Hall

10' clg.
11' clg.

1/2
Ba.

Ma. Bdrm.
13'-8" x 18'-10"

Kit.
13'-8" x 13'-6"

Porch
14' x 6'

Dining
12'-8" x 15'-6"

Foyer

Living
13'-6" x 12'-8"

Porch
14' x 6'

Porch
38' x 7'

**FIRST FLOOR**

Bdrm. 2
13'-6" x 12'

attic storage

Dr.

Ba. 2

Ba. 3

Dr.

Balcony
railing

attic storage

Bdrm. 3
13'-6" x 15'

Bdrm. 4
12'-8" x 13'-6"

open to below

**SECOND FLOOR**

# Isolated Master Suite

■ *Total living area  2,473 sq. ft.* ■ *Price Code D* ■

**SECOND FLOOR**

WIDTH 91'-8"
DEPTH 45'-8"

**FIRST FLOOR**

## No. 90420

### ■ This plan features:

— Three bedrooms

— Two full and one half baths

■ A spacious, sunken Living Room with a cathedral ceiling

■ An isolated Master Suite with a private bath and walk-in closet

■ Two additional bedrooms with a unique bath-and-a-half and ample storage space

■ An efficient U-shaped Kitchen with a double sink, ample cabinets, counter space and a Breakfast area

■ A second floor Studio overlooking the Living Room

■ An optional basement, slab or crawl space foundation — please specify when ordering

First floor — 2,213 sq. ft.
Second floor — 260 sq. ft.
Basement — 2,213 sq. ft.
Garage — 422 sq. ft.

# Illusion of Spaciousness

## No. 96484 ☒

**This plan features:**

- Three bedrooms
- Two full baths
- Open living spaces and vaulted ceilings creating an illusion of spaciousness
- Cathedral ceilings maximize space in Great Room and Dining Room
- Kitchen features skylight and breakfast bar
- Well equipped Master Suite in rear for privacy
- Two additional bedrooms in front share a full bath

Main floor — 1,246 sq. ft.
Garage — 420 sq. ft.

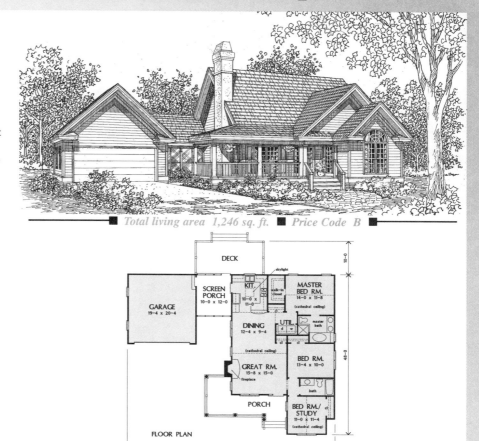

■ *Total living area  1,246 sq. ft.* ■ *Price Code  B* ■

FLOOR PLAN

© 1997 Donald A Gardner Architects, Inc.

# Elegant Exterior Attracts Attention

## No. 96530 ☒

**This plan features:**

- Three bedrooms
- Three full baths
- The exterior is highlighted by a high columned porch and many windows
- The Receiving Room is graced by a see-through fireplace that is shared with the Great Room
- The Great Room is spacious and opens onto the verandah
- The Kitchen/Dining Area adjoins the Great Room adding a spacious feeling to the home
- A vaulted ceiling, a private whirlpool bath and a Lounging Room are in the Master Suite
- Two additional bedrooms have access to a full bath

Main floor — 2,289 sq. ft.
Garage — 756 sq. ft.

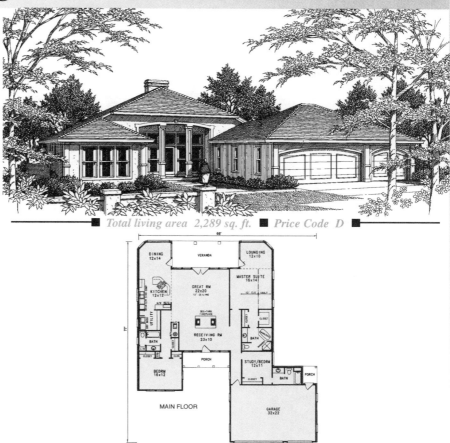

■ *Total living area  2,289 sq. ft.* ■ *Price Code  D* ■

MAIN FLOOR

# Extraordinary Elegance

© 1997 Donald A Gardner Architects, Inc.

■ *Total living area  2,916 sq. ft.* ■ *Price Code  E* ■

PATIO

SITTING
9-4 x 4-4

MASTER
BED RM.
14-0 x 16-0

FAMILY RM.
21-8 x 15-10
(two story ceiling)
fireplace

BRKFST.
9-4 x 10-4

PORCH

storage

KITCHEN
12-8 x 11-8

bath

master bath

walk-in closet

BED RM./
OFFICE
11-4 x 12-0

FOYER
8-8 x

DINING
12-8 x 13-8

UTIL
6-0
8-0

walk-in storage

LIVING RM./
STUDY
14-0 x 12-8
fireplace

PORCH

GARAGE
24-4 x 20-4

storage

FIRST FLOOR PLAN

65-4

© 1997 Donald A Gardner Architects, Inc.

SECOND FLOOR PLAN

family room below

BED RM.
14-0 x 14-8

attic storage

bath

attic storage

foyer below

BED RM.
12-8 x 13-8

walk-in closet

storage

down

down

BONUS RM.
14-1 x 19-5

attic storage

## No. 99821

### ■ This plan features:

- Four bedrooms
- Three full and one half baths
- ■ Stone and stucco exterior and contemporary interior offer class and convenience
- ■ Formal Dining and Living rooms at front of home, while casual areas located in back
- ■ Columns offer definition for open Family Room, Kitchen and breakfast bay
- ■ Master Bedroom suite features sitting bay, luxurious bath and walk-in closet
- ■ Second floor includes two more bedrooms, full bath and Bonus Room

First floor — 2,293 sq. ft.
Second floor — 623 sq. ft.
Bonus room — 359 sq. ft.
Garage & storage — 641 sq. ft.

# For Today's Sophisticated Homeowner

■ *Total living area  1,500 sq. ft.* ■ *Price Code  A* ■

WIDTH 59-10

MASTER
BATH

PORCH

BRKFST
8-0 X 11-6
10 FT CLG

FP

LIVING RM
16-0 X 13-8
10 FT CLG

KITCHEN
10-6 X 14-0

GARAGE

DEPTH 44-4

MASTER
BEDRM
11-4 X 14-6
10 FT CLG

SLOPE

BATH
2

ENTRY

PAN

BEDRM 2
12-0 X 13-0

BEDRM 3
11-0 X 13-8
10 FT
COFFERED CLG

PORCH

DINING RM
10-6 X 12-0

**MAIN FLOOR**

## No. 93027

### ■ This plan features:

- Three bedrooms
- Two full baths
- ■ A formal Dining Room that opens off the Foyer and has a classic bay window
- ■ A Kitchen notable for its angled eating bar that opens to the Living Room
- ■ A cozy fireplace in the Living Room, enjoyed also by the Kitchen
- ■ A Master Suite that includes a whirlpool tub/shower combination and a walk-in closet
- ■ Ten foot ceilings in the major living areas, including the Master Bedroom
- ■ No materials list is available for this plan

Main floor — 1,500 sq. ft.
Garage — 437 sq. ft.

216  © Larry E. Belk

# Comfortable Design Encourages Relaxation

© 1997 Donald A. Gardner Architects, Inc.

B. NATHAN

■ *Total living area  2,349 sq. ft.* ■ *Price Code  D* ■

# No. 96413

## ■ This plan features:

- Four bedrooms
- Three full baths
- ■ A wide front Porch providing a warm welcome
- ■ Center dormer lighting Foyer, as columns punctuate the entry to the Dining Room and Great Room
- ■ Spacious Kitchen with angled countertop and open to the Breakfast Bay
- ■ Tray ceilings add elegance to the Dining Room and the Master Suite
- ■ Master Suite, privately located, features an arrangement for the physically challenged

Main floor — 2,349 sq. ft.
Bonus — 435 sq. ft.
Garage — 615 sq. ft.

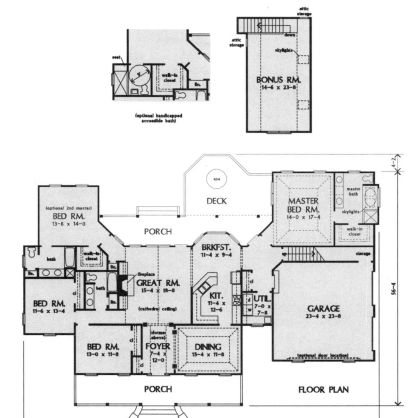

# Elegant Brick Two-Story

■ *Total living area  2,398 sq. ft.* ■ *Price Code D* ■

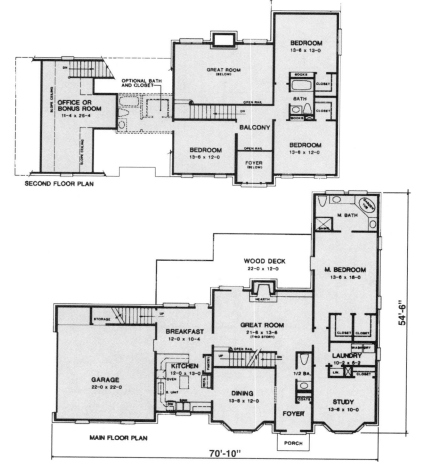

SECOND FLOOR PLAN

MAIN FLOOR PLAN

## No. 90450

■ **This plan features:**

— Four bedrooms

— Two or three full and one half baths

■ A two-story Great Room with a fireplace and access to a deck

■ Master Suite with two walk-in closets and a private master bath

■ A large island Kitchen serving the formal Dining Room and the sunny Breakfast Nook with ease

■ Three additional bedrooms, two with walk-in closets, sharing a full hall bath

■ An optional Bonus Room with a private entrance from below

■ An optional basement or crawl space foundation — please specify when ordering

First floor — 1,637 sq. ft.
Second floor — 761 sq. ft.
Bonus — 453 sq. ft.

# Classic Columns Accent Porch

## No. 94729

**This plan features:**

Three bedrooms

Two full baths

Classic columns accenting the entry Porch of this home achieving an elegant style

An open floor plan incorporating twelve foot ceilings in the main living rooms

Sliding glass doors opening to a rear Patio for expanded living space

Large kitchen including a peninsula counter/eating bar, convenient for meals on the go

Master Suite designed to take advantage of the rear views and has a large walk-in closet

Master bath with a garden tub and a double vanity

Two additional bedrooms sharing a full family bath

Main floor — 1,417 sq. ft.
Garage — 522 sq. ft.
Deck — 288 sq. ft.

*An*
**EXCLUSIVE DESIGN**
*By United Design Associates*

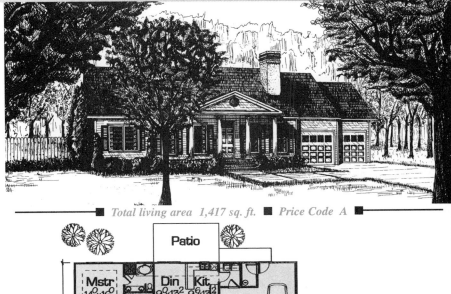

*Total living area 1,417 sq. ft.* ■ *Price Code A* ■

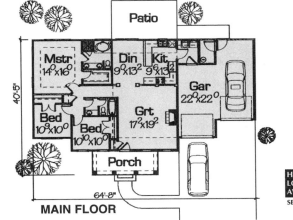

**MAIN FLOOR**

HIGH WIND LOAD ENGINEERING AVAILABLE
SEE PAGE 339 FOR DETAILS

---

# Stunning Brick and Siding Exterior

## No. 96414

**This plan features:**

Three bedrooms

Two full baths

Stunning brick and siding exterior surrounds well planned living spaces

Great Room open to the Breakfast Bay, Dining Room and Foyer

Bay window in the Master Bedroom creating a Great Master Suite sitting area as well as a dramatic rear elevation

Master Suite equipped with spacious pampering bath with corner shower, garden tub, enclosed toilet and huge walk-in closet

Bonus Room providing possibilities of expansion

Secondary bedrooms share full bath located between the rooms

Main floor — 2,196 sq. ft.
Garage & Storage — 575 sq. ft.
Bonus Room — 326 sq. ft.

*Total living area 2,196 sq. ft.* ■ *Price Code D* ■

**FLOOR PLAN**

# Farmhouse Romance

© 1991 Donald A. Gardner Architects, Inc.

■ *Total living area  1,936 sq. ft.*  ■ *Price Code  C* ■

FIRST FLOOR PLAN

© 1991 Donald A Gardner Architects, Inc.

SECOND FLOOR PLAN

## No. 99874

### ■ This plan features:

— Three bedrooms

— Two full and one half  baths

■ Windows and gables add a romantic feel to this farmhouse with a wrap-around Porch and expansive Deck area

■ The two-story Foyer has an upstairs balcony

■ The large Great Room with a dramatic fireplace features a box bay window at one end and access to a screened Porch at the other

■ The center island Kitchen opens to the Dining Room and large Breakfast Area for a real country feel

■ The Master Suite has double walk-in closets plus a whirlpool tub and a shower

First floor — 1,025 sq. ft.
Second floor — 911 sq. ft.
Bonus — 410 sq. ft.
Garage & storage — 520 sq. ft.

# Outstanding Appeal

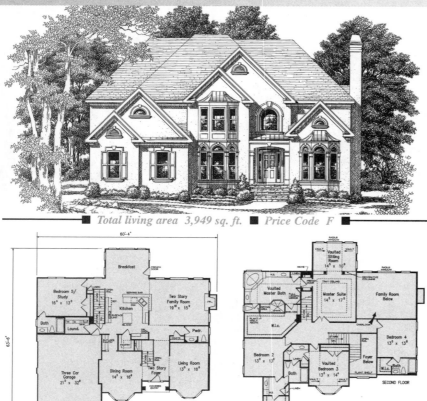

■ *Total living area  3,949 sq. ft.*  ■ *Price Code  F* ■

FIRST FLOOR PLAN

SECOND FLOOR

## No. 98437

### ■ This plan features:

— Five bedrooms

— Four full and one half baths

■ The Formal Dining and Living rooms are off the two-story Foyer

■ A Butler Pantry located between the Kitchen and formal Dining Room for convenience

■ An island Kitchen with a walk-in Pantry and a peninsula counter/serving bar highlight this room

■ The Breakfast Room accesses the rear yard through a French door

■ The second floor Master Suite is topped by tray ceiling in the bedroom and by a vaulted ceiling above the Sitting Room and bath

■ Three additional bedrooms with private access to full baths and closet space

■ An optional basement or crawl space foundation — please specify when ordering

First floor — 2,002 sq. ft.
Second floor — 1,947 sq. ft.
Basement — 2,002 sq. ft.
Garage — 737 sq. ft.

# Ultimate Master Suite

© Larry E. Belk

■ *Total living area  1,955 sq. ft.* ■ *Price Code  C* ■

# No. 93030

## This plan features:

- Three bedrooms

- Two full baths

■ A columned Dining Room and an expansive Great Room with a large hearth fireplace between sliding glass doors to a covered Porch and a Deck with hot tub

■ Kitchen with a built-in pantry, a peninsula sink and an octagon-shaped Breakfast area

■ A Master Bedroom wing with French doors, a vaulted ceiling, a plush master bath with a huge walk-in closet, a double vanity and a window tub

■ Two bedrooms with walk-in closets share a full hall bath

■ No materials list is available for this plan

Main floor — 1,955 sq. ft.
Garage — 561 sq. ft.

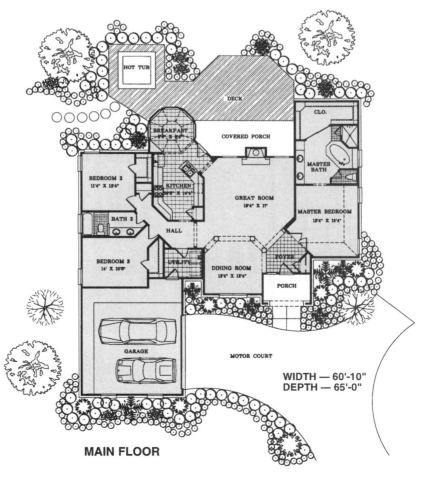

WIDTH — 60'-10"
DEPTH — 65'-0"

**MAIN FLOOR**

# Easy Everyday Living and Entertaining

■ *Total living area  1,664 sq. ft.* ■ *Price Code B* ■

## No. 92238

### ■ This plan features:

- Three bedrooms

- Two full baths

■ Front entrance accented by segmented arches, sidelight and transom windows

■ Open Living Room with focal point fireplace, wetbar and access to Patio

■ Dining area open to both the Living Room and the Kitchen

■ Efficient Kitchen with a cooktop island, walk-in pantry and Utility area with a Garage entry

■ Large walk-in closet, double vanity bath and access to Patio featured in the Master Bedroom suite

■ No materials list is available for this plan

Main floor — 1,664 sq. ft.
Basement — 1,600 sq. ft.
Garage — 440 sq. ft.

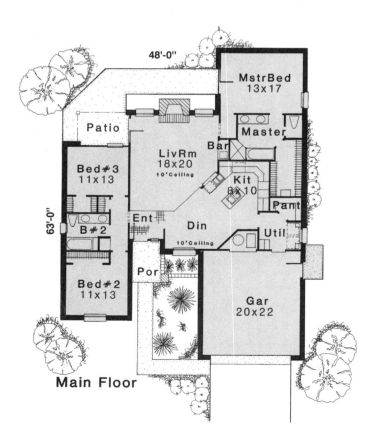

**Main Floor**

# Compact and Convenient Ranch

## No. 94208

**This plan features:**

Three bedrooms

Two full baths

Impressive Portico entry into Foyer with a decorative ceiling and formal Dining Room

Spacious Great Room with built-in entertainment center and cozy fireplace, opens through double French doors onto Veranda

Efficient Kitchen with a walk-in Pantry, serving/snack bar, and Eating Nook with bay window

Plush Master Suite with French doors to the Veranda, two walk-in closets and full bath

Two additional bedrooms, with large closets share a full bath

No materials list is available for this plan

Main floor — 1,795 sq. ft.

Garage — 465 sq. ft.

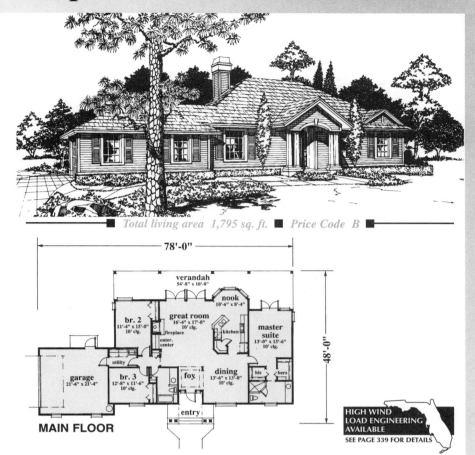

■ *Total living area  1,795 sq. ft.*  ■ *Price Code  B* ■

HIGH WIND LOAD ENGINEERING AVAILABLE
SEE PAGE 339 FOR DETAILS

**MAIN FLOOR**

# Classic Victorian

## No. 94721

**This plan features:**

Four bedrooms

Three full and one half baths

Large open areas that are bright and free flowing

Great Room accented by a fireplace and large front window

Sun Room off of the Great Room viewing the Porch

Dining Room in close proximity to the Kitchen

Efficient Kitchen flows into informal Breakfast Nook

Private first floor Master Suite highlighted by a plush master bath

Three bedrooms on the second floor, two with walk-in closets and one with a private bath

First floor — 1,868 sq. ft.

Second floor — 964 sq. ft.

Garage — 460 sq. ft.

■ *Total living area  2,832 sq. ft.*  ■ *Price Code  E* ■

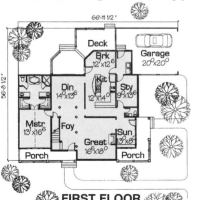

**FIRST FLOOR**

**SECOND FLOOR**

HIGH WIND LOAD ENGINEERING AVAILABLE
SEE PAGE 339 FOR DETAILS

*An* **EXCLUSIVE DESIGN**
*By United Design Associates*

# Open Spaces

## No. 96512

■ **This plan features:**

— Three bedrooms

— Two full and one half baths

■ Great Room opens to the Nook which adjoins the Kitchen creating a feeling of spaciousness

■ Cozy corner fireplace and two ceiling fans highlight the Great Room

■ The Kitchen is located between the Nook and the Dining Room for convenience in serving

■ Secluded Master Suite is enhanced by a five piece master bath and two walk-in closets

■ Two additional bedrooms on the second floor each have a walk-in closet and access to a full bath

First floor — 1,732 sq. ft.
Second floor — 544 sq. ft.
Garage — 460 sq. ft.

■ *Total living area 2,276 sq. ft.* ■ *Price Code D* ■

**WIDTH 60'-0"**
**DEPTH 59'-0"**

**FIRST FLOOR**

**SECOND FLOOR**

# Four Bedroom Beauty

## No. 98510

■ **This plan features:**

— Four bedrooms

— Two full baths

■ The formal Dining Room has a 9-foot ceiling, a bay window, and direct access to the Kitchen

■ A 10-foot ceiling continues from the entry into the Living Room that is accented by a fireplace and bookshelves

■ The Kitchen has an angled serving bar, a pantry, and is open to the Breakfast Nook

■ Three bedrooms all have 8-foot ceilings and large closets, they share a bath in the hall

■ The Master bedroom has a 9-foot ceiling, a private bath and a walk in closet

■ There is a patio in the rear of the home

■ No materials list is available for this plan

Main floor — 1,840 sq. ft.
Garage — 612 sq. ft.

■ *Total living area 1,840 sq. ft.* ■ *Price Code C* ■

**MAIN FLOOR**

# Symmetrical and Stately

■ *Total living area  2,387 sq. ft.* ■ *Price Code  E* ■

## No. 92546 ⚒

### This plan features:

- Four bedrooms
- Two full and one half baths
- Dining Room accented by an arched window and pillars
- Decorative ceiling crowns the Den which contains a hearth fireplace, built-in shelves and large double window
- Kitchen with a peninsula serving counter and Breakfast area, adjoining the Utility Room and Garage
- Master Bedroom Suite with a decorative ceiling, two vanities and a large walk-in closet
- Three additional bedrooms with double closets share a full bath
- An optional slab or crawl space foundation — please specify when ordering

Main floor — 2,387 sq. ft.
Garage — 505 sq. ft.

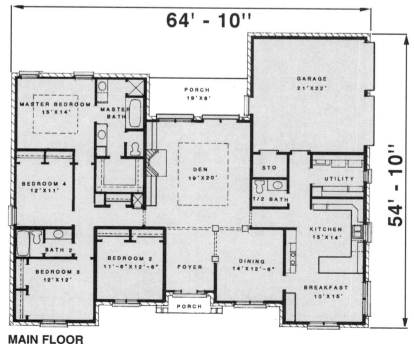

**MAIN FLOOR**

# Elegant Presence

■ *Total living area  2,980 sq. ft.* ■ *Price Code E* ■

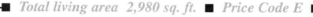

## No. 98231

### ■ This plan features:

— Four bedrooms

— Two full, one three-quarter and one half baths

■ A double door entrance into the grand Foyer, and an attached double door entry accesses the Library

■ The Living Room is to the left of the Foyer and steps up into the Dining Room

■ A vaulted ceiling crowns the Family Room and the Breakfast Room

■ The Master Suite is topped by a vaulted ceiling and includes a his-n-her bath

■ An optional basement or slab foundation — please specify when ordering

■ No material list is available for this plan

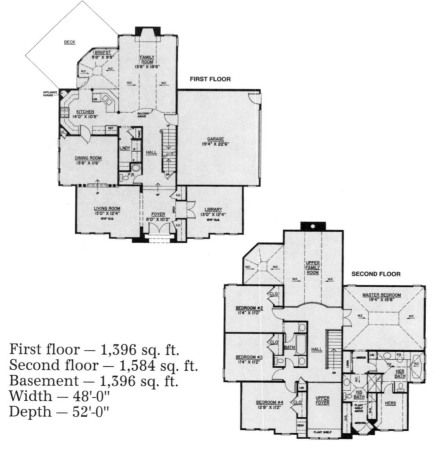

First floor — 1,396 sq. ft.
Second floor — 1,584 sq. ft.
Basement — 1,396 sq. ft.
Width — 48'-0"
Depth — 52'-0"

# Perfect Porch for a Swing

## No. 94603

**This plan features:**

Three bedrooms

Two full and one half baths

Friendly, country front Porch shelters entrance into central Foyer

An expansive Living Room with a massive fireplace below a two-story sloped ceiling and access to Patio

Convenient Kitchen with peninsula counter efficiently serve bright Breakfast Area and formal Dining Room

Bedroom featuring a dressing area with double vanity and a walk-in closet

Two additional second floor bedrooms with dormers and large closets, share a full bath and a large attic storage

An optional crawl space or slab foundation — please specify when ordering

No materials list is available for this plan

First floor — 1,238 sq. ft.

Second floor — 499 sq. ft.

Width — 38'-4"

Depth — 49'-0"

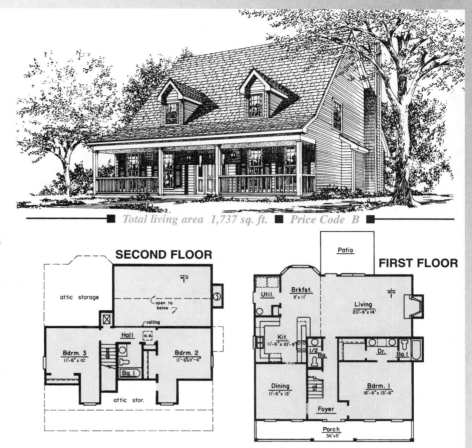

Total living area 1,737 sq. ft. ■ Price Code B

# Friendly Front Porch

## No. 96500

**This plan features:**

Three bedrooms

Two full and one half baths

Wrap-around front Porch and double French doors are an inviting sight

Central Foyer with a lovely landing staircase opens to the Dining and Great rooms

The fireplace is framed by a built-in credenza in the Great Room

Kitchen boasts a buffet, pantry and a peninsula counter/snack bar

Master Bedroom offers direct access to the Sun Room, a walk-in closet and a luxurious bath

First floor — 2,361 sq. ft.

Second floor — 650 sq. ft.

Detached Carport/Workshop — 864 sq. ft.

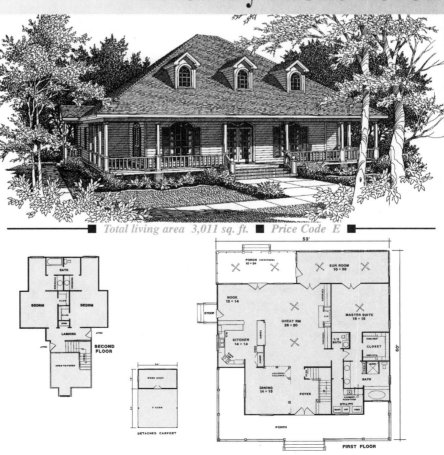

Total living area 3,011 sq. ft. ■ Price Code E

# Distinctive European Design

■ *Total living area  1,887 sq. ft.* ■ *Price Code D* ■

## No. 92516

■ **This plan features:**

— Three bedrooms

— Two full baths

■ The Living Room, topped by a vaulted ceiling

■ A gourmet Kitchen with a peninsula counter/snackbar and built-in Pantry

■ A large Master Bedroom, crowned by a raised ceiling, with French doors leading to a covered Porch, a luxurious bath and a walk-in closet

■ Two additional bedrooms with decorative windows and over-sized closets share a full hall bath

■ An optional crawl space or slab foundation — please specify when ordering

Main floor — 1,887 sq. ft.
Garage & Storage — 524 sq. ft.

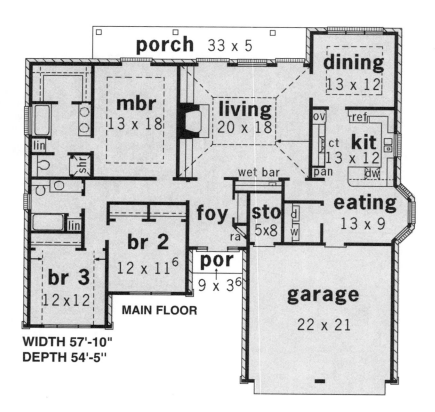

porch 33 x 5

dining 13 x 12

mbr 13 x 18

living 20 x 18

ov

ct

kit 13 x 12

ref

pan

dw

wet bar

lin

shr

lin

foy

sto 5x8

d w

eating 13 x 9

ra

br 2 12 x 11⁶

por 9 x 3⁶

garage 22 x 21

br 3 12 x 12

**MAIN FLOOR**

**WIDTH 57'-10"**
**DEPTH 54'-5"**

# Bay Windows and a Terrific Front Porch

■ *Total living area  1,778 sq. ft.* ■ *Price Code  B* ■

## No. 93261

An
## EXCLUSIVE DESIGN
*By Jannis Vann & Associates, Inc.*

**This plan features:**

– Three bedrooms

– Two full baths

■ A Country style front Porch

■ An expansive Living Area that includes a fireplace

■ A Master Suite with a private master bath and a walk-in closet, as well as a bay window view of the front yard

■ An efficient Kitchen that serves the sunny Breakfast Area and the Dining Room with equal ease

■ A built-in Pantry and a desk add to the conveniences in the Breakfast Area

■ Two additional bedrooms that share the full hall bath

■ A convenient main floor Laundry Room

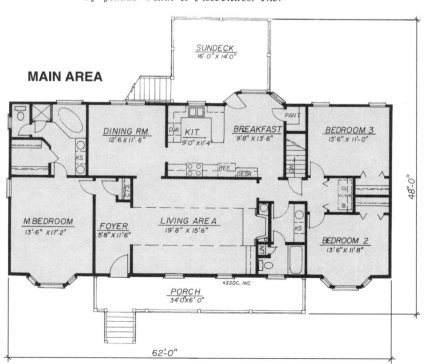

Main area — 1,778 sq. ft.
Basement — 1,008 sq. ft.
Garage — 728 sq. ft.

# Elegance And A Relaxed Lifestyle

© 1994 Donald A. Gardner Architects, Inc.

■ *Total living area  2,435 sq. ft.* ■ *Price Code  D* ■

## No. 99895

### ■ This plan features:

— Four bedrooms

— Three full baths

■ This family home has combined elegance with a relaxed lifestyle in an open plan full of surprises

■ Open two-level Foyer has a palladian window which visually ties in the formal Dining Area to the expansive Great Room

■ Windows all around, including bays in Master Bedroom and Breakfast Area provide natural light, while nine foot ceilings create volume

■ Master Bedroom features a whirlpool tub, separate shower and his-n-her vanities

First floor — 1,841 sq. ft.
Second floor — 594 sq. ft.
Bonus room — 411 sq. ft.
Garage & storage — 596 sq. ft.

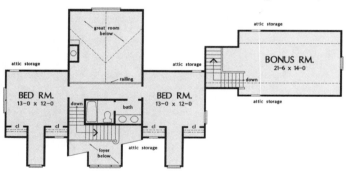

### SECOND FLOOR PLAN

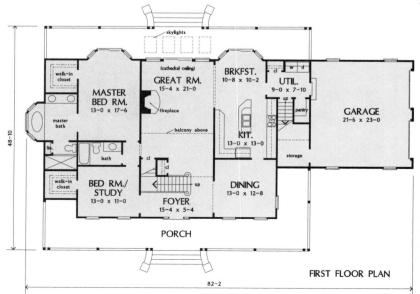

### FIRST FLOOR PLAN

# Turret Dining Views

■ *Total living area 1,742 sq. ft.* ■ *Price Code B* ■

# No. 93061

## ■ This plan features:

- Three bedrooms

- Two full baths

■ Great Room with a fireplace and access to the rear yard

■ Unique Dining Room with an alcove of windows, adjoins the Kitchen

■ Angled counter with an eating bar and a built-in pantry in the Kitchen easily serves the Breakfast area, and Great Room

■ Master bath with a corner whirlpool tub, a double vanity and a huge walk-in closet

■ An optional slab or crawl space foundation available — please specify when ordering

■ No materials list is available for this plan

Main floor — 1,742 sq. ft.
Garage — 566 sq. ft.

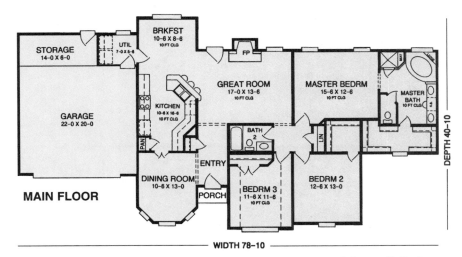

© Larry E. Belk

# Cozy Three-Bedroom

■ *Total living area  1,515 sq. ft.* ■ *Price Code B* ■

## No. 96522

■ **This plan features:**

— Three bedrooms

— Two full baths

■ The triple arched front Porch adds to the curb appeal of the home

■ The expansive Great Room is accented by a cozy gas fireplace

■ The efficient Kitchen includes an eating bar that separates it from the Great Room

■ The Master Bedroom is highlighted by a walk-in closet and a whirlpool bath

■ Two secondary bedrooms share use of the full hall bath

■ The rear Porch extends dining to the outdoors

Main floor — 1,515 sq. ft.
Garage — 528 sq. ft.

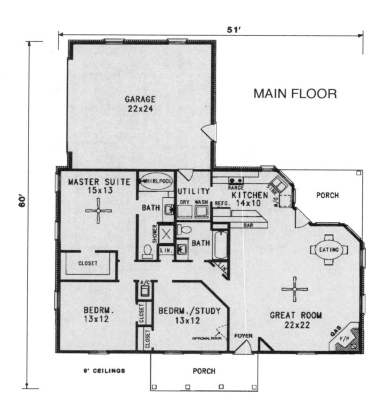

MAIN FLOOR

# Great Room With Columns

© 1995 Donald A Gardner Architects, Inc.

■ *Total living area  1,879 sq. ft.* ■ *Price Code  C* ■

## No. 99807

■ **This plan features:**

- Three bedrooms

- Two full baths

■ Great Room crowned with a cathedral ceiling and accented by columns and a fireplace

■ Tray ceilings and arched picture windows accent the front bedroom and the Dining Room

■ Secluded Master Suite highlighted by a tray ceiling and contains a bath with skylight, a garden tub and spacious walk-in closet

■ Two additional bedrooms share a full bath

■ An optional crawl space or basement foundation — please specify when ordering

Main floor — 1,879 sq. ft.
Bonus — 360 sq. ft.
Garage — 485 sq. ft.

**Floor Plan w/Basement Option**

© 1995 Donald A Gardner Architects, Inc.

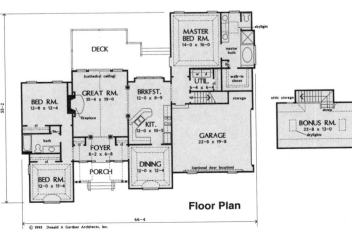

**Floor Plan**

© 1995 Donald A Gardner Architects, Inc.

# Farmhouse with Charm and Style

© 1993 Donald A. Gardner Architects, Inc.

■ *Total living area  2,308 sq. ft.* ■ *Price Code D* ■

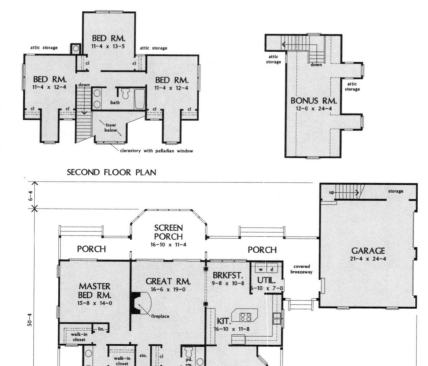

attic storage

**BED RM.**
11-4 x 13-5

attic storage

**BED RM.**
11-4 x 12-4

down

**BED RM.**
11-4 x 12-4

cl

cl

cl

cl

bath

foyer below

clerestory with palladian window

**SECOND FLOOR PLAN**

attic storage

down

attic storage

**BONUS RM.**
12-0 x 24-4

## No. 96439

### ■ This plan features:

— Four bedrooms

— Two full and one half baths

■ Arched windows, dormers and expansive Porches giving charm and style

■ Nine foot ceiling on the first floor expanding space visually

■ Great Room opening to a spacious screened Porch

■ Well planned Kitchen with an island cooktop and ample cabinet space

■ Deluxe Master Suite with a private bath and two walk-in closets

■ Bonus room adding extra storage or living space

First floor — 1,585 sq. ft.
Second floor — 723 sq. ft.
Bonus room — 419 sq. ft.
Garage & Storage — 594 sq. ft.

up

storage

**SCREEN PORCH**
16-10 x 11-4

**PORCH**

**PORCH**

**GARAGE**
21-4 x 24-4

**MASTER BED RM.**
15-8 x 14-0

fireplace

**GREAT RM.**
16-6 x 19-0

**BRKFST.**
9-8 x 10-8

**UTIL.**
5-10 x 7-0

w  d

covered breezeway

lin.

walk-in closet

**KIT.**
16-10 x 11-8

walk-in closet

sto.

cl

pd. rm.

master bath

**FOYER**
11-10 x 9-0

**DINING**
11-4 x 14-4

up

**PORCH**

**FIRST FLOOR PLAN**

6-4

50-4

50-4

30-0

© 1993  Donald A Gardner Architects, Inc.

# Bathed in Natural Light

■ *Total living area  1,619 sq. ft.* ■ *Price Code  B* ■

## No. 98416

■ **This plan features:**

- Three bedrooms

- Two full and one half baths

■ A high arched window illuminates the Foyer and adds style to the exterior of the home

■ Vaulted ceilings in the formal Dining Room, Breakfast Room and Great Room create volume

■ The Master Suite is crowned with a decorative tray ceiling

■ The Master Bath has a double vanity, oval tub, separate shower and a walk-in closet

■ The Loft, with the option of becoming a fourth bedroom, highlights the second floor

■ An optional basement or crawl space foundation — please specify when ordering

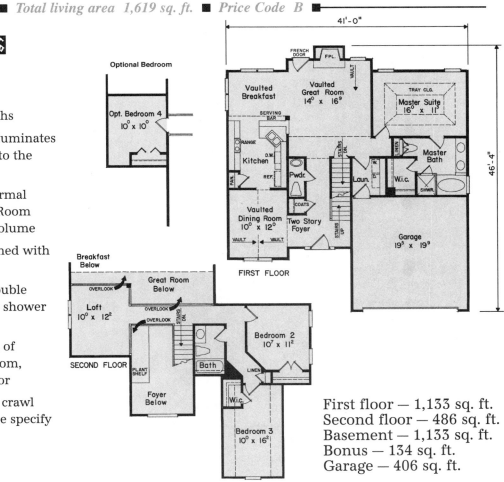

First floor — 1,133 sq. ft.
Second floor — 486 sq. ft.
Basement — 1,133 sq. ft.
Bonus — 134 sq. ft.
Garage — 406 sq. ft.

# Traditional Elegance

■ *Total living area  3,813 sq. ft.* ■ *Price Code F* ■

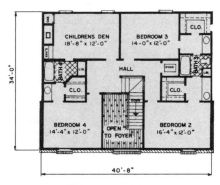

**SECOND FLOOR PLAN**

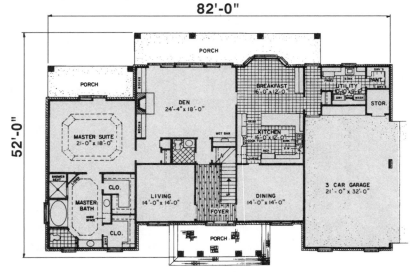

**FIRST FLOOR PLAN**

# No. 92504

## ■ This plan features:

— Four bedrooms

— Three full and one half baths

■ A elegant entrance leading into a two-story Foyer

■ Floor-to-ceiling windows in the formal Living and Dining rooms

■ A spacious Den with a hearth fireplace, built-in book shelves, a wetbar and a wall of windows

■ A Kitchen equipped with a bright Breakfast Area and a walk-in Pantry

■ A grand Master Suite with decorative ceilings, a private Porch and two walk-in closets

■ An optional crawl space or slab foundation — please specify when ordering

First floor — 2,553 sq. ft.
Second floor — 1,260 sq. ft.
Garage — 714 sq. ft.

# European Sophistication

© 1996 Donald A Gardner Architects, Inc.

■ *Total living area 1,699 sq. ft.* ■ *Price Code C* ■

## No. 99831 ⚒

### ■ This plan features:

- Three bedrooms

- Two full baths

■ Keystone arches, gables, and stucco give the exterior European sophistication

■ Large Great Room with fireplace, and U-shaped Kitchen with a large Utility Room nearby

■ Octagonal tray ceiling dresses up the Dining Room

■ Special ceiling treatments include a cathedral ceiling in the Great Room and tray ceilings in the Master and front bedrooms

■ Indulgent master bath with a separate toilet area, a garden tub, shower and twin vanities

Main floor — 1,699 sq. ft.
Bonus — 386 sq. ft.
Garage — 637 sq. ft.

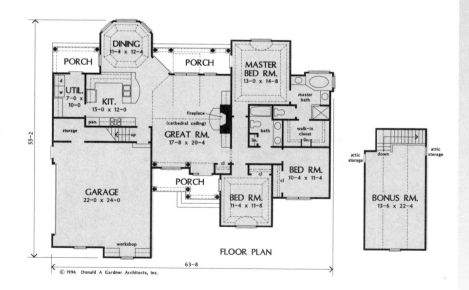

# Unique Combination Of Materials and Shapes

©1987 Donald A. Gardner Architects, Inc.

■ *Total living area  1,988 sq. ft.* ■ *Price Code C* ■

Main floor — 1,988 sq. ft.
Garage & Storage — 570 sq. ft.

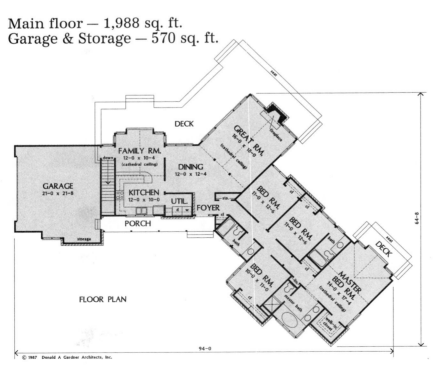

FLOOR PLAN

© 1987  Donald A Gardner Architects, Inc.

## No. 96430

■ **This plan features:**

— Four bedrooms

— Three full baths

■ The Foyer allows for easy access to all areas of the home, formal and informal

■ The Master Suite has a private Deck, cathedral ceiling and spacious bath

■ Two additional bedrooms share a hall bath

■ A third bedroom with private bath offers greater flexibility

■ The Family Room and Great Room gain added drama from cathedral ceilings

■ The Kitchen, efficiently laid out, has a snack bar for meals on the go

■ An optional basement or crawl space foundation — please specify when ordering

■ *Total living area 3,480 sq. ft.* ■ *Price Code F* ■

## No. 98508

### This plan features:

Four bedrooms

Three full and one half baths

Formal Living and Dining rooms gracefully defined with columns and decorative windows

Wood plank flooring and a massive fireplace accent the Great Room

Hub Kitchen with brick pavers and extended serving counter

Private Master Bedroom offers a Private Lanai and plush dressing area

Three second floor bedrooms with walk-in closets and private access to a full bath

No materials list is available for this plan

Main floor — 2,441 sq. ft.
Upper floor — 1,039 sq. ft.
Bonus — 271 sq. ft.
Garage — 660 sq. ft.

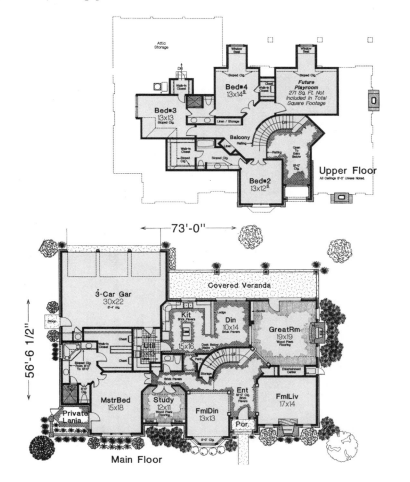

# Details Distinguish This Home Design

■ *Total living area  2,539 sq. ft.* ■ *Price Code E* ■

**SECOND FLOOR**

First floor — 1,809 sq. ft.
Second floor — 730 sq. ft.
Garage — 533 sq. ft.

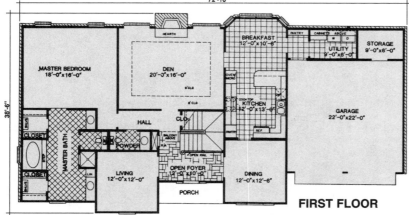

**FIRST FLOOR**

# No. 92537

## ■ This plan features:

— Four bedrooms

— Three full and one half baths

■ Entrance into Open Foyer is highlighted by an arched window

■ Formal Living and Dining rooms located off Foyer

■ Den has fireplace and access to backyard

■ Hub Kitchen with peninsula counter/snackbar, two Pantries, a Breakfast area, Utility room, and Garage entry

■ Spacious Master Bedroom suite with a large bath, two walk-in closets and dual vanity

■ Three additional bedrooms, one with a private bath, share second floor

■ An optional crawl space or slab foundation — please specify when ordering

# Attractive Ceiling Treatments and Open Layout

■ *Total living area  1,654 sq. ft.* ■ *Price Code B* ■

## No. 96506

### This plan features:

- Three bedrooms

- Two full and one half baths

- Great Room and Master Suite with step-up ceiling treatments

- A cozy fireplace providing warm focal point in the Great Room

- Open layout between Kitchen, Dining and Great Room lending a more spacious feeling

- Five-piece, private bath and walk-in closet pampering Master Suite

- Two additional bedrooms located at opposite end of home from Master Suite

Main floor — 1,654 sq. ft.
Garage — 480 sq. ft.

**MAIN FLOOR**

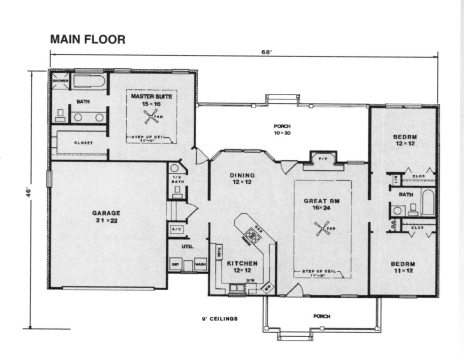

# Plan for the Future

■ *Total living area 1,325 sq. ft.* ■ *Price Code A* ■

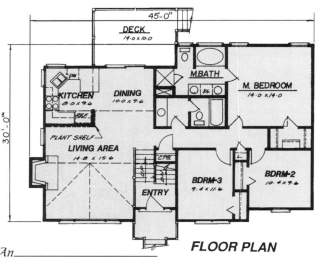

45'-0"

DECK
14·0 x 10·0

KITCHEN
8·0 x 9·6

DINING
10·0 x 9·6

M.BATH

M. BEDROOM
14·0 x 14·0

30'-0"

PLANT SHELF

LIVING AREA
14·8 x 15·6

BDRM-3
9·4 x 11·6

BDRM-2
10·4 x 9·6

ENTRY

**FLOOR PLAN**

*An*
EXCLUSIVE DESIGN
*By Jannis Vann & Associates, Inc.*

FUTURE PLAYROOM
15·0 x 22·8

DOUBLE GARAGE
22·0 x 26·0

**LOWER FLOOR**

## No. 93265

### ■ This plan features:

— Three bedrooms

— Two full baths

■ Entry leads up to Living area accented by a vaulted ceiling and arched window

■ Compact, efficient Kitchen with serving counter/snackbar

■ Comfortable Master Bedroom with a walk-in closet and bath

■ Two additional bedrooms with large closets, share a full bath

■ Entry leads down to Laundry, Garage and future Playroom

■ No materials list is available for this plan

Main floor — 1,269 sq. ft.
Lower level — 56 sq. ft.
Basement — 382 sq. ft.
Garage — 598 sq. ft.

# Country Cottage Charm

■ *Total living area  3,423 sq. ft.* ■ *Price Code  F* ■

# No. 98536

## This plan features:

- Four bedrooms
- Two full and one half baths
- Vaulted Master Bedroom has a private skylit bath
- Three more bedrooms have walk-in closets and share a full bath
- A Loft and Bonus Room above the Living Room
- Family Room has built-in book shelves, a fireplace, and overlooks the covered Verandah
- The huge three-car Garage has a separate Shop Area
- An optional slab or a crawl space foundation — please specify when ordering
- No materials list is available for this plan

Main floor — 2,787 sq. ft.
Upper floor — 636 sq. ft.
Garage — 832 sq. ft.

**Upper Floor**
Optional Bonus Room & Loft

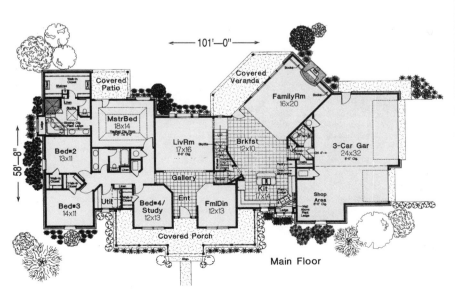

Main Floor

# Split Bedroom Plan

■ *Total living area  2,051 sq. ft.* ■ *Price Code  C* ■

## No. 98427

■ **This plan features:**

— Three bedrooms

— Two full baths

■ Dining Room is crowned by a tray ceiling

■ Living Room/Den privatized by double doors at its entrance, and is enhanced by a bay window

■ The Kitchen includes a walk-in pantry and a corner double sink

■ The vaulted Breakfast Room flows naturally from the Kitchen

■ The Master Suite is topped by a tray ceiling, and contains a compartmental bath plus two walk-in closets

■ An optional basement, slab or crawl space foundation — please specify when ordering

Main floor — 2,051 sq. ft.
Basement — 2,051 sq. ft.
Garage — 441 sq. ft.

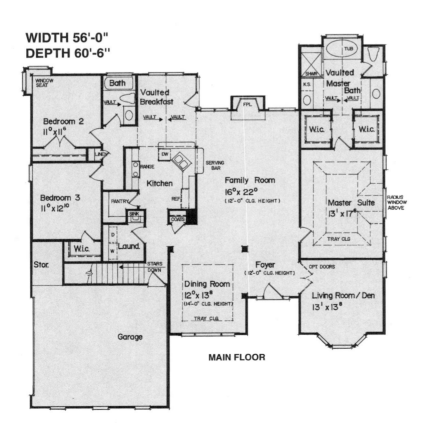

WIDTH 56'-0"
DEPTH 60'-6''

WINDOW SEAT

Bath

Vaulted Breakfast

Bedroom 2
11⁰ x 11⁶

Kitchen

RANGE

DW

SERVING BAR

Family Room
16⁰ x 22⁰
(12'-0" CLG. HEIGHT)

FPL

TUB

SHWR

Vaulted Master Bath

K.S.

W.i.c.

W.i.c.

Master Suite
13' x 17⁶
TRAY CLG

RADIUS WINDOW ABOVE

Bedroom 3
11⁰ x 12¹⁰

PANTRY

REF

SINK

COATS

LINEN

Foyer
(12'-0" CLG. HEIGHT)

OPT DOORS

W.i.c.

Laund.

D

W

Stor.

STAIRS DOWN

Dining Room
12⁰ x 13⁸
(14'-0" CLG. HEIGHT)
TRAY CLG.

Living Room / Den
13' x 13⁸

Garage

**MAIN FLOOR**

# Cathedral Ceiling Enlarges Great Room

© 1996 Donald A Gardner Architects, Inc.

■ *Total living area 1,699 sq. ft.* ■ *Price Code B* ■

# No. 99811

## This plan features:

- Three bedrooms

- Two full baths

- Two dormers add volume to the Foyer

- Great Room, topped by a cathedral ceiling, is open to the Kitchen and Breakfast area

- Accent columns define the Foyer, Great Room, Kitchen and Breakfast Area

- Private Master Suite crowned in a tray ceiling and highlighted by a skylit bath

- Front bedroom topped by a tray ceiling

Main floor — 1,699 sq. ft.
Garage — 498 sq. ft.
Bonus room — 336 sq. ft.

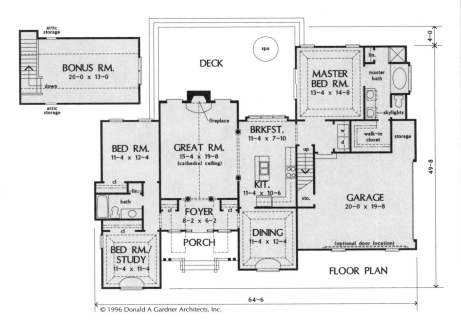

© 1996 Donald A Gardner Architects, Inc.

# Comfort Zone

■ *Total living area  1,908 sq. ft.* ■ *Price Code C* ■

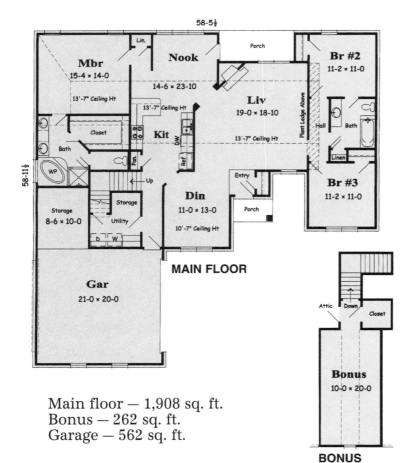

**MAIN FLOOR**

**BONUS**

Main floor — 1,908 sq. ft.
Bonus — 262 sq. ft.
Garage — 562 sq. ft.

## No. 91105

■ **This plan features:**

— Three bedrooms

— Two full baths

■ The stunning brick veneer, arched windows, gabled roof lines and herringbone patterns add plenty of character

■ The efficient Master bath includes a double vanity with knee space, a corner whirlpool tub, and a separate shower

■ Bonus area for future expansion is provided over the Garage accessed by a stairway near the Kitchen

■ Extra features include a Kitchen snack bar, a back Porch, an abundance of closets, and a large Living room

■ No materials list is available for this plan

# Traditional Ranch Plan

■ *Total living area 2,218 sq. ft.* ■ *Price Code D* ■

# No. 90454

## This plan features:

– Three bedrooms

– Two full baths

■ Large Foyer set between the formal Living and Dining rooms

■ Spacious Great Room adjacent to the open Kitchen/Breakfast area

■ Secluded Master Bedroom highlighted by the master bath with a garden tub, separate shower and his-n-her vanities

■ Bay window allows bountiful natural light into the Breakfast Area

■ Two additional bedrooms sharing a full bath

■ An optional basement or crawl space foundation — please specify when ordering

Main floor — 2,218 sq. ft.
Basement — 1,658 sq. ft.
Garage — 528 sq. ft.

# Classic Country Farmhouse

© 1995 Donald A Gardner Architects, Inc.

■ *Total living area  1,832 sq. ft.* ■ *Price Code C* ■

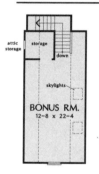

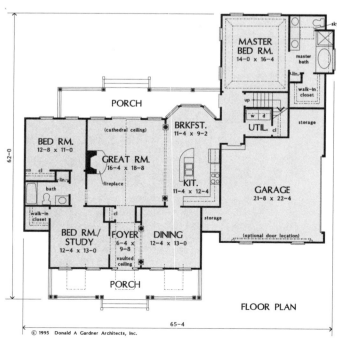

FLOOR PLAN

© 1995  Donald A Gardner Architects, Inc.

# No. 99808

## ■ This plan features:

— Three bedrooms

— Two full baths

■ Dormers, arched windows and multiple columns give this home country charm

■ Foyer, expanded by vaulted ceiling, accesses Dining Room, Bedroom/Study and Great Room

■ Expansive Great Room, with hearth fireplace topped by cathedral ceiling, opens to rear Porch and efficient Kitchen

■ Tray ceiling adds volume to private Master Bedroom with plush bath and walk-in closet

■ Extra room for growth offered by Bonus Room with skylight

Main floor — 1,832 sq. ft.
Bonus room — 425 sq. ft.
Garage & storage — 562 sq. ft.

# French Influenced One-Story

© 1990 Donald A. Gardner Architects, Inc.

■ *Total living area 2,045 sq. ft.* ■ *Price Code D* ■

## No. 96421

**This plan features:**

- Three bedrooms
- Two full baths
- Elegant details, arched windows, round columns and rich brick veneer creating curb appeal
- Arched clerestory window in the foyer introduces natural light to a large Great Room with cathedral ceiling and built-in cabinets
- Great Room adjoins a skylit Sun Room with a wetbar which then opens onto a spacious Deck
- Kitchen with cooking island centrally located with easy access to a large pantry and utility room
- Large Master Bedroom opening to the Deck and featuring a garden tub, separate shower and dual vanity
- An optional basement or crawl space foundation — please specify when ordering

Main floor — 2,045 sq. ft.
Garage & storage — 563 sq. ft.

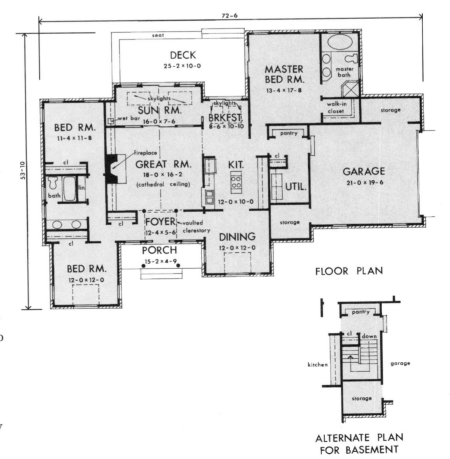

FLOOR PLAN

ALTERNATE PLAN
FOR BASEMENT

# Country Classic

©1995 Donald A. Gardner Architects, Inc.

■ *Total living area  1,838 sq. ft.* ■ *Price Code C* ■

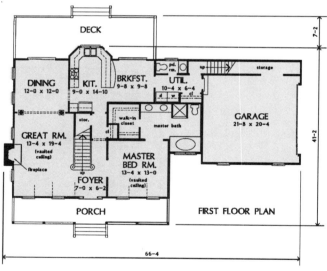

DECK

DINING
12-0 x 12-0

KIT.
9-0 x 14-10

BRKFST.
9-8 x 9-8

UTIL.
10-4 x 6-4

pd. rm.

up

storage

GREAT RM.
13-4 x 19-4
(vaulted ceiling)

fireplace

stor.

walk-in closet

master bath

GARAGE
21-8 x 20-4

MASTER
BED RM.
13-4 x 13-0
(vaulted ceiling)

FOYER
7-0 x 6-2

up

PORCH

FIRST FLOOR PLAN

7-2

41-2

66-4

BED RM.
12-0 x 12-0

walk-in closet

BED RM.
12-0 x 13-0

down

bath

walk-in closet

great room below

foyer below

master bedroom below

attic storage

BONUS RM.
13-4 x 23-8

skylights

SECOND FLOOR PLAN

## No. 96461

### ■ This plan features:

— Three bedrooms

— Two full and one half baths

■ Casually elegant exterior with dormers, gables and a charming front Porch

■ U-shaped Kitchen easily serves both adjacent eating areas

■ Nine foot ceilings amplify the first floor

■ Master Suite highlighted by a vaulted ceiling and dormer

■ Garden tub with a double window are focus of the master bath

■ Two bedrooms with walk-in closets sharing a hall bath, while back stairs lead to a spacious bonus room

First floor — 1,313 sq. ft.
Second floor — 525 sq. ft.
Bonus room — 367 sq. ft.
Garage — 513 sq. ft.

■ *Total living area  3,063 sq. ft.* ■ *Price Code  E* ■

## No. 98211

### This plan features:

- Four bedrooms

- Three full and one half baths

- High volume ceilings

- An extended staircase highlights the Foyer as columns define the Dining Room and the Grand Room

- A massive glass exterior rear wall and high ceiling in the Master Suite

- His-n-her walk-in closets and a five-piece lavish bath highlight the master bath

- The island Kitchen, Keeping Room and Breakfast Room create an open living space

- A fireplace accents both the Keeping Room and the two-story Grand Room

- An optional basement, slab or crawl space foundation — please specify when ordering

- No materials list is available for this plan

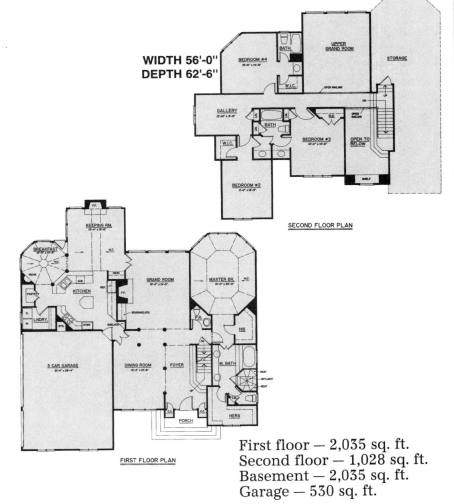

**WIDTH 56'-0"**
**DEPTH 62'-6"**

SECOND FLOOR PLAN

FIRST FLOOR PLAN

First floor — 2,035 sq. ft.
Second floor — 1,028 sq. ft.
Basement — 2,035 sq. ft.
Garage — 530 sq. ft.

# Old-Fashioned Country Porch

■ *Total living area  1,668 sq. ft.* ■ *Price Code B* ■

*An*
## EXCLUSIVE DESIGN
*By Jannis Vann & Associates, Inc.*

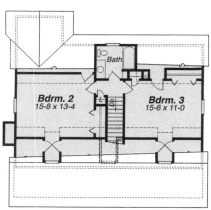

**SECOND FLOOR**

**FIRST FLOOR**

First floor — 1,057 sq. ft.
Second floor — 611 sq. ft.
Basement — 511 sq. ft.
Garage — 546 sq. ft.

# No. 93219

■ **This plan features:**

— Three bedrooms

— Two full and one half baths

■ A Traditional front Porch, with matching dormers above and a garage hidden below, leading into an open, contemporary layout

■ A Living Area with a cozy fireplace visible from the Dining Room for warm entertaining

■ An efficient U-shaped Kitchen featuring a corner, double sink and pass-thru to the Dining Room

■ A convenient half bath with a laundry center on the first floor

■ A spacious, first floor Master Suite with a lavish bath including a double vanity, walk-in closet and an oval, corner window tub

■ Two large bedrooms with dormer windows sharing a full hall bath

# Old-Fashioned With Contemporary Interior

— Total living area  2,052 sq. ft. ■ Price Code  C ■

## No. 98407 ⚒

### This plan features:

- Four bedrooms

- Three full baths

- A two-story Foyer is flanked by the Living Room and the Dining Room

- The Family Room features a fireplace and a French door

- The bayed Breakfast Nook and Pantry are adjacent to the Kitchen

- The Master Suite with a trayed ceiling has an attached bath with a vaulted ceiling

- Upstairs are two additional bedrooms, a full bath, a laundry closet and a Bonus Room

- An optional basement, slab or crawl space foundation — please specify when ordering

First floor — 1,135 sq. ft.
Second floor — 917 sq. ft.
Bonus — 216 sq. ft.
Basement — 1,135 sq. ft.
Garage — 452 sq. ft.

**SECOND FLOOR**

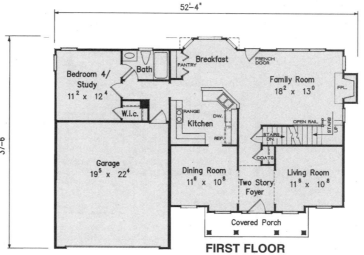

**FIRST FLOOR**

# Offering an Inviting Welcome

©1996 Donald A. Gardner Architects, Inc.

---

■ *Total living area  1,989 sq. ft.* ■ *Price Code C* ■

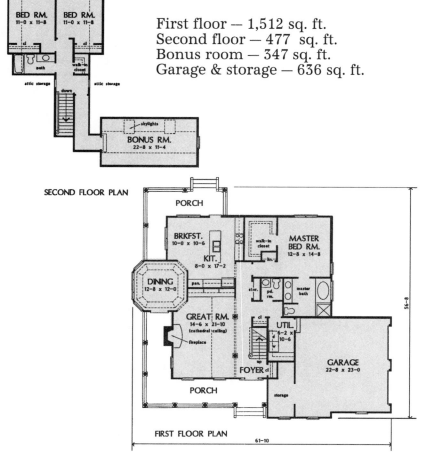

BED RM.
11-0 x 11-8

BED RM.
11-0 x 11-8

bath

walk-in closet

attic storage

down

attic storage

skylights

BONUS RM.
22-8 x 11-4

SECOND FLOOR PLAN

First floor — 1,512 sq. ft.
Second floor — 477  sq. ft.
Bonus room — 347 sq. ft.
Garage & storage — 636 sq. ft.

PORCH

BRKFST.
10-0 x 10-6

walk-in closet

lin.

MASTER
BED RM.
12-8 x 14-8

KIT.
8-0 x 17-2

pan.

stor.

pd. rm.

master bath

DINING
12-8 x 12-0

GREAT RM.
14-6 x 21-10
(cathedral ceiling)

cl

UTIL.
6-2 x 10-6

fireplace

FOYER

GARAGE
22-8 x 23-0

PORCH

storage

FIRST FLOOR PLAN

61-10

56-8

# No. 96472

■ **This plan features:**

— Three bedrooms

— Two full and one half baths

■ Triple gables and a wrapping front Porch

■ Cathedral ceiling highlights the Great Room which also includes defining columns and a cozy fireplace

■ Octagonal Dining Room with a tray ceiling and easy access to the Porch for summer dining outdoors

■ Kitchen equipped with a Pantry and a work island

■ Master Suite with a roomy walk-in closet and bath located downstairs for privacy

■ Upstairs, two bedrooms sharing a full bath and access to a skylit bonus room

# Family Room at Heart of the Home

■ *Total living area  2,558 sq. ft.* ■ *Price Code  D* ■

## No. 94640

■ **This plan features:**

- Four bedrooms

- Three full baths

■ The Living Room and Dining Room are to the left and right of the Foyer

■ The Dining Room with French doors opens to the Kitchen

■ An extended counter maximizes the workspace in the Kitchen

■ The Breakfast Room includes access to the Utility Room and to the secondary bedroom wing

■ The Master Bedroom is equipped with a double vanity bath, two walk-in closets and a linear closet

■ A cozy fireplace and a decorative ceiling highlight the Family Room

■ Secondary bedrooms have easy access to two full baths

■ No materials list is available for this plan

Main floor — 2,558 sq. ft.
Garage — 549 sq. ft.

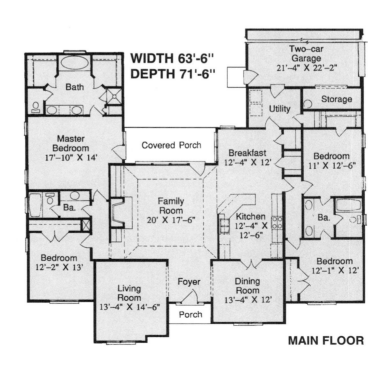

WIDTH 63'-6"
DEPTH 71'-6"

Two-car Garage 21'-4" X 22'-2"

Bath

Utility

Storage

Master Bedroom 17'-10" X 14'

Covered Porch

Breakfast 12'-4" X 12'

Bedroom 11' X 12'-6"

Ba.

Family Room 20' X 17'-6"

Kitchen 12'-4" X 12'-6"

Ba.

Bedroom 12'-2" X 13'

Living Room 13'-4" X 14'-6"

Foyer

Dining Room 13'-4" X 12'

Bedroom 12'-1" X 12'

Porch

**MAIN FLOOR**

# Victorian Details Add Visual Delight

— Total living area 1,920 sq. ft. ■ Price Code C ■

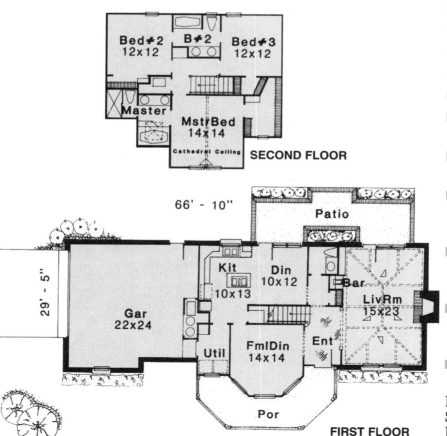

**Bed #2** 12x12
**B #2**
**Bed #3** 12x12
**Master**
**MstrBed** 14x14
**Cathedral Ceiling**
**SECOND FLOOR**

66' - 10"
29' - 5"

**Patio**
**Kit** 10x13
**Din** 10x12
**Bar**
**LivRm** 15x23
**Gar** 22x24
**Util**
**FmlDin** 14x14
**Ent**
**Por**
**FIRST FLOOR**

## No. 92218

■ **This plan features:**

— Three bedrooms

— Two full and one half baths

■ Quaint country porch

■ Expansive Living Room with a cozy fireplace and beamed ceiling

■ Formal Dining Room highlighted by an alcove of windows

■ An open Kitchen with cooktop work island, and nearby Utility Room with Garage entry

■ Master Bedroom suite offers a cathedral ceiling, huge walk-in closet and a pampering bath

■ Two secondary bedrooms with ample closets and private access to a full bath

■ No materials list is available for this plan

First floor — 1,082 sq. ft.
Second floor — 838 sq. ft.
Basement — 1,082 sq. ft.
Garage — 500 sq. ft.

*Total living area 1,683 sq. ft.* ■ *Price Code B* ■

# No. 93298

## This plan features:

- Three bedrooms

- Two full and one half baths

- Detailed gables and front Porch create a welcoming facade

- Open foyer features an angled staircase, a half bath and a coat closet

- The informal living area features a fireplace and opens onto the Sun Deck

- The Kitchen has access to both the formal and informal dining areas

- Master Bedroom includes a walk-in closet and compartmented private bath

- No materials list is available for this plan

First floor — 797 sq. ft.
Second floor — 886 sq. ft.
Basement — 797 sq. ft.
Garage — 414 sq. ft.

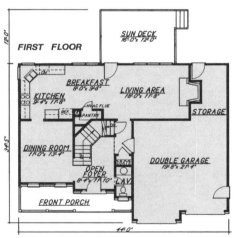

*An*
EXCLUSIVE DESIGN
*By Jannis Vann & Associates, Inc.*

# Perfect Home for Narrow Lot

© Donald A. Gardner Architects, Inc.

■ *Total living area  1,669 sq. ft.* ■ *Price Code C* ■

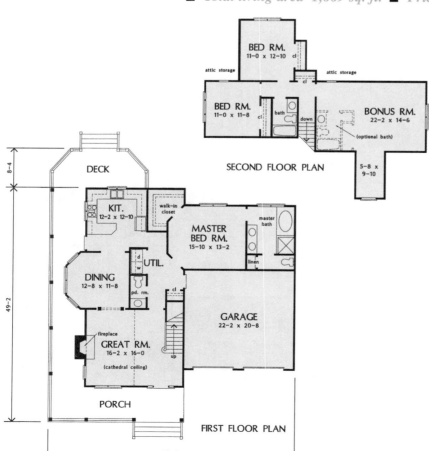

BED RM.
11-0 x 12-10 cl

attic storage

attic storage

cl

BED RM.
11-0 x 11-8  cl

bath

down

BONUS RM.
22-2 x 14-6

(optional bath)

5-8 x
9-10

SECOND FLOOR PLAN

8-4

DECK

walk-in
closet

KIT.
12-2 x 12-10

master
bath

MASTER
BED RM.
15-10 x 13-2

49-2

d
w

UTIL.

linen

DINING
12-8 x 11-8

pd. rm.

cl

GARAGE
22-2 x 20-8

fireplace

GREAT RM.
16-2 x 16-0

up

(cathedral ceiling)

PORCH

FIRST FLOOR PLAN

50-4

© 1997  Donald A Gardner Architects, Inc.

## No. 96487

### ■ This plan features:

— Three bedrooms

— Two full and one half baths

■ Wraparound Porch and two-car Garage features unusual for narrow lot floor plan

■ Alcove of windows and columns add distinction to Dining Room

■ Cathedral ceiling above inviting fireplace accent spacious Great Room

■ Efficient Kitchen with peninsula counter accesses side Porch and Deck

■ Master Suite on first floor and two additional bedrooms and Bonus Room on second floor

First floor — 1,219 sq. ft.
Second floor — 450 sq. ft.
Bonus Room — 406 sq. ft.
Garage — 473 sq. ft.

■ *Total living area  1,913 sq. ft.*  ■  *Price Code  C*  ■

# No. 98445

## This plan features:

Three bedrooms

Two full and one half baths

A two story Foyer

The Family Room is highlighted by a fireplace

The Dining Room adjoins the Family Room

The Master Bedroom is crowned by a tray ceiling

A balcony overlooks the Family Room and Foyer below

An optional basement, slab or crawl space foundation — please specify when ordering

No materials list is available for this plan

First floor — 1,398 sq. ft.
Second floor — 515 sq. ft.
Bonus room — 282 sq. ft.
Basement — 1,398 sq. ft.
Garage — 421 sq. ft.

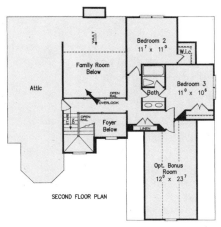

SECOND FLOOR PLAN

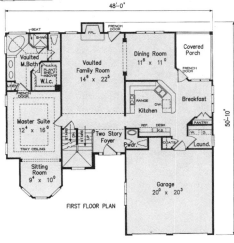

FIRST FLOOR PLAN

# Living Room Features Exposed Beams

■ *Total living area 1,876 sq. ft.* ■ *Price Code C* ■

Main floor — 1,876 sq. ft.
Garage — 619 sq. ft.

## No. 98503

■ **This plan features:**

— Three bedrooms

— Two full baths

■ A covered Porch shelters the entry to this home

■ The large Living room with exposed beams includes a fireplace and built-ins

■ The bright Dining Room is located next to the Kitchen which features a center island

■ The bedroom wing features three spacious bedrooms and two full baths

■ The two-car Garage has a handy workshop area

■ An optional crawl space or slab foundation available — please specify when ordering

■ No materials list is available for this plan

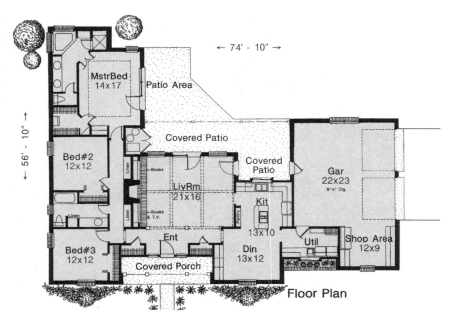

Floor Plan

■ *Total living area 2,263 sq. ft.* ■ *Price Code D* ■

# No. 90458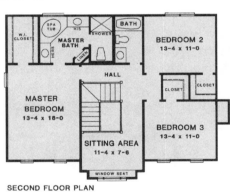

■ **This plan features:**

- Three bedrooms

- Two full and one half baths

■ The wrap-around Porch gives a nostalgic appeal to this home

■ The Great Room with fireplace is accessed directly from the Foyer

■ The formal Dining Room has direct access to the efficient Kitchen

■ An island, double sink, plenty of counter/cabinet space and a built-in Pantry complete the Kitchen

■ The second floor Master Suite has a five-piece, private bath and a walk-in closet

■ Two other bedrooms have walk-in closets and share a full bath

■ An optional basement or crawl space foundation — please specify when ordering

First floor — 1,125 sq. ft.
Second floor — 1,138 sq. ft.
Basement — 1,125 sq. ft.

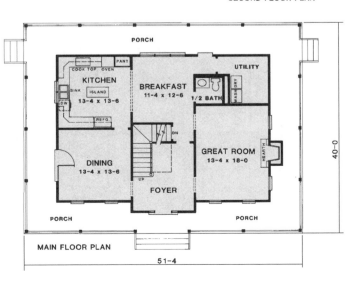

# Split Bedroom Floor Plan

■ *Total living area 1,243 sq. ft.* ■ *Price Code A* ■

## No. 96519

■ **This plan features:**

— Three bedrooms

— Two full baths

■ A split bedroom floor plan gives the Master Bedroom ultimate privacy

■ The Great room is highlighted by a fireplace and a vaulted ten-foot ceiling

■ A snack bar peninsula counter is one of the many conveniences of the Kitchen

■ The Patio is accessed from the Dining Room and expands dining to the outdoors

■ Two additional bedrooms share the full bath in the hall

■ No materials list is available for this plan

Main floor — 1,243 sq. ft.
Garage — 523 sq. ft.

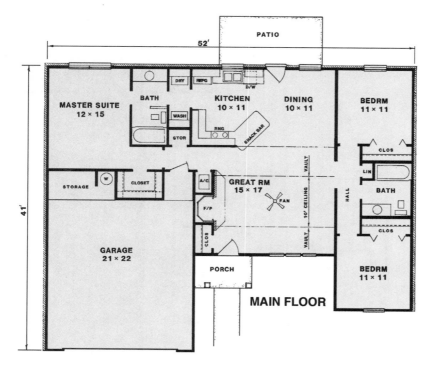

■ *Total living area  2,445 sq. ft.* ■ *Price Code  D* ■

# No. 98511

### This plan features:

- Four bedrooms

- Three full and one half baths

■ Entertaining in grand style in the formal Living Room, the Dining Room, or under the covered patio in the backyard

■ A Family Room crowned in a cathedral ceiling, enhanced by a center fireplace and built-in book shelves

■ An efficient Kitchen highlighted by a wall oven, plentiful counter space and a pantry

■ A Master Bedroom with a sitting area, huge walk in closet, private bath and access to a covered lanai

■ A secondary bedroom wing containing three additional bedrooms with ample closet space and two full baths

■ No materials list is available for this plan

Main floor — 2,445 sq. ft.
Garage — 630 sq. ft.

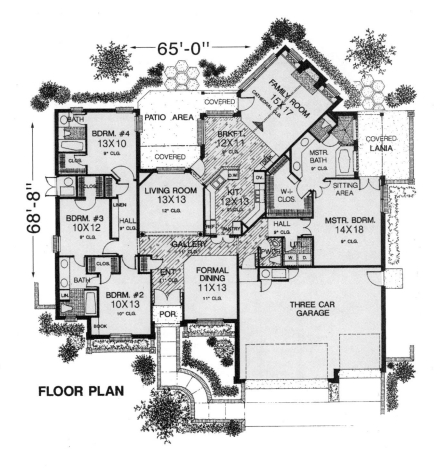

**FLOOR PLAN**

# Farmhouse Charm

©1995 Donald A. Gardner Architects, Inc.

B. NATHAN.

■ *Total living area  1,846 sq. ft.* ■ *Price Code C* ■

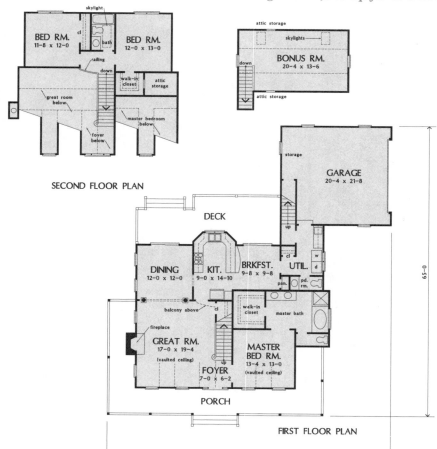

**SECOND FLOOR PLAN**

BED RM.
11-8 x 12-0

BED RM.
12-0 x 13-0

skylight

cl

bath

railing

down

walk-in closet

attic storage

great room below

master bedroom below

foyer below

**BONUS RM.**
20-4 x 13-6

attic storage

skylights

down

attic storage

storage

GARAGE
20-4 x 21-8

DECK

DINING
12-0 x 12-0

KIT.
9-0 x 14-10

BRKFST.
9-8 x 9-8

UTIL.

w

d

cl

pan.

pd. rm.

balcony above

cl

walk-in closet

master bath

fireplace

GREAT RM.
17-0 x 19-4
(vaulted ceiling)

MASTER BED RM.
13-4 x 13-0
(vaulted ceiling)

FOYER
7-0 x 6-2

up

PORCH

65-0

61-8

**FIRST FLOOR PLAN**

© 1995  Donald A Gardner Architects, Inc.

# No. 96462

## ■ This plan features:

— Three bedrooms

— Two full and one half baths

■ Nine foot ceilings and vaulted ceilings in Great Room and Master Bedroom add spaciousness

■ Dining Room accented by columns and accesses Deck for outdoor living

■ Efficient Kitchen features peninsula counter with serving bar for Breakfast Area

■ Master Suite includes a luxurious bath with walk-in closet, garden tub, shower and dual vanity

■ Two upstairs bedrooms, one with walk-in closet, share full bath with skylight

First floor — 1,380 sq. ft.
Second floor — 466 sq. ft.
Bonus room — 326 sq. ft.
Garage — 523 sq. ft.

# Details, Details, Details

■ *Total living area 2,155 sq. ft.* ■ *Price Code C* ■

# No. 98447

## This plan features:

- Three bedrooms

- Two full and one half baths

■ This elevation is highlighted by stucco, stone and detailing around the arched windows

■ The two-story Foyer allows access to the Dining Room and the Great Room

■ A vaulted ceiling and a fireplace can be found in the Great Room

■ The Breakfast Room has a vaulted ceiling and flows into the Kitchen and the Keeping Room

■ Two secondary bedrooms, each with a walk-in closet, share a full hall bath

■ The Master Suite has a tray ceiling a huge walk-in closet and a compartmental bath

■ An optional basement or crawl space foundation available — please specify when ordering

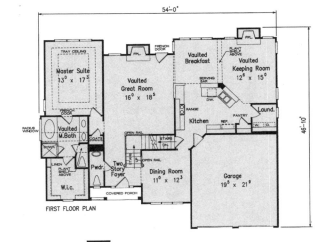

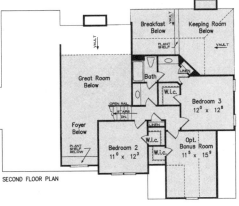

First floor — 1,628 sq. ft.
Second floor — 527 sq. ft.
Bonus room — 207 sq. ft.
Basement — 1,628 sq. ft.
Garage — 440 sq. ft.

# Didn't Waste An Inch of Space

© 1994 Donald A. Gardner Architects, Inc.

B. NATHAN

■ *Total living area  1,575 sq. ft.* ■ *Price Code C* ■

## No. 99834

■ **This plan features:**

— Three bedrooms

— Two full baths

■ Great Room with fireplace and built-in cabinets sharing a cathedral ceiling with angled Kitchen

■ Separate Dining Room allows for more formal entertaining

■ Master Bedroom topped by a cathedral ceiling, walk-in closet, and well-appointed bath

■ Front and rear covered Porches encourage relaxation

■ Skylit Bonus Room making a great Recreation Room or Office in the future

Main floor — 1,575 sq. ft.
Second floor — 276 sq. ft.
Garage — 536 sq. ft.

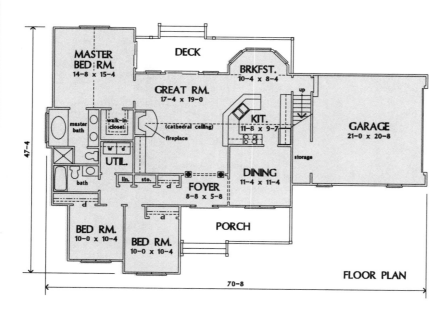

FLOOR PLAN

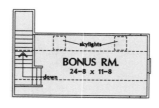

# Contemporary With Old World Charm

■ *Total living area 2,600 sq. ft.* ■ *Price Code D* ■

## No. 98417

■ **This plan features:**

- Four bedrooms

- Two full and one half baths

■ Entrance to Living Room is accented by three decorative columns

■ The Pantry and extended counter/serving bar highlight the Kitchen which is open to the Breakfast Area

■ Master Suite is enhanced by a two-sided fireplace, a sitting room with a bay window, and a luxurious private bath crowned by a vaulted ceiling

■ An optional basement or crawl space foundation available — please specify when ordering

First floor — 1,252 sq. ft.
Second floor — 1,348 sq. ft.
Basement — 1,252 sq. ft.
Garage — 483 sq. ft.

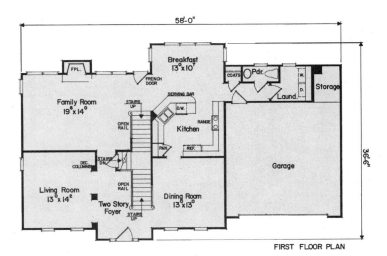

FIRST FLOOR PLAN

SECOND FLOOR PLAN

# A Modern Slant On A Country Theme

■ *Total living area 1,648 sq. ft.* ■ *Price Code B* ■

## No. 96513

**■ This plan features:**

— Three bedrooms

— Two full and one half baths

■ Country styled front Porch highlighting exterior which is enhanced by dormer windows

■ Modern open floor plan for a more spacious feeling

■ Great Room accented by a quaint corner fireplace and a ceiling fan

■ Dining Room flowing from the Great Room for easy entertaining

■ Kitchen graced by natural light from attractive bay window and a convenient snack bar for meals on the go

■ Master Suite secluded in separate wing for total privacy

■ Two additional bedrooms sharing full bath in the hall

Main floor — 1,648 sq. ft.
Garage — 479 sq. ft.

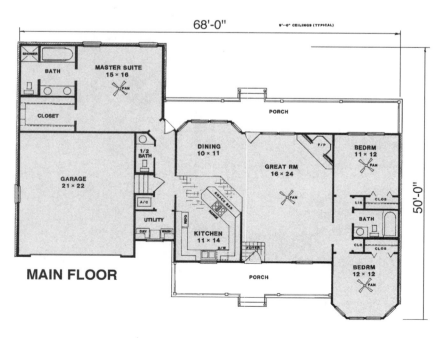

**MAIN FLOOR**

# Arched Windows Accent Sophisticated Design

■ *Total living area  2,551 sq. ft.* ■ *Price Code  E* ■

# No. 92509

## This plan features:

- Four bedrooms

- Two full and one half baths

■ Graceful columns and full-length windows highlight front Porch

■ Spacious Great Room with decorative ceiling over hearth fireplace between built-in cabinets

■ Kitchen with peninsula counter and breakfast alcove

■ Secluded Master Bedroom offers access to back Porch, and has a decorative ceiling and plush bath

■ Three additional bedrooms with loads of closets space share double vanity bath

■ An optional crawl space or slab foundation — please specify when ordering

Main area — 2,551 sq. ft.
Garage — 532 sq. ft.

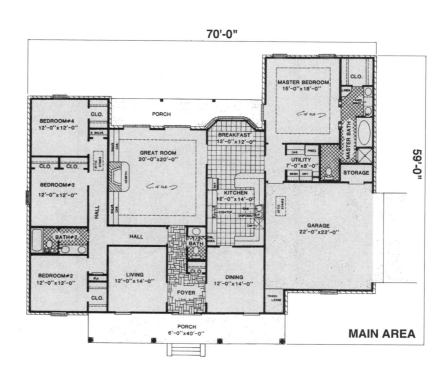

# Victorian Accents the Exterior

© 1991 Donald A. Gardner Architects, Inc.

■ *Total living area  1,865 sq. ft.* ■ *Price Code C* ■

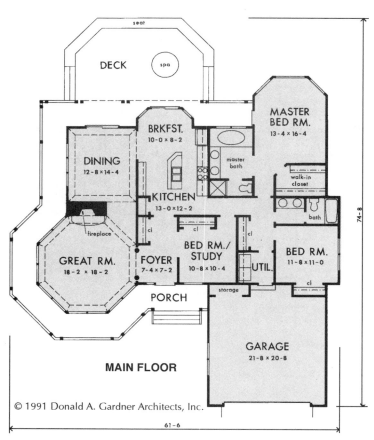

**MAIN FLOOR**

© 1991 Donald A. Gardner Architects, Inc.

# No. 99857

■ **This plan features:**

— Three bedrooms

— Two full baths

■ The covered wrap around Porch connects to the rear Deck

■ The foyer opens into the octagonal Great Room that is warmed by a fireplace

■ The Dining room has a tray ceiling and convenient access to the Kitchen

■ The galley Kitchen opens into the Breakfast bay

■ The Master bedroom has a bay area in the rear, a walk-in closet, and a fully appointed bath

■ Two more bedrooms complete this plan as does another full bath

Main floor — 1,865 sq. ft.
Garage — 505 sq. ft.

# Polished & Poised

B. NATHAN
© 1996 Donald A. Gardner Architects, Inc.

■ *Total living area 2,190 sq. ft.* ■ *Price Code D* ■

## No. 96471

**This plan features:**

Three bedrooms

Two full and one half baths

Hip roof, gables and brick accents add poise and polish to this traditional home

Curved transom window and sidelights illuminate the gracious Foyer

A curved balcony overlooks the Great Room which has a cathedral ceiling, fireplace and a wall of windows overlooking the Patio

Hub Kitchen easily serves the Dining Room, Breakfast Area and the Patio beyond

Master Bedroom wing is enhanced by a tray ceiling, walk-in closet and a deluxe bath

First floor — 1,577 sq. ft.
Second floor — 613 sq. ft.
Bonus room — 390 sq. ft.
Garage & storage — 634 sq. ft.

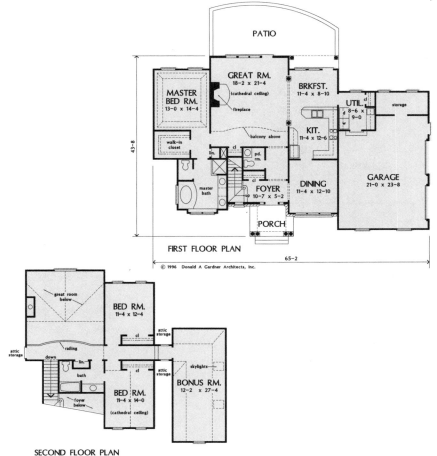

FIRST FLOOR PLAN

© 1996 Donald A Gardner Architects, Inc.

SECOND FLOOR PLAN

271

# Sunny Dormer Brightens Foyer

© 1996 Donald A Gardner Architects, Inc.

■ *Total living area  1,386 sq. ft.* ■ *Price Code B* ■

## No. 99812

■ **This plan features:**

— Three bedrooms

— Two full baths

■ Today's comforts with cost effective construction

■ Open Great room, Dining Room and Kitchen topped by a cathedral ceiling emphasizing spaciousness

■ Adjoining Deck providing extra living or entertaining room

■ Front bedroom crowned in cathedral ceiling and pampered by a private bath with garden tub, dual vanity and a walk-in closet

■ Skylit Bonus Room above the garage offering flexibility and opportunity for growth

Main floor — 1,386 sq. ft.
Garage — 517 sq. ft.
Bonus room — 314 sq. ft.

DECK

DINING
9-10 x 11-0
(cathedral ceiling)

GREAT RM.
15-10 x 16-10
(cathedral ceiling)

fireplace

MASTER
BED RM.
12-4 x 13-6
(cathedral ceiling)

walk-in closet

master bath

KIT.
9-10 x 11-8

d
w

FOYER
9-6 x 5-6

bath

cl

storage

up

cl

PORCH

cl

BED RM.
11-0 x 11-0

GARAGE
22-0 x 20-8

BED RM.
11-0 x 11-0
(cathedral ceiling)

FLOOR PLAN

54-10

10-0

48-0

© 1996  Donald A Gardner Architects, Inc.

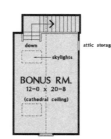

down

skylights

attic storage

BONUS RM.
12-0 x 20-8
(cathedral ceiling)

# Delightful Detailing

■ *Total living area  2,622 sq. ft.*  ■ *Price Code  E*  ■

## No. 98426

**This plan features:**

Three bedrooms

Two full and one half baths

The vaulted ceiling extends from the Foyer into the Living Room

The Dining Room is delineated by columns with a plant shelf above

Family Room has a vaulted ceiling, and a fireplace with radius windows on either side

The Kitchen equipped with an island serving bar, a desk, a wall oven, a Pantry and a Breakfast Bay

The Master Suite is highlighted by a Sitting Room, a walk-in closet and a private bath with a vaulted ceiling

An optional Bonus Room over the Garage

An optional basement or crawl space foundation — please specify when ordering

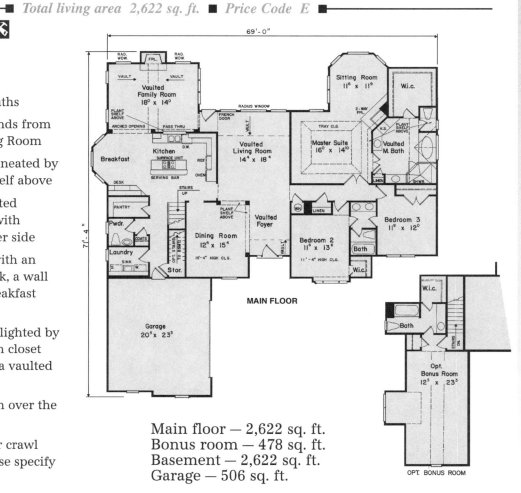

**MAIN FLOOR**

**OPT. BONUS ROOM**

Main floor — 2,622 sq. ft.
Bonus room — 478 sq. ft.
Basement — 2,622 sq. ft.
Garage — 506 sq. ft.

# An Estate of Epic Proportion

■ *Total living area  3,936 sq. ft.* ■ *Price Code F* ■

## No. 98539

■ **This plan features:**

— Four bedrooms

— Three full and one half baths

■ Front door opening into a grand Entry way with a 20' ceiling and a spiral staircase

■ Living Room with cathedral ceiling and fireplace

■ Walk down the Gallery to the Study with a full wall, built-in bookcase

■ The enormous Master Bedroom has a walk-in closet, sumptuous bath and a bayed Sitting Area

■ Family Room has a wetbar and a fireplace

■ An optional basement or slab foundation — please specify when ordering

■ No materials list is available for this plan

Main floor — 2,751 sq. ft.
Upper floor — 1,185 sq. ft.
Bonus — 343 sq. ft.
Garage — 790 sq. ft.

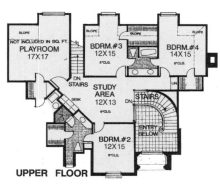

**UPPER FLOOR**

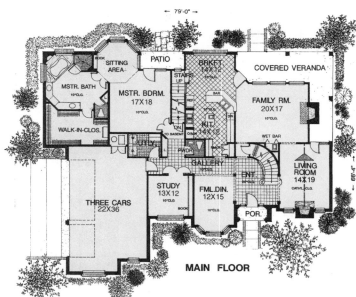

**MAIN FLOOR**

# Deck Includes Spa

© 1991 Donald A. Gardner Architects, Inc.

■ Total living area 1,778 sq. ft. ■ Price Code C ■

## No. 99873

### This plan features:

Three bedrooms

Two full and one half baths

An exterior Porch giving the home a traditional flavor

Great Room highlighted by a fireplace and a balcony above as well as a pass-through into the Kitchen

Kitchen eating area with skylights and bow windows overlooking the Deck with spa

Two additional bedrooms with a full bath on the second floor

Master Suite on the first floor is naturally illuminated by two skylights

An optional basement or crawl space foundation — please specify when ordering

First floor — 1,325 sq. ft.

Second floor — 453 sq. ft.

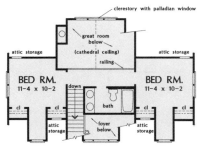

SECOND FLOOR PLAN

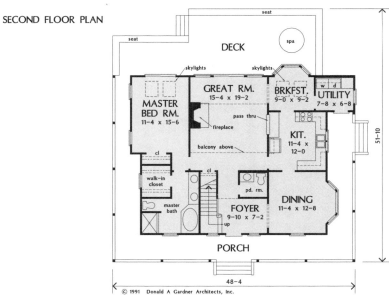

© 1991 Donald A Gardner Architects, Inc.

FIRST FLOOR PLAN

# Sunny Two-story Foyer

© 1994 Donald A. Gardner Architects, Inc.

B. NATIAN

■ *Total living area  1,823 sq. ft.* ■ *Price Code C* ■

DECK

SCREEN PORCH
12-0 x 12-0

(vaulted ceiling)

GREAT RM.
23-6 x 17-0

fireplace

plant shelf above

balcony above

BRKFST.
7-10 x 8-0

UTIL.
7-2 x 6-0

w  d

KIT.
11-4 x 10-0

storage

GARAGE
19-8 x 20-0

master bath

walk-in closet

plant shelf above

pd. rm.

cl

DINING
11-4 x 13-0

MASTER BED RM.
13-4 x 15-0

FOYER
9-10 x 5-4

up

PORCH

(cathedral ceiling)

54-0

61-6

FIRST FLOOR PLAN

great room below

skylight

attic storage

railing

BED RM.
12-2 x 12-0

cl

bath

down

foyer below

BED RM.
11-4 x 12-0

cl

cl

SECOND FLOOR PLAN

# No. 96476

## ■ This plan features:

— Three bedrooms

— Two full and one half baths

■ The two-story Foyer off the forma[l] Dining Room sets an elegant mood in this one-and-a-half story dormered home

■ The Great Room and Breakfast Area are both topped by a vaulte[d] ceiling

■ The screened Porch has a relaxing atmosphere

■ The Master Suite on the first floo[r] includes a cathedral ceiling and an elegant bath with whirlpool tub and separate shower

■ There is plenty of Attic and Garag[e] storage space available

First floor — 1,335 sq. ft.
Second floor — 488 sq. ft.
Garage & Storage — 465 sq. ft.

# A Comfortable Informal Design

■ *Total living area  1,300 sq. ft.*  ■  *Price Code  B*  ■

# No. 94801

## This plan features:

- Three bedrooms

- Two full baths

■ Warm, Country style front Porch with wood details

■ Spacious Activity Room enhanced by a pre-fab fireplace

■ Open and efficient Kitchen/ Dining area highlighted by bay window, adjacent to Laundry and Garage entry

■ Corner Master Bedroom offers a pampering bath with a garden tub and double vanity topped by a vaulted ceiling

■ Two additional bedrooms with ample closets, share a full bath

■ An optional crawl space or slab foundation available — please specify when ordering

Main floor — 1,300 sq. ft.
Garage — 576 sq. ft.

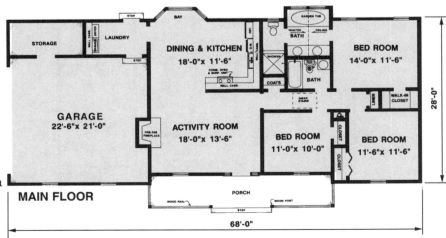

# Quaint Starter Home

■ *Total living area  1,050 sq. ft.* ■ *Price Code A* ■

## No. 92400

■ **This plan features:**

— Three bedrooms

— Two full baths

■ A vaulted ceiling giving an airy feeling to the Dining and Living Rooms

■ A streamlined Kitchen with a comfortable work area, a double sink and ample cabinet space

■ A cozy fireplace in the Living Room

■ A Master Suite with a large closet, French doors leading to the Patio and a private bath

■ Two additional bedrooms sharing a full bath

■ No materials list is available for this plan

Main area — 1,050 sq. ft.
Garage — 261 sq. ft.

*Floor plan labels:*

36

42

MASTER BEDROOM 11 X 12

BEDROOM 9 X 12

PATIO

BEDROOM 9 X 10

W D

KITCHEN 9 X 11

GARAGE 12 X 24

VAULT

VAULT

DINING 9 X 10

LIVING 14 X 14

MAIN AREA

# Grace with an Elegant Front Porch

■ *Total living area  1,750 sq. ft.* ■ *Price Code  B* ■

## No. 98462

### ■ This plan features:

- Three bedrooms

- Two full and one half baths

■ The two-story Foyer accesses the living areas

■ The Kitchen flows into the Breakfast Area

■ The Family Room is enhanced by a fireplace

■ A work island adds counter space to the Kitchen

■ The Master Suite has a private bath

■ The front secondary bedroom has a window seat

■ An optional basement, slab or crawl space foundation — please specify when ordering

■ No materials list is available for this plan

First floor — 926 sq. ft.
Second floor — 824 sq. ft.
Bonus room — 282 sq. ft.
Basement — 926 sq. ft.
Garage — 440 sq. ft.

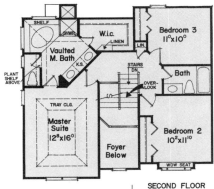

SECOND FLOOR

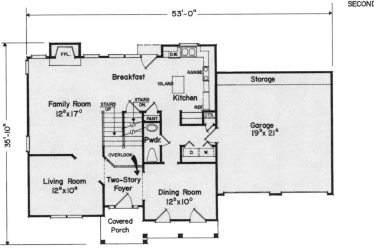

FIRST FLOOR

# For the Growing Family

■ *Total living area 1,862 sq. ft.* ■ *Price Code C* ■

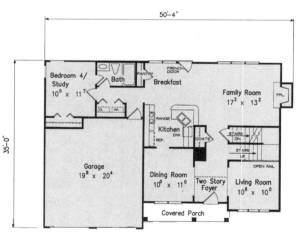

**FIRST FLOOR**

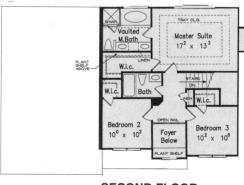

**SECOND FLOOR**

# No. 98473

## ■ This plan features:

— Three bedrooms

— Three full baths

■ Formal areas are located to either side of the Foyer

■ Kitchen equipped with a corner double sink and a wrap-around snack bar

■ Fireplace in the Family Room adds warmth

■ Master Suite decorated by a tray ceiling in the bedroom

■ An optional basement or crawl space foundation available — please specify when ordering

■ No materials list is available for this plan

First floor — 1,103 sq. ft.
Second floor — 759 sq. ft.
Basement — 1,103 sq. ft.
Garage — 420 sq. ft.

© 1997 Donald A. Gardner Architects, Inc.

■ *Total living area  1,515 sq. ft.* ■ *Price Code  C* ■

# No. 99835

## This plan features:

- Three bedrooms

- Two full baths

■ Working at the Kitchen island focuses your view to the Great Room with its vaulted ceiling and a fireplace

■ Clerestory dormers emanate light into the Great Room

■ Both the Dining Room and Master Suite are enhanced by tray ceilings

■ Skylights flood natural light into the Bonus space

■ The private Master Suite has its own bath and an expansive walk-in closet

Main floor — 1,515 sq. ft.
Bonus — 288 sq. ft.
Garage — 476 sq. ft.

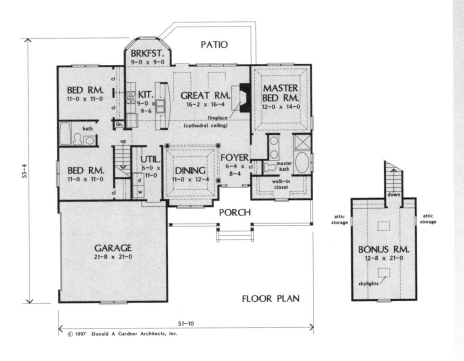

# Four Bedroom Country Classic

© 1994 Donald A. Gardner Architects, Inc.

B. NATHAN

■ *Total living area  2,164 sq. ft.* ■ *Price Code D* ■

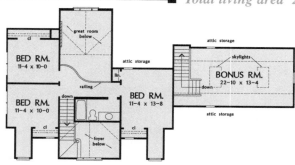

SECOND FLOOR PLAN

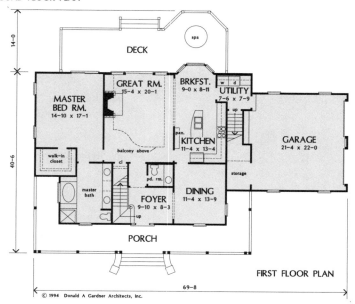

FIRST FLOOR PLAN

69-8

© 1994 Donald A Gardner Architects, Inc.

## No. 96408

■ **This plan features:**

— Four bedrooms

— Two full and one half baths

■ Foyer open to the Dining Room creating a hall with a balcony over the vaulted Great Room

■ Great Room opens to the Deck and to the island Kitchen with convenient pantry

■ Nine foot ceilings on the first floor expand volume

■ Master Suite pampered by a whirlpool tub, double vanity, separate shower and Deck access

■ Bonus Room to be finished now or later

First floor — 1,499 sq. ft.
Second floor — 665 sq. ft.
Garage & storage — 567 sq. ft.
Bonus room — 380 sq. ft.

# Towering Windows Enhance Elegance

© Larry E. Belk

■ *Total living area 2,838 sq. ft.* ■ *Price Code E* ■

## No. 93034

■ **This plan features:**

- Four bedrooms
- Three full baths
- Designed for a corner or pie-shaped lot
- Spectacular split staircase highlights Foyer
- Expansive Great Room with hearth fireplace opens to formal Dining Room and Patio
- Quiet Study can easily convert to another bedroom or home office
- Secluded Master Suite offers private Porch, two walk-in closets two vanities and a corner whirlpool tub
- Three second floor bedrooms with walk-in closets, share a balcony and double vanity bath
- No materials list is available for this plan

First floor — 1,966 sq. ft.
Second floor — 872 sq. ft.
Garage — 569 sq. ft.

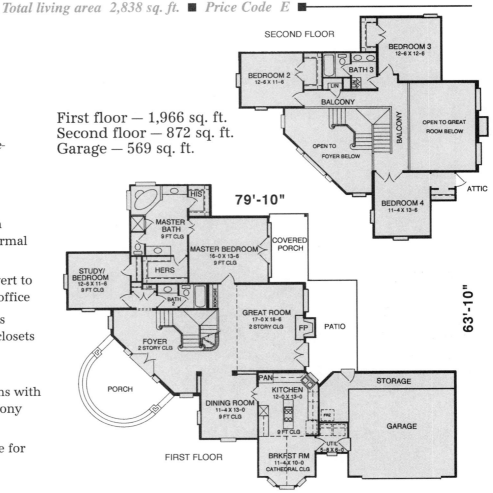

# Traditional Two-Story Home

© 1997 Donald A. Gardner Architects, Inc.

■ *Total living area  2,250 sq. ft.* ■ *Price Code D* ■

**SECOND FLOOR**

**FIRST FLOOR**

© 1997 Donald A. Gardner Architects, Inc.

# No. 96491

■ **This plan features:**

— Three bedrooms

— Two full and two half baths

■ Facade handsomely accented by multiple gables, keystone arches and transom windows

■ Arched clerestory window lights two-story Foyer for a dramatic entrance

■ Two-story Great Room with inviting fireplace, wall of windows and back Porch access

■ Great cooks will enjoy open Kitchen with easy access to Screen Porch and Dining Room

■ Private Master Bedroom has two walk-in closets and deluxe bath

First floor — 1,644 sq. ft.
Second floor — 606 sq. ft.
Bonus room — 548 sq. ft.
Garage & storage — 657 sq. ft.

■ *Total living area 2,891 sq. ft.* ■ *Price Code E* ■

## No. 94231

### This plan features:

- Three bedrooms

- Two full and one three-quarter baths

- Glass arch entrance leads into Foyer and Grand Room

- Decorative windows highlight Study and formal Dining Room

- Spacious Kitchen with walk-in pantry and peninsula serving counter easily serves Nook, Veranda and Dining Room

- Luxurious Master Suite with step ceiling, sitting area, his-n-her closets and pampering bath

- Two additional bedrooms, one with a private Deck, have bay windows and walk-in closets

- No materials list is available for this plan

First floor — 2,181 sq. ft.
Second floor — 710 sq. ft.
Garage — 658 sq. ft.

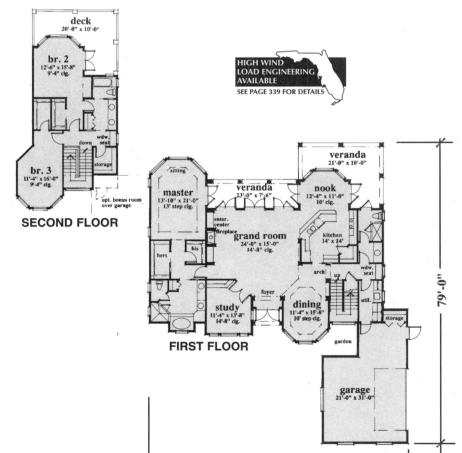

HIGH WIND LOAD ENGINEERING AVAILABLE
SEE PAGE 339 FOR DETAILS

SECOND FLOOR

FIRST FLOOR

# Warm and Inviting

■ *Total living area  1,363 sq. ft.* ■ *Price Code B* ■

## No. 92528

■ **This plan features:**

— Three bedrooms

— Two full baths

■ A Den with a cozy fireplace and vaulted ceiling

■ A well-equipped Kitchen with a window above a double sink, and a built-in Pantry

■ A spacious Master Bedroom with a private master bath and walk-in closet

■ Additional bedrooms sharing full hall bath

■ An optional crawl space or slab foundation — please specify when ordering

Main floor — 1,363 sq. ft.
Garage — 434 sq. ft.

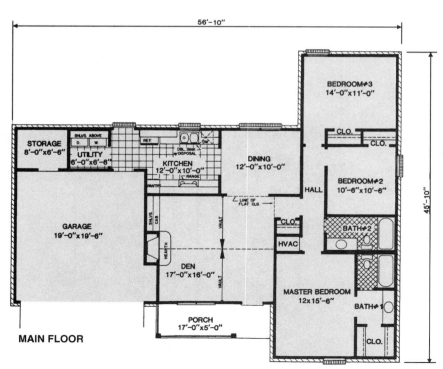

MAIN FLOOR

# Splendid Appointments

■ *Total living area 3,083 sq. ft.* ■ *Price Code E* ■

# No. 98452

## This plan features:

Three bedrooms

Three full and one half baths

The two story Foyer is highlighted by a staircase with an open rail

The formal Dining Room opens onto a terrace for expanded dining options

A two-story Family Room is accented by arched openings from the Dining Room and Foyer

The spacious Kitchen/Breakfast Room includes a cook top island and a built-in Pantry

The Keeping room with a vaulted ceiling and a cozy fireplace adjoins the Breakfast area

An optional basement or crawl space foundation — please specify when ordering

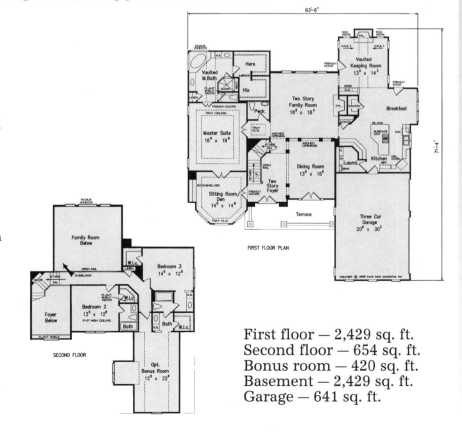

First floor — 2,429 sq. ft.
Second floor — 654 sq. ft.
Bonus room — 420 sq. ft.
Basement — 2,429 sq. ft.
Garage — 641 sq. ft.

# Spectacular Stucco and Stone

■ *Total living area 4,106 sq. ft.* ■ *Price Code F* ■

## SECOND FLOOR

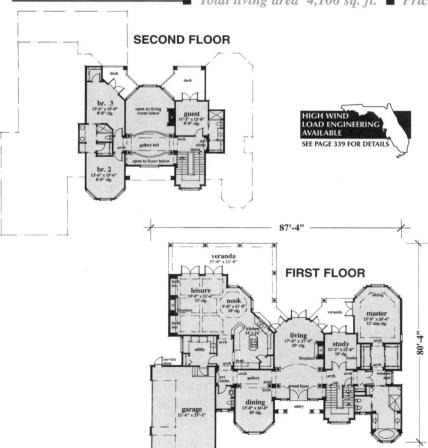

br. 3
13'-6" x 15'-0"
8'-8" clg.

open to living room below

guest
11'-2" x 12'-8"
8'-8" clg.

gallery loft

niche
down

br. 2
13'-4" x 15'-6"
8'-8" clg.

open to foyer below

deck

deck

arch

arch

HIGH WIND
LOAD ENGINEERING
AVAILABLE
SEE PAGE 339 FOR DETAILS

## FIRST FLOOR

87'-4"

80'-4"

veranda
37'-6" x 11'-0"

leisure
19'-0" x 21'-6"
12' clg.

nook
9'-4" x 11'-0"
10' clg.

kitchen
14' x 16'

utility

living
17'-0" x 17'-0"
20' clg.

sitting

master
15'-8" x 20'-6"
12' step clg.

veranda

study
11'-2" x 12'-4"
10' clg.

fireplace

gallery

desk

arch

grand foyer

dining
13'-0" x 16'-0"
10' clg.

entry

garage
21'-6" x 35'-2"

service door

art niche

window seat

## No. 94239

### ■ This plan features:

— Four bedrooms

— One full, two three-quarter and one half baths

■ Arches and columns accent Entry Grand Foyer, Gallery, Living and Dining rooms

■ Open Living Room with fireplace and multiple glass doors

■ Formal Dining Room with bay windows conveniently located

■ Angled Kitchen with walk-in Pantry and peninsula counter

■ Master wing offers a step ceiling, two walk-in closets and a lavish bath

■ No materials list is available for this plan

First floor — 3,027 sq. ft.
Second floor — 1,079 sq. ft.
Basement — 3,027 sq. ft.
Garage — 802 sq. ft.

# Country French Design

■ *Total living area 2,714 sq. ft.* ■ *Price Code E* ■

## No. 90470

### This plan features:

- Three bedrooms
- Two full and one half baths
- Open Foyer receives light from the dormer above
- Great Room features rear wall hearth fireplace and a built-in media center
- Breakfast bay is open into the fully equipped U-shaped Kitchen
- First floor Master Bedroom encompasses entire private wing
- An optional basement or a crawl space foundation — please specify when ordering

First floor — 1,997 sq. ft.
Second floor — 717 sq. ft.
Bonus room — 541 sq. ft.
Basement – 1,997 sq. ft.
Garage – 575 sq. ft.

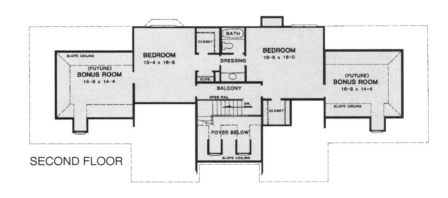

SECOND FLOOR

FIRST FLOOR

# Delightful Home

■ *Total living area  1,853 sq. ft.* ■ *Price Code C* ■

**observation deck**

**master**
13'-0" x 14'-0"
vault. clg.

**am kitchen**

**open to grand room below**

**down**

**SECOND FLOOR**

HIGH WIND
LOAD ENGINEERING
AVAILABLE
SEE PAGE 339 FOR DETAILS

← 44'-0" →

**deck**
17'-0" x 9'-0"

**dining**
12'-8" x 11'-0"
8' clg.

**deck**

**grand room**
20'-0" x 18'-0"
vault. clg.

fireplace

**kitchen**
11' x 12'

**br. 2**
12'-0" x 11'-8"
8' clg.

40'-0"

**up  down**

**foyer**

**down**

**entry porch**

**br. 3**
12'-0" x 10'-0"
8' clg.

**FIRST FLOOR**

## No. 94248

■ **This plan features:**

— Three bedrooms

— Two full baths

■ Grand Room with a fireplace, vaulted ceiling and double French doors to the rear Deck

■ Kitchen has a large walk-in pantry, island with a sink and dishwasher creating a perfect triangular workspace

■ Dining Room with doors to both decks, has expanses of glass looking out to the rear yard

■ Master Bedroom features a double door entry, private bath and a morning kitchen

■ No materials list is available for this plan

■ No materials list is available for this plan

First floor — 1,342 sq. ft.
Second floor — 511 sq. ft.
Garage — 1,740 sq. ft.

# Two-Story Foyer Adds to Elegance

■ *Total living area 2,454 sq. ft.* ■ *Price Code D* ■

## No. 93240

### This plan features:

- Four bedrooms

- Two full and one half baths

- Two-story entrance with lovely curved staircase

- Family Room enhanced by fireplace and access to Sundeck

- Country-sized Kitchen with bright Breakfast area, adjoins Dining Room and Utility/Garage entry

- French doors lead into plush Master Bedroom with decorative ceiling and large master bath

- Three additional bedrooms with ample closets share a full bath and Bonus Room

- An optional basement, crawl space or slab foundation — please specify when ordering

First floor — 1,277 sq. ft.
Second floor — 1,177 sq. ft.
Bonus room — 392 sq. ft.
Basement — 1,261 sq. ft.
Garage — 572 sq. ft.

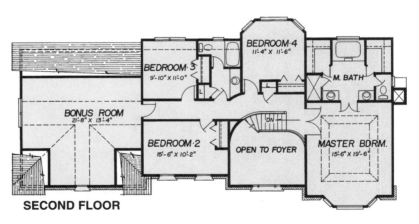

**SECOND FLOOR**

*An*
## EXCLUSIVE DESIGN
*By Jannis Vann & Associates, Inc.*

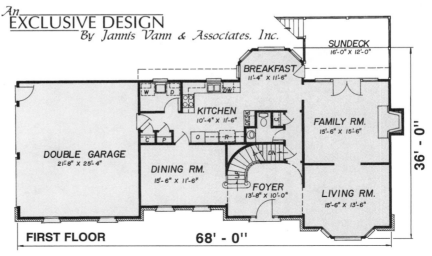

**FIRST FLOOR**    68' - 0"

# Attractive Exterior

■ *Total living area  2,167 sq. ft.* ■ *Price Code C* ■

## No. 98512

### ■ This plan features:

— Three bedrooms

— Two full baths

■ In the Gallery, columns separate space between the Great Room and the Dining Room

■ Access to backyard covered Patio from bayed Breakfast Nook

■ The large Kitchen is a chef's dream with lots of counter space and a Pantry

■ The Master Bedroom is removed from traffic areas and contains a luxurious master bath

■ A hall connects the two secondary bedrooms which share a full sky bath

■ No materials list is available for this plan

Main floor — 2,167 sq. ft.
Garage — 690 sq. ft.

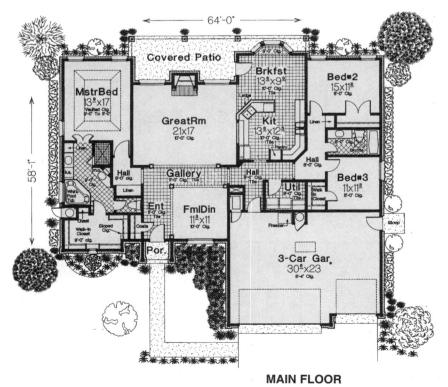

**MAIN FLOOR**

# A Magnificent Manor

■ *Total living area  2,389 sq. ft.* ■ *Price Code  D* ■

## No. 98410 ⊠

### This plan features:

- Three bedrooms

- Three full baths

- The formal Living Room is located directly off the Foyer

- An efficient Kitchen accesses the formal Dining Room for ease in serving

- The Breakfast Area is separated from the Kitchen by an extended counter/serving bar

- The two-story Family Room is highlighted by a fireplace that is framed by windows

- A tray ceiling crowns the Master Bedroom while a vaulted ceiling tops the master bath

- Two additional bedrooms share the full double vanity hall bath

- An optional basement or crawl space foundation available — please specify when ordering

First floor — 1,428 sq. ft.
Second floor — 961 sq. ft.
Bonus — 472 sq. ft.
Basement — 1,428 sq. ft.
Garage — 507 sq. ft.

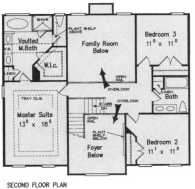

SECOND FLOOR PLAN

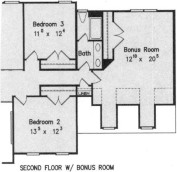

SECOND FLOOR W/ BONUS ROOM

FIRST FLOOR PLAN

# Secluded Master Suite

■ *Total living area 1,680 sq. ft.* ■ *Price Code C* ■

## No. 92527

### ■ This plan features:

— Three bedrooms

— Two full baths

■ A convenient one-level design with an open floor plan between the Kitchen, Breakfast Area and Great Room

■ A vaulted ceiling and a cozy fireplace in the spacious Great Room

■ A well-equipped Kitchen using a peninsula counter as an eating bar

■ A Master Suite with a luxurious master bath

■ Two additional bedrooms having use of a full hall bath

■ An optional crawl space or slab foundation — please specify when ordering

Main area — 1,680 sq. ft.
Garage — 538 sq. ft.

**MAIN AREA**

66'-10"

44'-10"

CLO.

MASTER BEDROOM
13'-0"x16'-0"

MASTER BATH

60"x42" TUB

BEDROOM #3
11'-0"x12'-0"

CLO.

LINEN

BREAKFAST
11'-0"x9'-6"

UTILITY
6'-0"x6'-0"

STORAGE
12'-0"x4'-0"

GREAT ROOM
17'-0"x16'-0"

BATH #2

LINEN

HALL

KITCHEN
11'-0"x12'-6"

DBL. SNK w/DISPOSAL

REF.

COOKTOP

DBL OVEN

FOYER
6'-0"x8'-0"

DINING
12'-0"x12'-0"

BEDROOM #2
11'-0"x12'-6"

CLO.

CLO.

PORCH

GARAGE
22'-0"x22'-0"

# Celebrate the Outdoors

© 1990 Donald A. Gardner Architects, Inc.

■ *Total living area  2,218 sq. ft.* ■ *Price Code  D* ■

# No. 96423

## ■ This plan features:

– Three bedrooms

– Two full and one half baths

■ Country classic celebrating the outdoors with a wrap-around Porch, Sun Room and spacious rear Deck

■ Palladian window in front, a grand arched window in the rear and skylights in the Sun Room

■ Second floor balcony overlooking the generous Great Room with a cathedral ceiling and clerestory

■ Large country Kitchen with a pass-through to the Great Room and a center island

■ Private Master Suite with access to the Sun Room through a luxurious master bath

■ An optional basement or crawl space foundation — please specify when ordering

SECOND FLOOR PLAN

First floor — 1,651 sq. ft.
Second floor — 567 sq. ft.

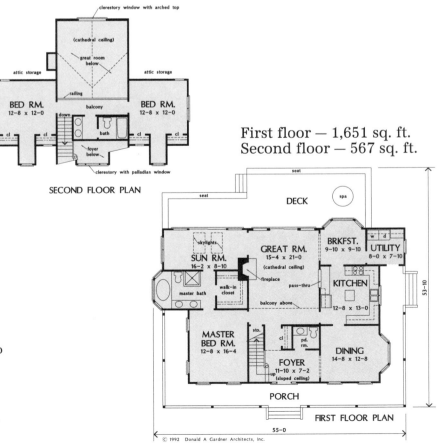

FIRST FLOOR PLAN

© 1992 Donald A Gardner Architects, Inc.

# Easy, Economical Building

© 1996 Donald A Gardner Architects, Inc.

■ *Total living area 1,959 sq. ft.* ■ *Price Code C* ■

## No. 99813

### ■ This plan features:

— Three bedrooms

— Two full baths

■ Many architectural elements offer efficient and economical design

■ Great Room vaulted ceiling gracefully arches to include arched window dormer

■ Open Kitchen with angled counter easily serves Breakfast area

■ Tray ceilings enhance Dining Room, front bedroom and Master Bedroom

■ Private master bath includes garden tub, double vanity and skylight

■ An optional basement or crawl space foundation — please specify when ordering

Main floor — 1,959 sq. ft.
Bonus room — 385 sq. ft.
Garage & storage — 484 sq. ft.

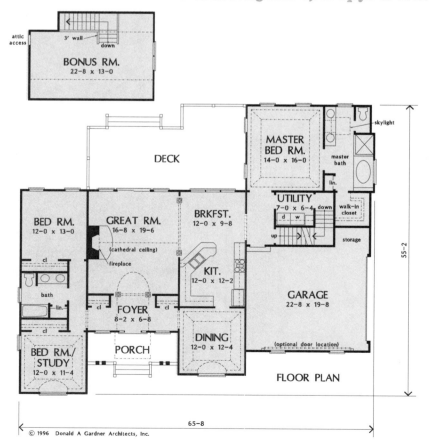

BONUS RM.
22-8 x 13-0

attic access

3' wall

down

MASTER BED RM.
14-0 x 16-0

skylight

master bath

DECK

UTILITY
7-0 x 6-4

down

walk-in closet

lin.

storage

up

BED RM.
12-0 x 13-0

GREAT RM.
16-8 x 19-6
(cathedral ceiling)

fireplace

BRKFST.
12-0 x 9-8

KIT.
12-0 x 12-2

GARAGE
22-8 x 19-8

bath

lin.

cl

FOYER
8-2 x 6-8

cl

DINING
12-0 x 12-4

(optional door location)

BED RM./STUDY
12-0 x 11-4

PORCH

FLOOR PLAN

55-2

65-8

© 1996 Donald A Gardner Architects, Inc.

# Easy-Living Plan

©1996 Donald A. Gardner Architects, Inc.

B.NATHAN

■ *Total living area  1,864 sq. ft.*  ■  *Price Code  C*  ■

# No. 96468

### This plan features:

- Three bedrooms
- Two full baths
- Sunlit Foyer flows easily into the generous Great Room
- Great Room crowned in a cathedral ceiling and accented by a fireplace
- Accent columns define the open Kitchen and Breakfast Bay
- Master Bedroom topped by a tray ceiling and highlighted by a well-appointed master bath
- Two additional bedrooms, sharing a skylit bath in the hall, create the children's wing

Main floor — 1,864 sq. ft.
Bonus room — 319 sq. ft.
Garage — 503 sq. ft.

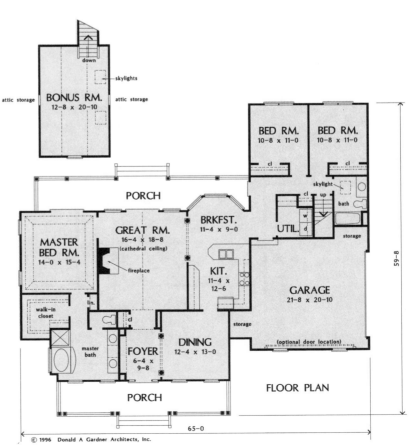

© 1996  Donald A Gardner Architects, Inc.

# For First Time Buyers

■ *Total living area  1,310 sq. ft.* ■ *Price Code A* ■

## No. 93048

■ **This plan features:**

— Three bedrooms

— Two full baths

■ An efficiently designed Kitchen with a corner sink, ample counter space and a peninsula counter

■ A sunny Breakfast Room with a convenient hide-away laundry center

■ An expansive Living Room with a corner fireplace and direct access to the rear yard

■ A private Master Suite with a walk-in closet and a double vanity bath

■ Two additional bedrooms, both with walk-in closets, that share a full hall bath

■ No materials list is available for this plan

Main floor — 1,310 sq. ft.
Garage — 449 sq. ft.

WIDTH 49–10

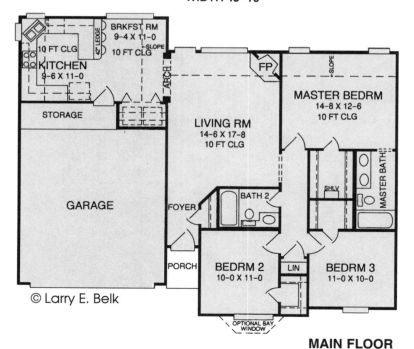

BRKFST RM
9–4 X 11–0
10 FT CLG
42" LEDGE
SLOPE

10 FT CLG
KITCHEN
9–6 X 11–0

STORAGE

ARCH

FP

SLOPE

MASTER BEDRM
14–8 X 12–6
10 FT CLG

LIVING RM
14–6 X 17–8
10 FT CLG

GARAGE

FOYER

BATH 2

SHLV

MASTER BATH

DEPTH 40–6

PORCH

BEDRM 2
10–0 X 11–0

LIN

BEDRM 3
11–0 X 10–0

© Larry E. Belk

OPTIONAL BAY WINDOW

**MAIN FLOOR**

298

# Simply Cozy

■ *Total living area  1,325 sq. ft.* ■ *Price Code  A* ■

# No. 98912 ✕

■ **This plan features:**

— Three bedrooms

— Two full baths

■ Quaint front Porch sheltering
Entry into the Living Area
showcased by a massive fireplace
and built-ins below a vaulted
ceiling

■ Formal Dining Room accented by
a bay of glass with Sun Deck
access

■ Efficient, galley Kitchen with
Breakfast Area, laundry facilities
and outdoor access

■ Secluded Master Bedroom offers a
roomy walk-in closet and plush
bath with a dual vanity and a
garden window tub

■ Two additional bedrooms with
ample closets share a full skylit
bath

Main floor — 1,325 sq. ft.

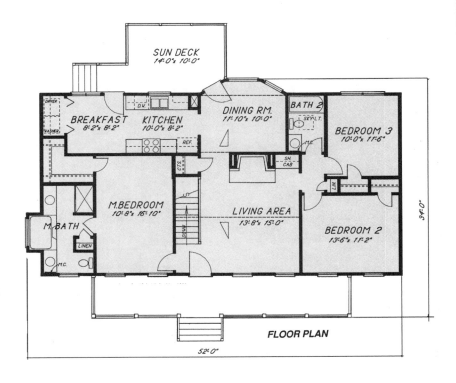

FLOOR PLAN

*An*
EXCLUSIVE DESIGN
*By Jannis Vann & Associates, Inc.*

# Small, Yet Lavishly Appointed

■ Total living area 1,845 sq. ft. ■ Price Code C ■

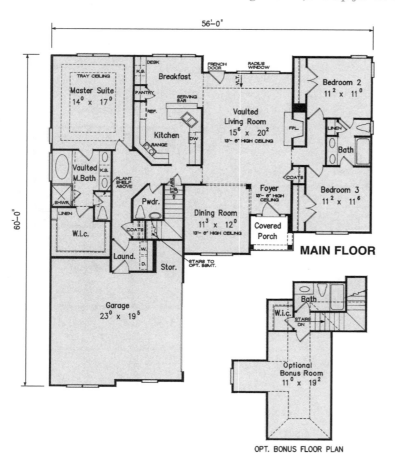

**MAIN FLOOR**

- TRAY CEILING
- Master Suite 14⁰ x 17⁰
- Breakfast
- DESK
- K.S.
- FRENCH DOOR
- RADIUS WINDOW
- PANTRY
- SERVING BAR
- REF.
- Kitchen
- DW
- RANGE
- Vaulted Living Room 15⁶ x 20² 13'- 6" HIGH CEILING
- Bedroom 2 11² x 11⁰
- FPL
- LINEN
- Bath
- Vaulted M.Bath
- K.S.
- PLANT SHELF ABOVE
- SHWR
- LINEN
- Pwdr.
- COATS
- Foyer 13'- 6" HIGH CEILING
- COATS
- Bedroom 3 11² x 11⁶
- W.i.c.
- COATS
- Dining Room 11³ x 12⁰ 13'- 6" HIGH CEILING
- Covered Porch
- Laund.
- W.
- D.
- Stor.
- STAIRS TO OPT. BSMT.
- Garage 23⁰ x 19⁵

- Bath
- W.i.c.
- STAIRS DN
- Optional Bonus Room 11⁰ x 19²

**OPT. BONUS FLOOR PLAN**

56'-0"
60'-0"

## No. 98425

### ■ This plan features:

— Three bedrooms

— Two full and one half baths

■ The Dining Room, Living Room, Foyer and master bath all topped by high ceilings

■ Master Bedroom includes a decorative tray ceiling and a walk-in closet

■ Kitchen open to the Breakfast Room and enhanced by a serving bar and a Pantry

■ Living Room with a large fireplace and a French door to the rear yard

■ An optional basement or crawl space foundation — please when ordering

Main floor — 1,845 sq. ft.
Bonus — 409 sq. ft.
Basement — 1,845 sq. ft.
Garage — 529 sq. ft.

# Stature and Dignity

© 1997 Donald A. Gardner Architects, Inc.

B. NATHAN.

■ *Total living area  2,682 sq. ft.* ■  *Price Code  E* ■

## No. 96490

### This plan features:

- Four bedrooms
- Three full baths
- Multiple columns and gables add appeal to traditional style
- Foyer and Great Room both have two-story ceilings and clerestory windows
- Great Room highlighted by fireplace, built-in shelves and French doors to back Porch
- Bright Breakfast Bay accesses efficient Kitchen and back stairway to bedrooms and Bonus Room
- Bedroom/Study and full bath near Master Bedroom suite offers multiple uses

First floor — 2,067 sq. ft.
Second floor — 615 sq. ft.
Bonus room — 433 sq. ft.
Garage & storage — 729 sq. ft.

FIRST FLOOR PLAN

© 1997  Donald A Gardner Architects, Inc.

SECOND FLOOR PLAN

# Quality Inside and Out

■ *Total living area  2,835 sq. ft.* ■ *Price Code E* ■

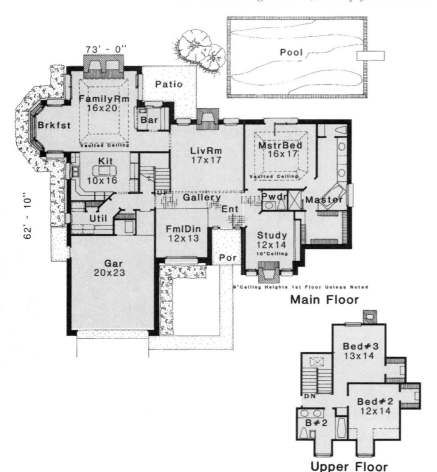

**Main Floor**

73' - 0"

62' - 10"

Pool

Patio

FamilyRm
16x20
Vaulted Ceiling

Brkfst

Bar

LivRm
17x17

MstrBed
16x17
Vaulted Ceiling

Kit
10x16

up

Gallery

Pwdr

Master

Util

Ent

FmlDin
12x13

Study
12x14
10'Ceiling

Gar
20x23

Por

9'Ceiling Heights 1st Floor Unless Noted

**Upper Floor**

Bed#3
13x14

DN

Bed#2
12x14

B#2

## No. 92269

■ **This plan features:**

— Three bedrooms

— Two full and one half baths

■ The entry/Gallery opens to the Living Room

■ Convenient Study offers built-ins and another fireplace

■ Country Kitchen with work island opens to Breakfast bay, Family Room and Dining Room

■ Expansive Family Room offers access to the Patio

■ Private Master Bedroom suite with a lavish bath and walk-in closet

■ Two second floor bedrooms share a double vanity bath

■ No materials list is available for this plan

Main floor — 2,273 sq. ft.
Upper floor — 562 sq. ft.
Garage — 460 sq. ft.

■ *Total living area  3,335 sq. ft.* ■ *Price Code  F* ■

## No. 92219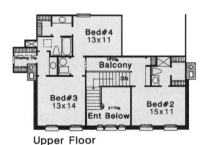

### This plan features:

Four bedrooms

Two full, one three-quarter and one half baths

Entry hall with a graceful landing staircase, flanked by formal areas

Fireplaces highlight the Living Room/Parlor and Dining Room

Kitchen with an island cooktop, built-in pantry and Breakfast area

Cathedral ceiling crowns Family Room and is accented by a fireplace

Lavish Master Bedroom wing with plenty of storage space

Three bedrooms, one with a private bath

No materials list is available for this plan

ain floor — 2,432 sq. ft.
pper floor — 903 sq. ft.
asement — 2,432 sq. ft.
arage — 742 sq. ft.

Upper Floor

Bed#4 13x11
Balcony
Bed#3 13x14
Ent Below
Bed#2 15x11

Main Floor

Pool
90' - 0"
45' - 4"
Gar 22x23
Covered Patio
Covered Patio
FamilyRm 18x22
MstrBed 15x21
Kit
Brkfst 10x15
Powdr
GolfCart Stor. 15x20
Rear Entry
Bar
Util
FmlDin 13x15
LivRm/ Parlor 15x17
WorkShop
Ent
Covered Por

# Quaint and Cozy

© 1993 Donald A. Gardner Architects, Inc.

B. NATHAN

■ *Total living area  1,864 sq. ft.*  ■ *Price Code C* ■

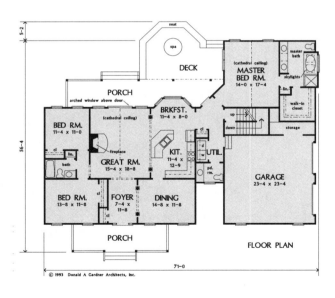

DECK

PORCH

arched window above door

BED RM.
11-4 x 11-0

GREAT RM.
15-4 x 18-8
(cathedral ceiling)

fireplace

bath

BED RM.
13-8 x 11-8

FOYER
7-4 x
11-8

DINING
14-8 x 11-8

PORCH

seat

spa

BRKFST.
11-4 x 8-0

KIT.
11-4 x
12-9

UTIL.

pd. rm.

MASTER BED RM.
14-0 x 17-4
(cathedral ceiling)

master bath

skylights

walk-in closet

up

down

storage

GARAGE
23-4 x 23-4

FLOOR PLAN

56-4

5-2

71-0

© 1993 Donald A Gardner Architects, Inc.

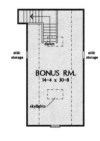

attic storage

BONUS RM.
14-4 x 30-8

down

skylights

attic storage

# No. 99878

## ■ This plan features:

— Three bedrooms

— Two full and one half baths

■ Spacious floor plan with large Great Room crowned by cathedral ceiling

■ Central Kitchen with angled counter opens to the Breakfast Area and Great Room

■ Privately located Master Bedroom has a cathedral ceiling

■ Operable skylights over the tub accent the luxurious master bath

■ Bonus Room over the Garage makes expanding easy

■ An optional crawl space or basement foundation — please specify when ordering

Main floor — 1,864 sq. ft.
Garage — 614 sq. ft.
Bonus — 420 sq. ft.

■ *Total living area  2,978 sq. ft.* ■ *Price Code  E* ■

## No. 94242

**This plan features:**

- Three bedrooms

- Two full, one three-quarter and one half baths

- Wonderfully balanced exterior highlighted by triple arched glass in Entry Porch, leading into the Gallery Foyer

- Triple arches lead into Formal Living and Dining Room, Verandah and beyond

- Kitchen, Nook and Leisure Room easily flow together

- Owners' wing has a Master Suite with glass alcove to rear yard, a lavish bath and a Study offering many uses

- No materials list is available for this plan

Main floor — 2,978 sq. ft.
Garage — 702 sq. ft.

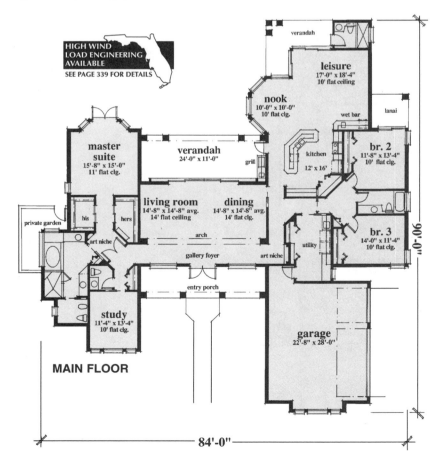

HIGH WIND
LOAD ENGINEERING
AVAILABLE
SEE PAGE 339 FOR DETAILS

**MAIN FLOOR**

verandah

leisure
17'-0" x 18'-4"
10' flat ceiling

nook
10'-0" x 10'-0"
10' flat clg.

wet bar

lanai

master
suite
15'-8" x 15'-0"
11' flat clg.

verandah
24'-0" x 11'-0"

grill

kitchen
12' x 16'

br. 2
11'-8" x 13'-4"
10' flat clg.

private garden

his

hers

art niche

living room
14'-8" x 14'-8" avg.
14' flat ceiling

dining
14'-8" x 14'-8" avg.
14' flat clg.

arch

gallery foyer

art niche

utility

br. 3
14'-0" x 11'-4"
10' flat clg.

study
11'-4" x 13'-4"
10' flat clg.

entry porch

garage
22'-8" x 28'-0"

90'-0"

84'-0"

# Rewards of Success

■ *Total living area  2,965 sq. ft.* ■ *Price Code F* ■

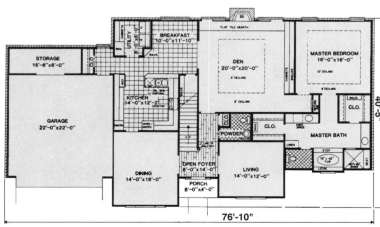

## No. 92535

■ **This plan features:**

— Four bedrooms

— Three full and one half baths

■ An open Foyer flanked by the Dining Room and the Living Room

■ Den with a large fireplace, and built-in cabinets and shelves

■ A well-appointed Kitchen serving the Dining Room

■ A Master Bedroom with a lavish bath and a walk-in closet

■ Three additional bedrooms and two full baths occupying the second floor

■ An optional crawl space or slab foundation — please specify when ordering

First floor — 2,019 sq. ft.
Second floor — 946 sq. ft.
Garage — 577 sq. ft.

■ *Total living area  2,425 sq. ft.* ■ *Price Code  E* ■

## No. 98419

### This plan features:

- Three bedrooms

- Two full and one half baths

- Vaulted Great Room is highlighted by a fireplace

- Decorative columns define the Dining Room

- A built-in Pantry and a radius window in the Kitchen

- The Breakfast Bay is crowned by a vaulted ceiling

- A tray ceiling over the Master Bedroom and Sitting Area

- Two additional bedrooms, each with a walk-in closet, share the full, double vanity bath in the hall

- An optional basement, crawl space or slab foundation — please specify when ordering

- No materials list is available for this plan

First floor — 1,796 sq. ft.
Second floor — 629 sq. ft.
Bonus room — 208 sq. ft.
Basement — 1,796 sq. ft.
Garage — 588 sq. ft.

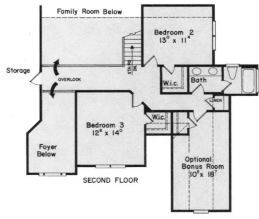

SECOND FLOOR

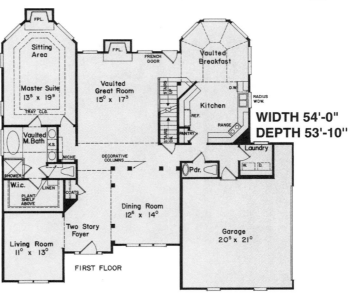

WIDTH 54'-0"
DEPTH 53'-10"

FIRST FLOOR

# Small Yet Sophisticated

■ *Total living area  1,360 sq. ft.* ■ *Price Code A* ■

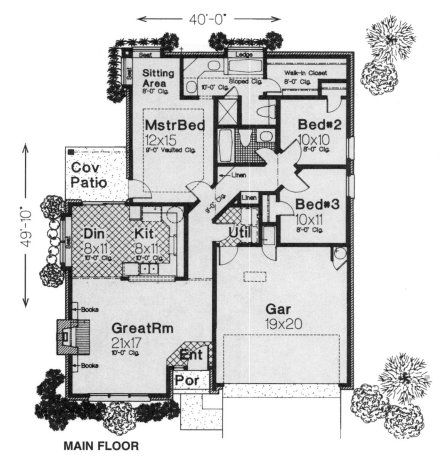

**MAIN FLOOR**

## No. 92281

■ **This plan features:**

— Three bedrooms

— Two full baths

■ Spacious Great Room highlighted by a fireplace and built-in shelving

■ Efficient, U-shaped Kitchen with ample work and storage space, sliding glass door to Covered Patio and a Dining area with a window seat

■ Spacious Master Bedroom suite enhanced by window seats, vaulted ceiling, a lavish bath and large walk-in closet

■ Two additional bedrooms share a full bath

■ Convenient Utility area and Garage entry

■ No materials list is available for this plan

Main floor — 1,360 sq. ft.
Garage — 380 sq. ft.

# Larger Feeling than Square Footage Indicates

© 1991 Donald A. Gardner Architects, Inc.

■ *Total living area  1,541 sq. ft.* ■ *Price Code  C* ■

# No. 96419 ✂

■ **This plan features:**

- Three bedrooms

- Two full baths

■ Arched windows, dormers, front and side Porches, rear Deck, and an open interior give this home a larger feeling

■ Elegant columns define the Dining Room, while the Great Room gains an open and airy feeling from the cathedral ceiling and arched window above the sliding door

■ Master Suite pampers the owner with a private bath which includes a whirlpool tub, separate shower, double vanity, linen closet, and walk-in closet

■ An optional crawl space or basement foundation — please specify when ordering

Main floor — 1,541 sq. ft.
Garage & Storage — 446 sq. ft.

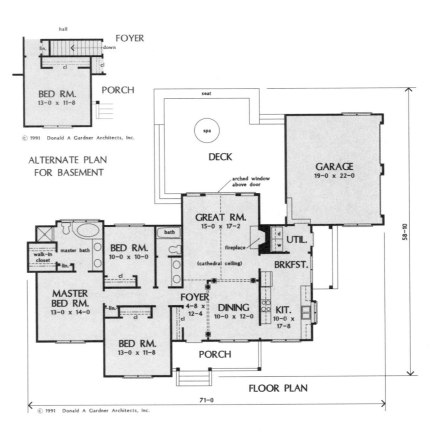

# Designed For Easy Building And Easy Living

© 1996 Donald A Gardner Architects, Inc.

■ *Total living area  1,800 sq. ft.* ■ *Price Code C* ■

## No. 99814

■ **This plan features:**

— Three bedrooms

— Two full baths

■ Refined, traditional exterior created by brick, double dormers and a hip roof

■ Foyer opens to a generous Great Room with cathedral ceiling and fireplace

■ Columns define entrance to Kitchen with a center island

■ Master Bedroom, Dining Room, and front Bedroom/Study receive distinction from tray ceilings

Main floor — 1,800 sq. ft.
Garage — 477 sq. ft.

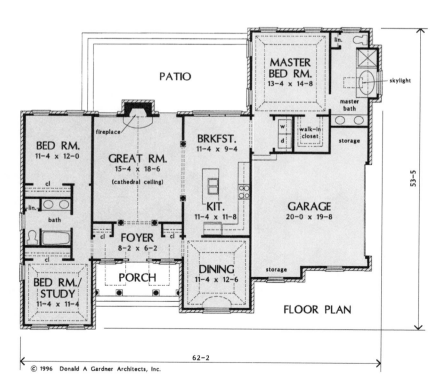

© 1996  Donald A Gardner Architects, Inc.

# Columned Elegance

■ Total living area 2,485 sq. ft. ■ Price Code D ■

# No. 90461

■ **This plan features:**

- Three bedrooms

- Two full baths

■ Elegant columns on the front Porch

■ The Study and the Dining room both overlook the front Porch

■ The Great room has a fireplace, built-in book shelves and access to the rear Deck

■ The Kitchen has an angled serving bar with a double sink

■ The secluded Master suite has dual walk-in closets, and a bath with a spa tub

■ An optional basement or crawl space foundation available — please specify when ordering

Main floor — 2,485 sq. ft.
Basement — 2,485 sq. ft.
Garage — 484 sq. ft.

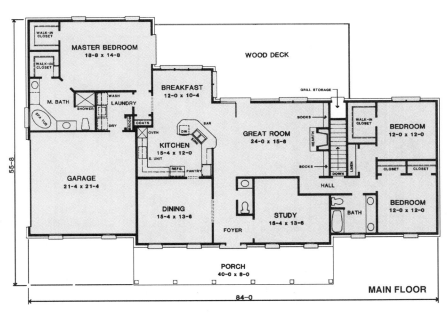

# Outstanding Four Bedroom

■ *Total living area  1,945 sq. ft.* ■ *Price Code C* ■

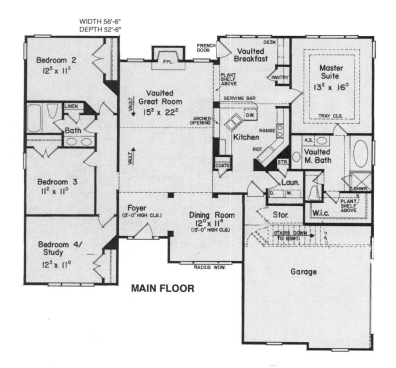

WIDTH 56'-6"
DEPTH 52'-6"

Bedroom 2
12⁵ x 11³

Vaulted
Great Room
15³ x 22²

Bedroom 3
11² x 11⁰

Foyer
(13'-0" HIGH CLG.)

Bedroom 4/
Study
12⁵ x 11⁰

LINEN

Bath

VAULT

VAULT

ARCHED
OPENING

COATS

Dining Room
12⁰ x 11⁴
(13'-0" HIGH CLG.)

RADIUS WDW.

FRENCH
DOOR

FPL.

Vaulted
Breakfast

PLANT
SHELF
ABOVE

SERVING BAR

DESK

PANTRY

Kitchen

D.W.

RANGE

REF.

STR.

Laun.

D.   W.

Stor.

STAIRS DOWN
TO BSMT.

Master
Suite
13² x 16⁰

TRAY CLG.

K.S.

Vaulted
M. Bath

SHWR.

W.i.c.

PLANT
SHELF
ABOVE

Garage

**MAIN FLOOR**

## No. 98435

### ■ This plan features:

— Four bedrooms

— Two full baths

■ A radius window highlights the Dining Room

■ The Great Room accented by a fireplace

■ Arched opening to the Kitchen

■ Breakfast Room has a French door to the rear yard

■ Tray ceiling and a five-piece bath in the Master Suite

■ An optional basement or crawl space foundation available — please specify when ordering

Main floor — 1,945 sq. ft.

# Brick Beauty

■ *Total living area  2,685 sq. ft.* ■ *Price Code  E* ■

## No. 98525

■ **This plan features:**

– Four bedrooms

– Three full and one half baths

■ Living Room and the Dining Room are each distinguished by their impressive front windows

■ Kitchen with center island and opens into the Breakfast Nook which has sliding doors to the backyard Patio

■ Enormous Family Room with fireplace, will be the central location of family activities

■ First floor Master Bedroom is removed from high traffic areas, and is complimented by a spacious bath and walk-in closet

■ Connected by the upstairs hallway are three bedrooms and two full baths

■ No materials list is available for this plan

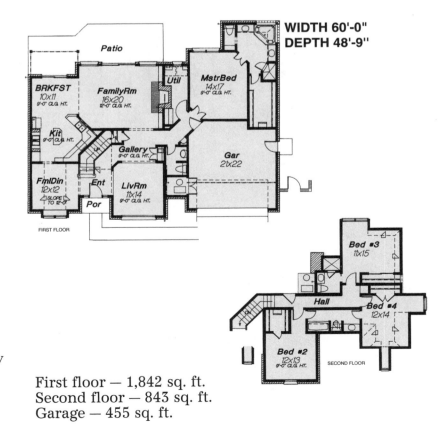

**WIDTH 60'-0"**
**DEPTH 48'-9"**

First floor — 1,842 sq. ft.
Second floor — 843 sq. ft.
Garage — 455 sq. ft.

# Appealing Farmhouse Design

© 1995 Donald A. Gardner Architects, Inc.

■ *Total living area 1,792 sq. ft.* ■ *Price Code C* ■

## SECOND FLOOR PLAN

attic storage

BED RM.
10-4 x 10-0

bath

MASTER BED RM.
13-6 x 15-8

BONUS RM.
20-0 x 14-2

cl

down

attic storage

BED RM.
11-4 x 11-10

walk-in closet

master bath

walk-in closet

© 1995 Donald A Gardner Architects, Inc.

First floor — 959 sq. ft.
Second floor — 833 sq. ft.
Bonus room — 344 sq. ft.
Garage & storage — 500 sq. ft.

## FIRST FLOOR PLAN

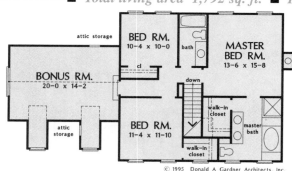

storage

d w UTIL.
7-0 x 6-0

BRKFST.
9-8 x 9-2

PORCH

KIT.
11-4 x 11-4

GREAT RM.
14-4 x 20-0

fireplace

GARAGE
20-0 x 20-0

pan.

42-8

(optional door location)

DINING
11-4 x 14-4

up

FOYER
10-6 x 7-8

cl

pd. rm.

PORCH

52-6

© 1995 Donald A Gardner Architects, Inc.

## No. 99836

### ■ This plan features:

— Three bedrooms

— Two full and one half baths

■ Comfortable farmhouse features an easy to build floor plan with all the extras

■ Active families will enjoy the Great Room which is open to the Kitchen and Breakfast Bay, as well as expanded living space provided by the full back Porch

■ For narrower lot restrictions, the Garage can be modified to open in front

■ Second floor Master Bedroom contains a walk-in closet and a private bath with a garden tub and separate shower

■ Two more bedrooms on the second floor, one with a walk-in closet, share a full bath

# French Flavor

■ *Total living area  2,490 sq. ft.* ■ *Price Code  F* ■

## No. 92549

■ **This plan features:**

- Four bedrooms

- Three full baths

■ Porch entry into open Foyer with a lovely, landing staircase

■ Elegant columns define Dining and Den area for gracious entertaining

■ Efficient, U-shaped Kitchen with a serving counter, Eating bay, and nearby Utility and Garage

■ Decorative ceiling tops Master Bedroom offering a huge walk-in closet and plush bath

■ An optional crawl space or slab foundation — please specify when ordering

First floor — 1,911 sq. ft.
Second floor — 579 sq. ft.
Garage — 560 sq. ft..

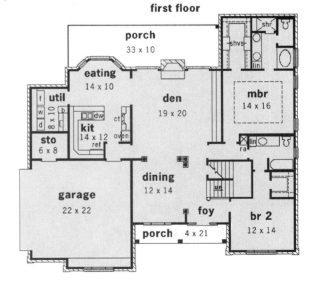

first floor

porch
33 x 10

eating
14 x 10

util
8 x 10

kit
14 x 12

sto
6 x 8

garage
22 x 22

den
19 x 20

mbr
14 x 16

dining
12 x 14

foy

porch
4 x 21

br 2
12 x 14

WIDTH 57'-10"
DEPTH 56'-10"

second floor

br 3
13⁶ x 12

br 4
12 x 12

open to foyer

# Country Charmer

■ *Total living area 1,438 sq. ft.* ■ *Price Code A* ■

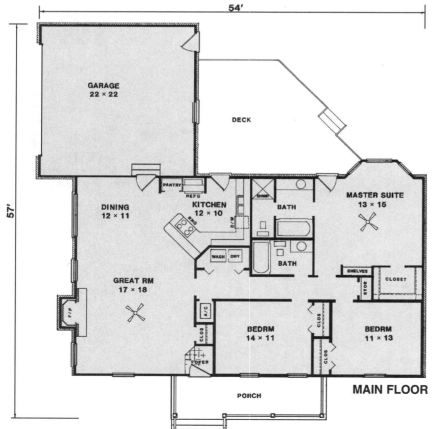

**MAIN FLOOR**

## No. 96509

■ **This plan features:**

—Three bedrooms

—Two full baths

■ Quaint front Porch is perfect for sitting and relaxing

■ Great Room opening into Dining Area and Kitchen

■ Corner Deck in rear of home accessed from Kitchen and Master Suite

■ Master Suite with a private bath, walk-in closet and built-in shelves

■ Two large secondary bedrooms in the front of the home share a hall bath

■ Two-car Garage located in the rear of the home

Main floor — 1,438 sq. ft.
Garage — 486 sq. ft.

316

■ *Total living area  3,352 sq. ft.* ■ *Price Code  F* ■

# No. 98513

## This plan features:

- Three bedrooms

- Three full and one half baths

- Brick and stone blend masterfully for an impressive French country exterior

- Separate Master Suite with expansive bath and closet

- Study containing a built-in desk and bookcase

- Angled island Kitchen highlighted by walk-in Pantry and open to the Breakfast Bay

- Fantastic Family Room including a brick fireplace and a built-in entertainment center

- Three additional bedrooms with private access to a full bath

- No materials list is available for this plan

Main floor — 3,352 sq. ft.
Garage — 672 sq. ft.

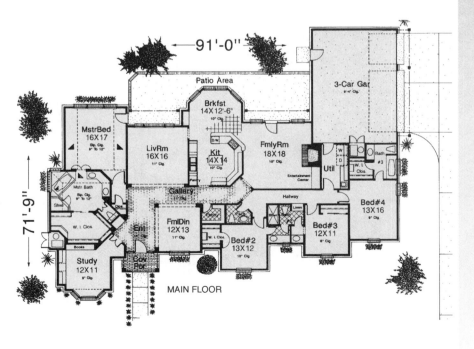

# One-Story Home Brimming With Amenities

■ *Total living area  2,079 sq. ft.* ■ *Price Code C* ■

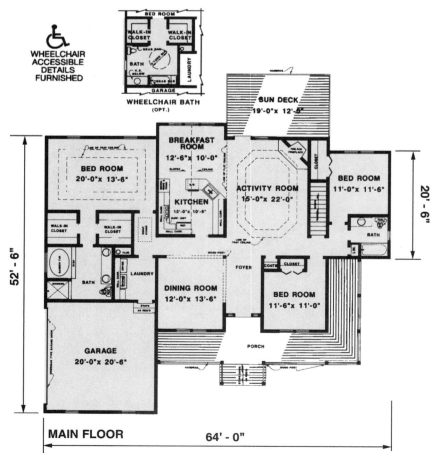

WHEELCHAIR ACCESSIBLE DETAILS FURNISHED

BED ROOM

WALK-IN CLOSET  WALK-IN CLOSET

BATH  GRAB BAR

GARAGE  LAUNDRY

**WHEELCHAIR BATH**
(OPT.)

SUN DECK
19'-0"x 12'-6"

BED ROOM
20'-0"x 13'-6"

BREAKFAST ROOM
12'-6"x 10'-0"

KITCHEN
12'-0"x 10'-6"

ACTIVITY ROOM
15'-0"x 22'-0"

BED ROOM
11'-0"x 11'-6"

BATH

WALK-IN CLOSET  WALK-IN CLOSET

BATH  LAUNDRY

20' - 6"

52' - 6"

DINING ROOM
12'-0"x 13'-6"

FOYER  COATS  CLOSET

BED ROOM
11'-6"x 11'-0"

GARAGE
20'-0"x 20'-6"

PORCH

**MAIN FLOOR**  64' - 0"

# No. 94805

## ■ This plan features:

— Three bedrooms

— Two full baths

■ Pleasant Country look with doubl[e] dormer windows and wrap-around Porch

■ Foyer opens to Dining Room and Activity Room enhanced by tray ceiling, corner fireplace and Sun Deck access

■ Kitchen/Breakfast Room topped by a sloped ceiling, offers an angular serving counter and lots of storage space

■ Secluded Master Bedroom graced with twin walk-in closets and a garden tub bath

■ Two additional bedrooms with easy access to full bath

Main floor — 2,079 sq. ft.
Garage — 438 sq. ft.
Basement — 2,079 sq. ft.

# Brick Detail with Arches

■ *Total living area  1,987 sq. ft.* ■ *Price Code  D* ■

## No. 92544

### This plan features:

Four bedrooms

Two full and one half baths

Front and back Porches expand the living space and provide inviting access to the open layout

Spacious Den with a fireplace flanked by built-in shelves and double access to the rear Porch

Formal Dining Room with an arched window

Efficient, U-shaped Kitchen with a snackbar counter, a bright Breakfast area and an adjoining laundry and Garage

Secluded Master Bedroom suite

Three additional bedrooms with walk-in closets, share one and half baths

An optional slab or crawl space foundation available — please specify when ordering

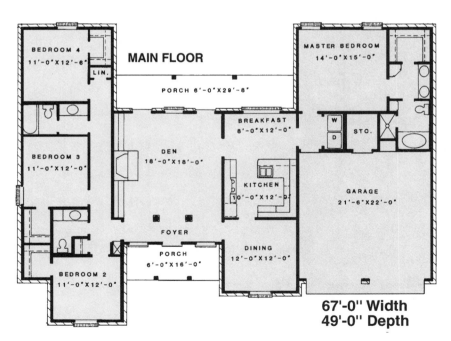

Main floor — 1,987 sq. ft.
Garage/Storage — 515 sq. ft.

# Classic Country Farmhouse

© 1992 Donald A Gardner Architects, Inc.

■ *Total living area 1,663 sq. ft.* ■ *Price Code C* ■

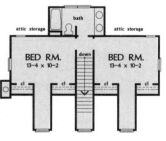

SECOND FLOOR PLAN

First floor — 1,145 sq. ft.
Second floor — 518 sq. ft.
Bonus room — 380 sq. ft.
Garage & storage — 509 sq. ft.

## No. 99800

### ■ This plan features:

— Three bedrooms

— Two full and one half baths

■ Covered Porch gives classic country farmhouse look, and includes multiple dormers, a great layout for entertaining, and a Bonus Room

■ Clerestory dormer window bathe the two-story Foyer in natural light

■ Large Great Room with fireplace opens to the Dining/Breakfast/ Kitchen space, which leads to a spacious Deck with optional spa and seating for easy indoor/ outdoor entertaining

■ First floor Master Suite offers privacy and luxury with a separate shower, whirlpool tub and a dual vanity

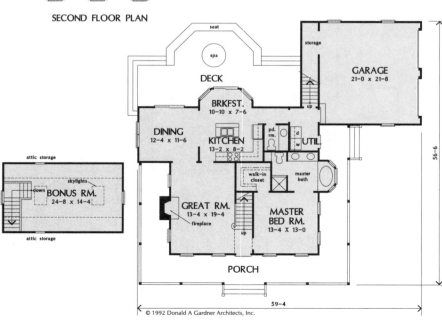

FIRST FLOOR PLAN

© 1992 Donald A Gardner Architects, Inc.

# Stone and Siding

■ *Total living area  2,690 sq. ft.* ■ *Price Code  E* ■

## No. 94810 ✖

### This plan features:

- Four bedrooms

- Three full and one half baths

- Attractive styling using a combination of stone and siding and a covered Porch add to the curb appeal

- Formal foyer giving access to the bedroom wing, Library or Activity room

- Activity room showcasing a focal point fireplace and including direct access to the rear Deck and the Breakfast Room

- Breakfast Room is topped by a vaulted ceiling and flows into the kitchen

- A secluded Guest Suite is located off the kitchen area

- Master Suite topped by a tray ceiling and pampered by five-piece bath

Main floor — 2,690 sq. ft.
Basement — 2,690 sq. ft.
Garage — 660 sq. ft.

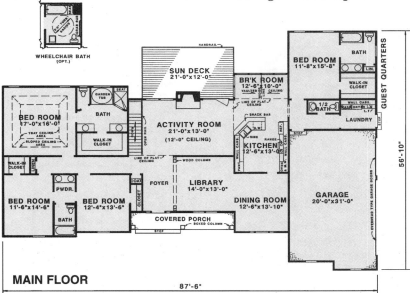

# Cozy Three Bedroom

■ *Total living area  1,199 sq. ft.* ■ *Price Code B* ■

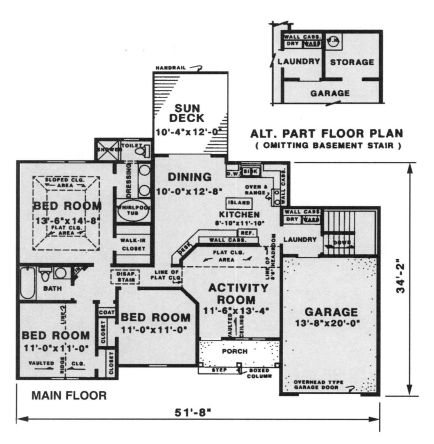

**ALT. PART FLOOR PLAN**
( OMITTING BASEMENT STAIR )

**MAIN FLOOR**

# No. 94800

■ **This plan features:**

— Three bedrooms

— Two full baths

■ Covered Entry leads into Activity Room highlighted by a double window and a vaulted ceiling

■ Kitchen with work island opens t Dining Area

■ Master Bedroom offers a decorative ceiling and whirlpool tub

■ Garage with entry into Laundry Room serving as a Mud Room

■ An optional basement, slab or crawl space foundation — please specify when ordering

Main floor — 1,199 sq. ft.
Basement — 1,199 sq. ft.
Garage — 287 sq. ft.

# Great As A Mountain Retreat

© 1996 Donald A Gardner Architects, Inc.

■ *Total living area 1,912 sq. ft.* ■ *Price Code D* ■

## No. 99815

### This plan features:

- Three bedrooms

- Two full baths

- Board and batten siding, stone, and stucco combine to give this popular plan a casual feel

- User friendly Kitchen with huge Pantry for ample storage and island counter

- Casual family meals in sunny Breakfast Bay; formal gatherings in the columned Dining area

- Master Suite is topped by a deep tray ceiling, has a large walk-in closet, an extravagant private bath and direct access to back Porch

Main floor — 1,912 sq. ft.
Garage — 580 sq. ft.
Bonus — 398 sq. ft.

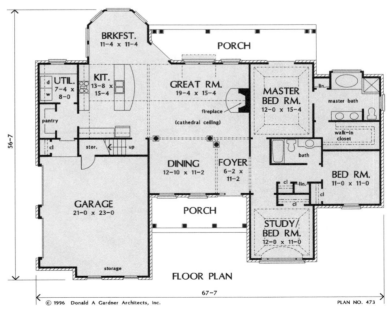

FLOOR PLAN

© 1996 Donald A Gardner Architects, Inc.

PLAN NO. 473

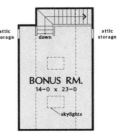

# Easy One Floor Living

■ *Total living area  1,671 sq. ft.* ■ *Price Code  B* ■

**WIDTH 50'-0"**
**DEPTH 51'-0"**

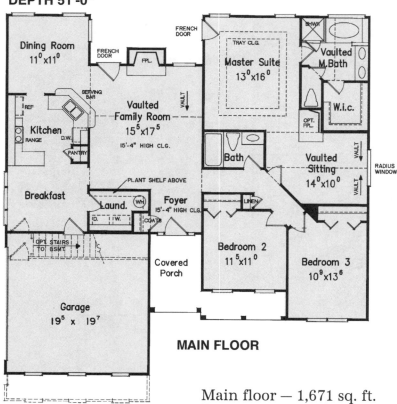

**MAIN FLOOR**

Main floor — 1,671 sq. ft.
Basement — 1,685 sq. ft.
Garage — 400 sq. ft.

## No. 98423

■ **This plan features:**

— Three bedrooms

— Two full baths

■ A spacious Family Room topped by a vaulted ceiling and highlighted by a large fireplace and a French door to the rear yard

■ A serving bar open to the Family Room and the Dining Room, a Pantry and a peninsula counter adding more efficiency to the Kitchen

■ A crowning tray ceiling over the Master Bedroom and a vaulted ceiling over the Master Bath

■ A vaulted ceiling over the cozy Sitting Room in the Master Suite

■ Two additional bedrooms, roomy in size, sharing the full bath in the hall

■ An optional basement, crawl space or slab foundation — please specify when ordering

# Roomy, Yet Practical Home

© 1997 Donald A. Gardner Architects, Inc.

■ *Total living area 2,023 sq. ft.* ■ *Price Code D* ■

## No. 96406

### This plan features:

– Three bedrooms

– Two full and one half baths

■ A smart exterior conceals an economical use of interior space

■ The two-story Foyer leads to the Great Room with a fireplace, a wall of windows and access to the back Porch

■ Columns divide the Great Room from the Breakfast Room which is open to an angled Kitchen with Pantry

■ A handy Utility Room leads to a two-car Garage with ample storage space

■ A split bedroom plan places the Master Suite with two walk-in closets on the second floor

First floor — 1,489 sq. ft.
Second floor — 534 sq. ft.
Garage & Storage — 568 sq. ft.
Bonus — 393 sq. ft.

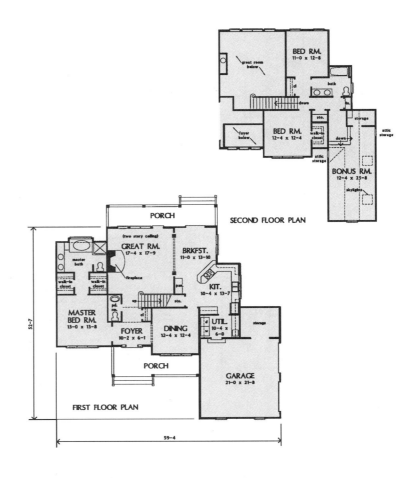

# Triple Arched Porch

■ *Total living area  1,744 sq. ft.* ■ *Price Code B* ■

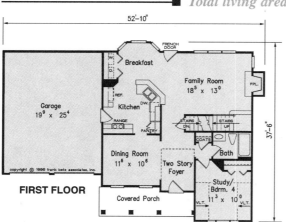

**FIRST FLOOR**

Garage
19⁹ x 25⁴

Breakfast

Family Room
18⁵ x 13⁰

FPL.

REF.

Kitchen
DW.

RANGE

PANTRY

STAIRS DN

STAIRS UP

COATS

Bath

Dining Room
11⁶ x 10⁶

Two Story Foyer

Study/Bdrm. 4
11³ x 10⁰

Covered Porch

FRENCH DOOR

VLT.

VLT.

copyright © 1996 frank betz associates, inc.

52'-10"

37'-6"

**SECOND FLOOR**

PLANT SHELF ABOVE

SHWR.

Vaulted M.Bath

FRENCH DOOR

W.I.C.

Bath

LINEN

Master Suite
18² x 13⁰

TRAY CEILING

STAIRS DN

W.I.C.

Bedroom 3
11⁶ x 11²

Foyer Below

Bedroom 2
11³ x 10²

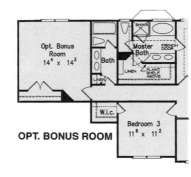

**OPT. BONUS ROOM**

Opt. Bonus Room
14⁴ x 14³

Bath

SHWR.

Master Bath

FRENCH DOOR

LINEN

LINEN

PLANT SHELF ABOVE

W.I.C.

Bedroom 3
11⁶ x 11²

# No. 98474

## ■ This plan features:

— Four bedrooms

— Three full baths

■ A triple arched front Porch

■ An open layout in the rear living area

■ The Study/Bedroom four is topped by a vaulted ceiling

■ The Master Suite has a vaulted ceiling over the bath

■ An optional Bonus Room offers expansion for future needs

■ An optional basement or crawl space foundation — please specify when ordering

■ No materials list is available for this plan

First floor — 972 sq. ft.
Second floor — 772 sq. ft.
Bonus room — 358 sq. ft.
Basement — 972 sq. ft.
Garage — 520 sq. ft.

© 1995 Donald A. Gardner Architects, Inc.    B. NATHAN

■ *Total living area  1,883 sq. ft.* ■ *Price Code  C* ■

## No. 96479

### This plan features:

- Three bedrooms
- Two full baths
- Unlimited options on the second floor Bonus Area
- Columns accenting the Dining Room, adjacent to the Foyer
- Great room, open to the Kitchen and Breakfast Room, enlarged by a cathedral ceiling
- Living and entertaining space expands to the Deck
- Master Suite topped by a tray ceiling and including a walk-in closet, skylit bath with garden tub and a double vanity
- Flexible Bedroom/Study shares a bath with another bedroom

First floor — 1,803 sq. ft.
Second floor — 80 sq. ft.
Garage & storage — 569 sq. ft.
Bonus Space — 918 sq. ft.

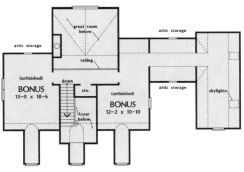

SECOND FLOOR PLAN

FIRST FLOOR PLAN

© 1995 Donald A Gardner Architects, Inc.

# Designed for Today's Family

— S. NATHAN.

■ *Total living area  2,192 sq. ft.* ■ *Price Code D* ■

## No. 99838

### ■ This plan features:

— Three bedrooms

— Two full and one half baths

■ Volume and 9' ceilings add elegance to a comfortable, open floor plan

■ Secluded bedrooms designed for pleasant retreats at the end of the day

■ Airy Foyer topped by a vaulted dormer allows natural light to stream in

■ Formal Dining Room delineated from the Foyer by columns topped with a tray ceiling

■ Extra flexibility in the front bedroom which could double as a Study

■ Tray ceiling in the bedroom and skylights and a garden tub in the bath highlight the Master Suite

Main floor — 2,192 sq. ft.
Garage & Storage — 582 sq. ft.
Bonus — 390 sq. ft.

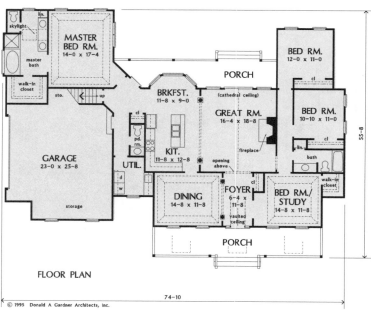

FLOOR PLAN

BONUS RM.
14-4 x 21-8

# For an Established Neighborhood

■ *Total living area 1,292 sq. ft.* ■ *Price Code A* ■

# No. 93222

## This plan features:

- Three bedrooms
- Two full baths
- An expansive Living Room enhanced by natural light streaming in from the large front window
- A bayed formal Dining Room with direct access to the Sun Deck and the Living Room for entertainment ease
- An efficient, galley Kitchen, convenient to both formal and informal eating areas
- An informal Breakfast Room with direct access to the Sun Deck
- A large Master Suite equipped with a walk-in closet and a full private bath

Main area — 1,276 sq. ft.
Finished staircase — 16 sq. ft.
Basement — 392 sq. ft.
Garage — 728 sq. ft.

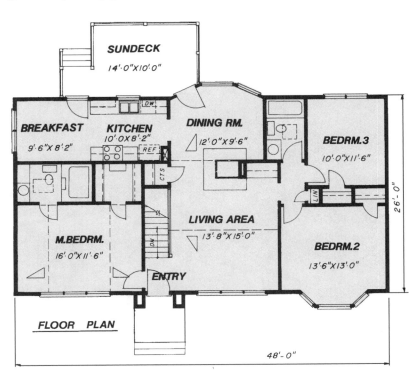

SUNDECK
14'-0"X10'-0"

BREAKFAST
9'-6"X8'-2"

KITCHEN
10'-0X8'-2"

DINING RM.
12'-0"X9'-6"

BEDRM.3
10'-0"X11'-6"

M.BEDRM.
16'-0"X11'-6"

LIVING AREA
13'-8"X15'-0"

BEDRM.2
13'-6"X13'-0"

ENTRY

FLOOR PLAN

26'-0"

48'-0"

An
EXCLUSIVE DESIGN
By *Jannis Vann & Associates, Inc.*

# Separate Guest Quarters

**Total living area 3,792 sq. ft.** ■ **Price Code F** ■

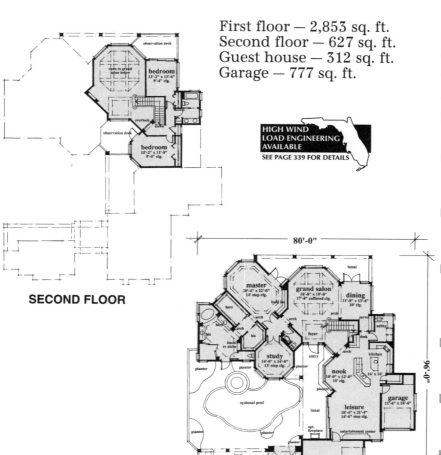

**SECOND FLOOR**

80'-0"

**FIRST FLOOR**

First floor — 2,853 sq. ft.
Second floor — 627 sq. ft.
Guest house — 312 sq. ft.
Garage — 777 sq. ft.

**HIGH WIND LOAD ENGINEERING AVAILABLE**
**SEE PAGE 339 FOR DETAILS**

# No. 94246

## ■ This plan features:

— Four bedrooms

— Three full and one half baths

■ Portico Entry way opens up to a unique courtyard plan

■ Octagon-shaped Grand Salon overlooks Lanai and opens to formal Dining Area

■ An efficient Kitchen with a walk-in Pantry, built-in desk, island sink and expansive snack bar

■ Open Leisure room with a high ceiling, offers an entertainment center, sliding glass doors to lanai and courtyard

■ Master wing has a large bedroom with a stepped ceiling, a bayed sitting area and lavish bath area

■ Two upstairs bedrooms with private decks, share a double vanity bath

■ Private Guest House offers luxurious accommodations

■ No materials list is available for this plan

■ *Total living area  3,381 sq. ft.* ■ *Price Code  F* ■

## No. 98514

**This plan features:**

- Five bedrooms
- Two full, one three-quarter and one half baths
- The Entry/Gallery features a grand spiral staircase
- The Study has built-in bookcases
- Formal Living and Dining Rooms each have palladian windows
- The large Family Room has a fireplace
- The first floor Master Bedroom contains a luxurious bath with a cathedral ceiling
- An optional slab or crawl space foundation — please specify when ordering
- No materials list is available for this plan

Main floor — 2,208 sq. ft.
Upper floor — 1,173 sq. ft.
Bonus — 224 sq. ft.
Garage — 520 sq. ft.

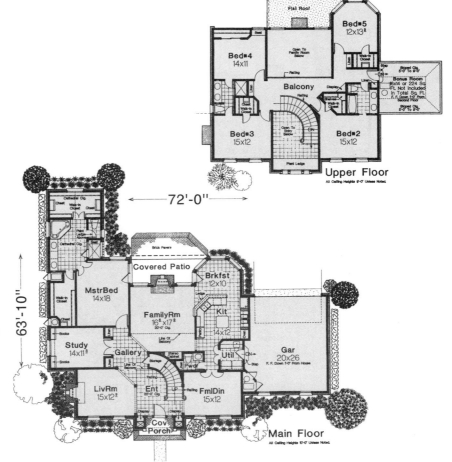

Upper Floor

72'-0"

63'-10"

Main Floor

# Stunning First Impression

■ *Total living area 2,464 sq. ft.* ■ *Price Code D* ■

## No. 98540

### ■ This plan features:

— Four bedrooms

— Two full and one half baths

■ Dormer windows on the second floor, arched windows and entrance, brick quoin corners come together for a stunning first impression

■ Large Living Room with a fireplace and an open formal Dining Area

■ Family Room at the rear of home containing a bar

■ Huge island Kitchen with a Breakfast area and plenty of work and storage space

■ Luxurious Master Suite occupying an entire wing of the home and providing a quiet retreat

■ Three additional bedrooms on the second floor sharing a large bath

■ No materials list is available for this plan

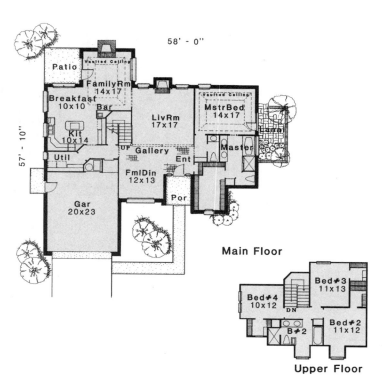

**Main Floor**

**Upper Floor**

Main floor — 1,805 sq. ft.
Upper floor — 659 sq. ft.
Basement — 1,800 sq. ft.
Garage — 440 sq. ft.

# Wrapping Front Porch and Gabled Dormers

©1997 Donald A. Gardner Architects, Inc.

■ *Total living area 2,596 sq. ft.* ■ *Price Code E* ■

## No. 96411

### This plan features:

Four bedrooms

Three full baths

Generous Great Room with a fireplace, cathedral ceiling and a balcony above

Flexible Bedroom/Study having a walk-in closet and an adjacent full bath

Master Suite with a sunny bay window and a private bath topped by a cathedral ceiling and highlighted by his-n-her vanities, and a separate tub and shower

Two additional bedrooms, each with dormer windows, sharing a full bath with a cathedral ceiling, palladian window and double vanity

Bonus Room over the Garage for future expansion

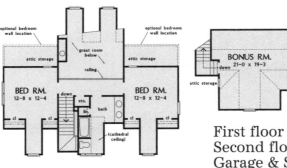

SECOND FLOOR PLAN

First floor — 1,939 sq. ft.
Second floor — 657 sq. ft.
Garage & Storage — 526 sq. ft.
Bonus room — 386 sq. ft.

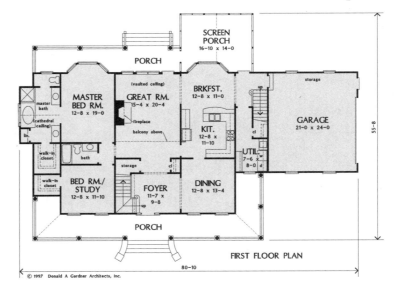

FIRST FLOOR PLAN

© 1997 Donald A Gardner Architects, Inc.

# Distinctive Windows Add to Curb Appeal

■ *Total living area  2,735 sq. ft.* ■ *Price Code F* ■

## No. 92550

**■ This plan features:**

— Four bedrooms

— Three full baths

■ A private Master Bedroom with a raised ceiling and attached bath with a spa tub

■ A wing of three bedrooms on the right side of the home sharing two full baths

■ An efficient Kitchen is straddled by an Eating Nook and a Dining Room

■ A cozy Den with a raised ceiling and a fireplace that is the focal point of the home

■ A two-car Garage with a storage area

■ An optional crawl space or slab foundation — please specify when ordering

Main floor — 2,735 sq. ft.
Garage — 561 sq. ft.

**WIDTH 68'-10"**
**DEPTH 67'-4"**

**mbr**
15 x 21⁴
raised clg

**porch**
8 x 30⁸

**br 4**
14 x 12

**sto**
8⁶ x 8

**util** 8⁶ x 9

**eating**
13 x 11

**den**
18 x 24

**garage**
21 x 22

**kit**
13 x 13

**br 3**
14 x 12

raised clg

**pan**

ledge

**dining**
14 x 12

**foy**

**porch**

**br 2**
14 x 12

**MAIN FLOOR**

# Impressive Entrance

■ *Total living area  4,125 sq. ft.* ■ *Price Code  F* ■

## No. 98439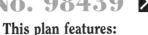

### This plan features:

Four bedrooms

Three full baths

Two-story Foyer leads through arched openings to the formal Living Room and Dining Room

An Island Kitchen offers a Pantry and serving bar

The Breakfast Room opens to the Kitchen and has a French door to the rear yard

A fireplace and built-in shelving highlight the Family Room

A home Office or secondary bedroom has a double door entrance for privacy as well as a private full bath

The Master Suite has a Sitting Room and lavish bath

An optional basement or crawl space foundation — please specify when ordering

First floor — 2,058 sq. ft.
Second floor — 2,067 sq. ft.
Basement — 2,058 sq. ft.
Garage — 819 sq. ft.

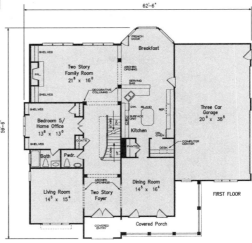

# First Floor Master Suite

■ *Total living area 2,357 sq. ft.* ■ *Price Code D* ■

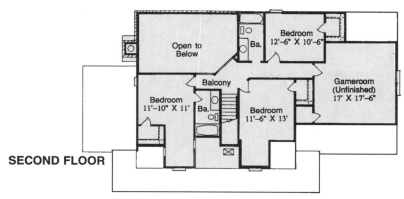

**SECOND FLOOR**

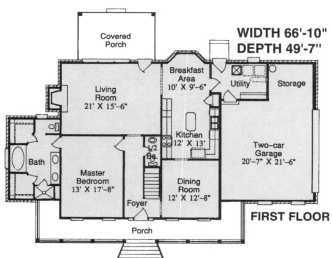

**WIDTH 66'-10"**
**DEPTH 49'-7"**

**FIRST FLOOR**

## No. 94613

■ **This plan features:**

— Four bedrooms

— Three full and one half baths

■ Spacious Living Room enhanced by fireplace

■ Kitchen with work island, built-in pantry, Utility room, Garage entry and Breakfast Area

■ Spacious Master Bedroom suite with a private bath

■ Three second floor bedrooms with walk-in closets, share two full baths and a Game Room

■ An optional crawl space or slab foundation — please specify when ordering

■ No materials list is available for this plan

First floor — 1,492 sq. ft.
Second floor — 865 sq. ft.
Bonus room — 303 sq. ft.
Garage — 574 sq. ft.

# Moderate Ranch Has Features of a Larger Plan

■ *Total living area  1,811 sq. ft.* ■ *Price Code  C* ■

## No. 90441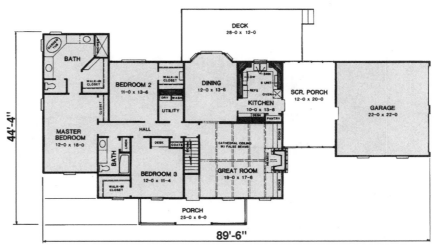

**This plan features:**

Three bedrooms

Two full baths

A large Great Room with a vaulted ceiling and a stone fireplace with bookshelves on either side

A spacious Kitchen with ample cabinet space conveniently located next to the large Dining Room

A Master Suite having a large bath with a garden tub, double vanity and a walk-in closet

Two other large bedrooms, each with a walk-in closet and access to the full bath

An optional basement, slab or crawl space combination — please specify when ordering

Main floor — 1,811 sq. ft.

**MAIN FLOOR**

# Traditional Ranch

■ *Total living area 2,275 sq. ft.* ■ *Price Code D* ■

## No. 92404

■ **This plan features:**

— Three bedrooms

— Two full baths

■ A tray ceiling in the Master Suite that is equipped with his-n-her walk-in closets and a private master bath with a cathedral ceiling

■ A formal Living Room with a cathedral ceiling

■ A decorative tray ceiling in the elegant formal Dining Room

■ A spacious Family Room with a vaulted ceiling and a fireplace

■ A modern, well-appointed Kitchen with snack bar and bayed Breakfast Area

■ Two additional bedrooms, each with a walk-in closet, share a full hall bath

Main floor — 2,275 sq. ft.
Basement — 2,207 sq. ft.
Garage — 512 sq. ft.

# Hurricane Engineering for Florida!

HIGH WIND LOAD ENGINEERING AVAILABLE

The Garlinghouse Company has teamed with The Sater Design Collection and United Design Associates, not only to supply our Sunbelt Home Plans publication with stunning home designs, but to provide structural wind load engineering services for the Florida building market. We are now able to provide high wind load engineering for any design from The Sater Design Collection and United Design Associates that appears in this publication.

Our extensive engineering packages will come to you complete with 3 sets of signed and sealed blueprints along with the modified reproducible vellums. Many localities will require energy calculations in addition to the engineered plans. The energy calculations can often be obtained from a reputable HVAC contractor free of charge as an incentive to use their service or we can provide them for a fee of $150.00. Check with your local building department to find out your exact requirements before ordering.

The Sater Design Collection, from Bonita Springs, Florida and United Design Associates from Auburn, AL will help make building your dream home a reality. Through this exclusive offer, we are able to provide these high wind load engineering services at very reasonable prices.

| Price Code | High Wind Load Engineering Fees |
|------------|---------------------------------|
| A | $650 |
| B | $775 |
| C | $900 |
| D | $1025 |
| E | $1150 |
| F | $1275 |
| G | $1400 |
| H | $1525 |

**NOTE:** High wind load engineering pricing is in addition to the cost of a reproducible vellum and is only available for plans with this symbol... HIGH WIND LOAD ENGINEERING AVAILABLE

Once you have placed your order, please allow 7-10 additional business days for delivery after we have received all of your applicable site information. This includes a copy of your site plan and legal description of your property.

High wind load engineering is a custom professional service and is locally specific. Please note that all fees for this service are non-refundable upon commencement of any engineering. The above pricing includes shipping from The Sater Design Collection or United Design Associates to you.

We are proud to offer these engineering services to you at these very competitive rates.

# Everything You Need...
## ...to Make Your Dream Come True

*You pay only a fraction of the original cost for home designs by respected professionals.*

**You've Picked Your Dream Home!**

You can imagine your new home situated on your lot in the morning sunlight. You can visualize living there, enjoying your family, entertaining friends and celebrating holidays. All that remains are the details. That's where we can help. Whether you plan to build it yourself, act as your own general contractor or hire a professional builder, your Garlinghouse Co. home plans will provide the perfect design and specifications to help make your dream home a reality.

We can offer you an array of additional products and services to help you with your planning needs. We can supply materials lists, construction cost estimates based on your local material and labor costs and modifications to your selected plan if you would like.

For over 90 years, homeowners and builders have relied on us for accurate, complete, professional blueprints. Our plans help you get results fast... and save money, too! These pages will give you all the information you need to order. So get started now... We know you'll love your new Garlinghouse home!

Sincerely,

*Bradford Fishing*    *James D. McNair III*

President      Chief Executive Officer

## EXTERIOR ELEVATIONS

Elevations are scaled drawings of the front, rear, left, and right sides of a home. All of the necessary information pertaining to the exterior finish materials, roof pitches, and exterior height dimensions of your home are defined.

## CABINET PLANS

These plans, or in some cases elevations, will detail the layout of the kitchen and bathroom cabinets at a larger scale. This gives you an accurate layout for your cabinets or an ideal starting point for a modified custom cabinet design. Available for most plans. You may also show the floor plan without a cabinet layout. This will allow you to start from scratch and design your own dream kitchen.

## TYPICAL WALL SECTION

This section is provided to help your builder understand the structural components and materials used to construct the exterior walls of your home. This section will address insulation, roof components, and interior and exterior wall finishes. Your plans will be designed with either 2x4 2x6 exterior walls, but most professional contractors can easily adapt the plans to the wall thickness you require.

## FIREPLACE DETAILS

If the home you have chosen includes a fireplace, the fireplace detail will show typical methods to construct the firebox, hearth and flue chase for masonry units, or a wood frame chase for a zero-clearance unit. Available for most plans.

## FOUNDATION PLAN

These plans will accurately dimension the footprint of your home including load bearing points and beam placement if applicable. The foundation style will vary from plan to plan. Your local climatic conditions will dictate whether a basement, slab or crawlspace is best suited for your area. In most cases, if your plan comes with one foundation style, a professional contractor can easily adapt the foundation plan to an alternate style.

## ROOF PLAN

The information necessary to construct the roof will be included with your home plans. Some plans will reference roof trusses, while many others contain schematic framing plans. These framing plans will indicate the lumber sizes necessary for the rafters and ridgeboards based on the designated roof loads.

## TYPICAL CROSS SECTION

A cut-away cross-section through the entire home shows your building contractor the exact correlation of construction components at all levels of the house. It will help to clarify the load bearing points from the roof all the way down to the basement. Available for most plans.

## DETAILED FLOOR PLANS

The floor plans of your home accurately dimension the positioning of all walls, doors, windows, stairs and permanent fixtures. They will show you the relationship and dimensions of rooms, closets and traffic patterns. The schematic of the electrical layout may be included in the plan. This layout is clearly represented and does not hinder the clarity of other pertinent information shown. All these details will help your builder properly construct your new home.

## STAIR DETAILS

If stairs are an element of the design you have chosen, the plans will show the necessary information to build these, either through a stair cross section, or on the floor plans. Either way, the information provides your builders the essential reference points that they need to build the stairs.

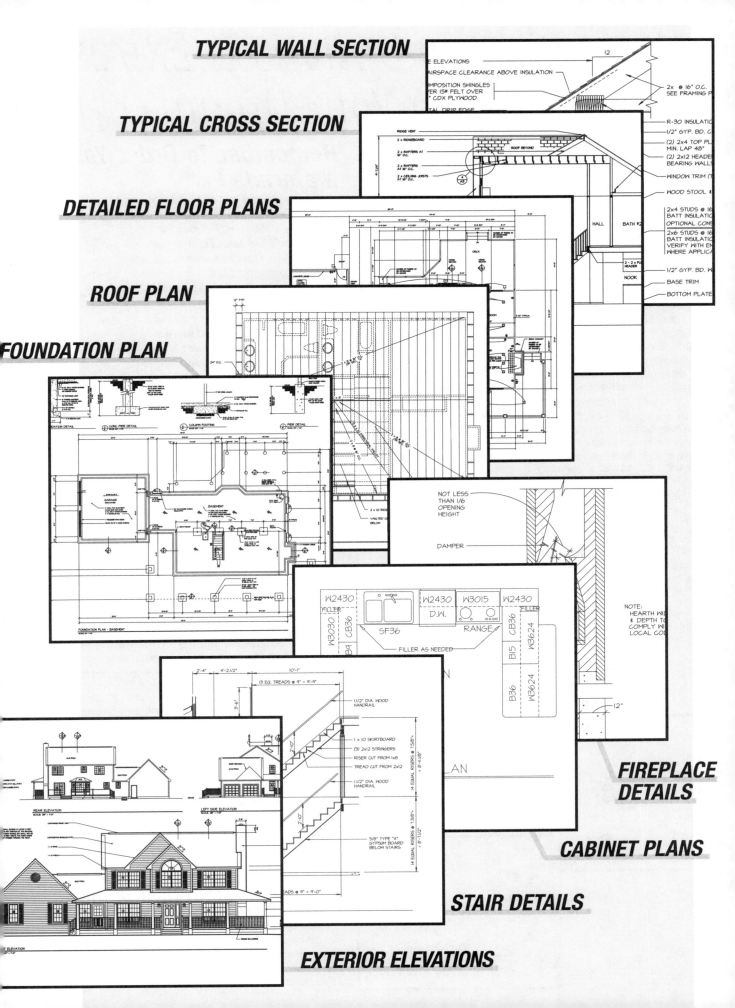

# TYPICAL WALL SECTION

# TYPICAL CROSS SECTION

# DETAILED FLOOR PLANS

# ROOF PLAN

# FOUNDATION PLAN

# FIREPLACE DETAILS

# CABINET PLANS

# STAIR DETAILS

# EXTERIOR ELEVATIONS

# Garlinghouse Options & Extras
## ...Make Your Dream A Home

## Reversed Plans Can Make Your Dream Home Just Right!

*"That's our dream home...if only the garage were on the other side!"*
You could have exactly the home you want by flipping it end-for-end. Check it out by holding your dream home page of this book up to a mirror. Then simply order your plans "reversed." We'll send you one full set of mirror-image plans (with the writing backwards) as a master guide for you and your builder.

The remaining sets of your order will come as shown in this book so the dimensions and specifications are easily read on the job site...but most plans in our collection come stamped "REVERSED" so there is no construction confusion.

As Shown          Reversed

We can only send reversed plans with multiple-set orders. There is a $50 charge for this service.

Some plans in our collection are available in Right Reading Reverse. Right Reading Reverse plans will show your home in reverse, with the writing on the plan being readable. This easy-to-read format will save you valuable time and money. Please contact our Customer Service Department at (860) 343-5977 to check for Right Reading Reverse availability. (There is a $150 charge for plan series 964, 980, & 998. $125 for all other plans.)

## Specifications & Contract Form

We send this form to you free of charge with your home plan order. The form is designed to be filled in by you or your contractor with the exact materials to use in the construction of your new home. Once signed by you and your contractor it will provide you with peace of mind throughout the construction process.

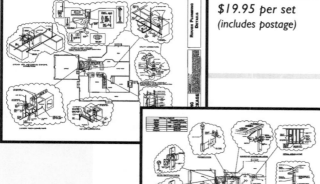

**$19.95** per set
(includes postage)

## Remember To Order Your Materials List

It'll help you save money. Available at a modest additional charge, the Materials List gives the quantity, dimensions, and specifications for the major materials needed to build your home. You will get faster, more accurate bids from your contractors and building suppliers — and avoid paying for unused materials and waste. Materials Lists are available for all home plans except as otherwise indicated, but can only be ordered with a set of home plans. Due to differences in regional requirements and homeowner or builder preferences... electrical, plumbing and heating/air conditioning equipment specifications are not designed specifically for each plan. However, non-plan specific detailed typical prints of residential electrical, plumbing and construction guidelines can be provided. Please see below for additional information.

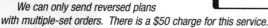

## Detail Plans Provide Valuable Information About Construction Techniques

Because local codes and requirements vary greatly, we recommend that you obtain drawings and bids from licensed contractors to do your mechanical plans. However, if you want to know more about techniques — and deal more confidently with subcontractors — we offer these remarkably useful detail sheets. These detail sheets will aid in your understanding of these technical subjects. **The detail sheets are not specific to any one home plan and should be used only as a general reference guide.**

### RESIDENTIAL CONSTRUCTION DETAILS

Ten sheets that cover the essentials of stick-built residential home construction. Details foundation options — poured concrete basement, concrete block, or monolithic concrete slab. Shows all aspects of floor, wall and roof framing. Provides details for roof dormers, overhangs, chimneys and skylights. Conforms to requirements of Uniform Building code or BOCA code. Includes a quick index and a glossary of terms.

### RESIDENTIAL PLUMBING DETAILS

Eight sheets packed with information detailing pipe installation methods, fittings, and sized. Details plumbing hook-ups for toilets, sinks, washers, sump pumps, and septic system construction. Conforms to requirements of National Plumbing code. Color coded with a glossary of terms and quick index.

### RESIDENTIAL ELECTRICAL DETAILS

Eight sheets that cover all aspects of residential wiring, from simple switch wiring to service entrance connections. Details distribution panel layout with outlet and switch schematics, circuit breaker and wiring installation methods, and ground fault interrupter specifications. Conforms to requirements of National Electrical Code. Color coded with a glossary of terms.

# Modifying Your Favorite Design, Made *EASY!*

## OPTION #1

### Modifying Your Garlinghouse Home Plan

*Simple modifications to your dream home, including minor non-structural changes and material substitutions, can be made between you and your builder by marking the changes directly on your blueprints. However, if you are considering making significant changes to your chosen design, we recommend that you use the services of The Garlinghouse Design Staff. We will help take your ideas and turn them into a reality, just the way you want. Here's our procedure!*

*When you place your Vellum order, you may also request a free Garlinghouse Modification Kit. In this kit, you will receive a red marking pencil, furniture cut-out sheet, ruler, a self addressed mailing label and a form for specifying any additional notes or drawings that will help us understand your design ideas. Mark your desired changes directly on the Vellum drawings. NOTE: Please use only a **red pencil** to mark your desired changes on the Vellum. Then, return the redlined Vellum set in the original box to us. **IMPORTANT:** Please **roll** the Vellums for shipping, **do not fold** the Vellums for shipping.*

*We also offer modification estimates. We will provide you with an estimate to draft your changes based on your specific modifications before you purchase the vellums, for a $50 fee. After you receive your estimate, if you decide to have us do the changes, the $50 estimate fee will be deducted from the cost of your modifications. If, however, you choose to use a different service, the $50 estimate fee is non-refundable. (Note: Personal checks cannot be accepted for the estimate.)*

*Within 5 days of receipt of your plans, you will be contacted by the Design Staff with an estimate for the design services to draw those changes. A 50% deposit is required before we begin making the actual modifications to your plans.*

*Once the design changes have been completed to your vellum plan, a representative will call to inform you that your modified Vellum plan is complete and will be shipped as soon as the final payment has been made. For additional information call us at 1-860-343-5977. Please refer to the Modification Pricing Guide for estimated modification costs.*

## OPTION #2

### Reproducible Vellums for Local Modification Ease

*If you decide not to use Garlinghouse for your modifications, we recommend that you follow our same procedure of purchasing our Vellums. You then have the option of using the services of the original designer of the plan, a local professional designer, or architect to make the modifications to your plan.*

*With a Vellum copy of our plans, a design professional can alter the drawings just the way you want, then you can print as many copies of the modified plans as you need to build your house. And, since you have already started with our complete detailed plans, the cost of those expensive professional services will be significantly less than starting from scratch. Refer to the price schedule for Vellum costs.*

***IMPORTANT RETURN POLICY:*** *Upon receipt of your Vellums, if for some reason you decide you do not want a modified plan, then simply return the Kit and the unopened Vellums. Reproducible Vellum copies of our home plans are copyright protected and only sold under the terms of a license agreement that you will receive with your order. Should you not agree to the terms, then the Vellums may be returned, **unopened,** for a full refund less the shipping and handling charges, plus a 20% restocking fee. For any additional information, please call us at 1-860-343-5977.*

| CATEGORIES | ESTIMATED COST |
|---|---|
| KITCHEN LAYOUT — PLAN AND ELEVATION | $175.00 |
| BATHROOM LAYOUT — PLAN AND ELEVATION | $175.00 |
| FIREPLACE PLAN AND DETAILS | $200.00 |
| INTERIOR ELEVATION | $125.00 |
| EXTERIOR ELEVATION — MATERIAL CHANGE | $140.00 |
| EXTERIOR ELEVATION — ADD BRICK OR STONE | $400.00 |
| EXTERIOR ELEVATION — STYLE CHANGE | $450.00 |
| NON BEARING WALLS (INTERIOR) | $200.00 |
| BEARING AND/OR EXTERIOR WALLS | $325.00 |
| WALL FRAMING CHANGE — 2X4 TO 2X6 OR 2X6 TO 2X4 | $240.00 |
| ADD/REDUCE LIVING SPACE — SQUARE FOOTAGE | QUOTE REQUIRED |
| NEW MATERIALS LIST | QUOTE REQUIRED |
| CHANGE TRUSSES TO RAFTERS OR CHANGE ROOF PITCH | $300.00 |
| FRAMING PLAN CHANGES | $325.00 |
| GARAGE CHANGES | $325.00 |
| ADD A FOUNDATION OPTION | $300.00 |
| FOUNDATION CHANGES | $250.00 |
| RIGHT READING PLAN REVERSE | $575.00 |
| ARCHITECTS SEAL (Available for most states.) | $300.00 |
| ENERGY CERTIFICATE | $150.00 |
| LIGHT AND VENTILATION SCHEDULE | $150.00 |

## Questions?

Call our customer service department at 1-860-343-5977

# "How to obtain a construction cost calculation based on labor rates and building material costs in <u>your</u> Zip Code area!"

# ZIP-QUOTE!
## HOME COST CALCULATOR

## WHY?

Do you wish you could quickly find out the building cost for your new home without waiting for a contractor to compile hundreds of bids? Would you like to have a benchmark to compare your contractor(s) bids against? *Well, Now You Can!!,* with **Zip-Quote** Home Cost Calculator. Zip-Quote is only available for zip code areas within the United States.

## HOW?

Our new **Zip-Quote** Home Cost Calculator will enable you to obtain the calculated building cost to construct your new home, based on labor rates and building material costs within your zip code area, without the normal delays or hassles usually associated with the bidding process. Zip-Quote can be purchased in two separate formats, an itemized or a bottom line format.

"How does **Zip-Quote** actually work?" When you call to order, you must choose from the options available, for your specific home, in order for us to process your order. Once we receive your **Zip-Quote** order, we process your specific home plan building materials list through our Home Cost Calculator which contains up-to-date rates for all residential labor trades and building material costs in your zip code area. "The result?" A calculated cost to build your dream home in your zip code area. This calculation will help you (as a consumer or a builder) evaluate your building budget. This is a valuable tool for anyone considering building a new home.

All database information for our calculations is furnished by Marshall & Swift, L.P. For over 60 years, Marshall & Swift L.P. has been a leading provider of cost data to professionals in all aspects of the construction and remodeling industries.

## OPTION 1

The **Itemized Zip-Quote** is a detailed building material list. Each building material list line item will separately state the labor cost, material cost and equipment cost (if applicable) for the use of that building material in the construction process. Each category within the building material list will be subtotaled and the entire Itemized cost calculation totaled at the end. This building materials list will be summarized by the individual building categories and will have additional columns where you can enter data from your contractor's estimates for a cost comparison between the different suppliers and contractors who will actually quote you their products and services.

## OPTION 2

The **Bottom Line Zip-Quote** is a one line summarized total cost for the home plan of your choice. This cost calculation is also based on the labor cost, material cost and equipment cost (if applicable) within your local zip code area.

## COST

The price of your **Itemized Zip-Quote** is based upon the pricing schedule of the plan you have selected, in addition to the price of the materials list. Please refer to the pricing schedule on our order form. The price of your initial **Bottom Line Zip-Quote** is $29.95. Each additional **Bottom Line Zip-Quote** ordered in conjunction with the initial order is only $14.95. **Bottom Line Zip-Quote** may be purchased separately and does NOT have to be purchased in conjunction with a home plan order.

## FYI

An **Itemized Zip-Quote** Home Cost Calculation can ONLY be purchased in conjunction with a Home Plan order. The **Itemized Zip-Quote** can not be purchased separately. The **Bottom Line Zip-Quote** can be purchased separately and doesn't have to be purchased in conjunction with a home plan order. Please consult with a sales representative for current availability. If you find within 60 days of your order date that you will be unable to build this home, then you may exchange the plans and the materials list towards the price of a new set of plans (see order info pages for plan exchange policy). The **Itemized Zip-Quote** and the **Bottom Line Zip-Quote** are NOT returnable. The price of the initial **Bottom Line Zip-Quote** order can be credited towards the purchase of an **Itemized Zip-Quote** order only. Additional **Bottom Line Zip-Quote** orders, within the same order can not be credited. Please call our Customer Service Department for more information.

**Itemized Zip-Quote** is available for plans where you see this symbol. 🔳

**Bottom Line Zip-Quote** is available for all plans under 4,000 square feet.

## SOME MORE INFORMATION

Itemized and Bottom Line Zip-Quotes give you approximated costs for constructing the particular house in your area. These costs are not exact and are only intended to be used as a preliminary estimate to help determine the affordability of a new home and/or as a guide to evaluate the general competitiveness of actual price quotes obtained through local suppliers and contractors. However, Zip-Quote cost figures should never be relied upon as the only source of information in either case. Land, sewer systems, site work, landscaping and other expenses are not included in our building cost figures. Garlinghouse and Marshall & Swift L.P. can not guarantee any level of data accuracy or correctness in a Zip-Quote and disclaim all liability for loss with respect to the same, in excess of the original purchase price of the Zip-Quote product. All Zip-Quote calculations are based upon the actual blueprints and do not reflect any differences or options that may be shown on the published house renderings, floor plans, or photographs.

# Ignoring Copyright Laws Can Be
# A $1,000,000 Mistake

Recent changes in the US copyright laws allow for statutory penalties of up to **$100,000** per incident for copyright infringement involving any of the copyrighted plans found in this publication. The law can be confusing. So, for your own protection, take the time to understand what you can and cannot do when it comes to home plans.

## ···WHAT YOU CANNOT DO···

### You Cannot Duplicate Home Plans

Purchasing a set of blueprints and making additional sets by reproducing the original is **illegal**. If you need multiple sets of a particular home plan, then you must purchase them.

### You Cannot Copy Any Part of a Home Plan to Create Another

Creating your own plan by copying even part of a home design found in this publication is called "creating a derivative work" and is **illegal** unless you have permission to do so.

### You Cannot Build a Home Without a License

You must have specific permission or license to build a home from a copyrighted design, even if the finished home has been changed from the original plan. It is **illegal** to build one of the homes found in this publication without a license.

# What Garlinghouse Offers

## Home Plan Blueprint Package

By purchasing a multiple set package of blueprints or a vellum from Garlinghouse, you not only receive the physical blueprint documents necessary for construction, but you are also granted a license to build one, and only one, home. You can also make simple modifications, including minor non-structural changes and material substitutions, to our design, as long as these changes are made directly on the blueprints purchased from Garlinghouse and no additional copies are made.

## Home Plan Vellums

By purchasing vellums for one of our home plans, you receive the same construction drawings found in the blueprints, but printed on vellum paper. Vellums can be erased and are perfect for making design changes. They are also semi-transparent making them easy to duplicate. But most importantly, the purchase of home plan vellums comes with a broader license that allows you to make changes to the design (ie, create a hand drawn or CAD derivative work), to make an unlimited number of copies of the plan, and to build one home from the plan.

## License To Build Additional Homes

With the purchase of a blueprint package or vellums you automatically receive a license to build one home and only one home, respectively. If you want to build more homes than you are licensed to build through your purchase of a plan, then additional licenses may be purchased at reasonable costs from Garlinghouse. Inquire for more information.

# IMPORTANT INFORMATION TO READ BEFORE YOU PLACE YOUR ORDER

## How Many Sets Of Plans Will You Need?

### The Standard 8-Set Construction Package

Our experience shows that you'll speed every step of construction and avoid costly building errors by ordering enough sets to go around. Each tradesperson wants a set — the general contractor and all subcontractors; foundation, electrical, plumbing, heating/air conditioning and framers. Don't forget your lending institution, building department and, of course, a set for yourself. * Recommended For Construction *

### The Minimum 4-Set Construction Package

If you're comfortable with arduous follow-up, this package can save you a few dollars by giving you the option of passing down plan sets as work progresses. You might have enough copies to go around if work goes exactly as scheduled and no plans are lost or damaged by subcontractors. But for only $50 more, the 8-set package eliminates these worries. * Recommended For Bidding *

### The Single Study Set

We offer this set so you can study the blueprints to plan your dream home in detail. They are stamped "study set only-not for construction", and you cannot build a home from them. In pursuant to copyright laws, it is <u>illegal</u> to reproduce any blueprint.

## An Important Note About Building Code Requirements:

All plans are drawn to conform to one or more of the industry's major national building standards. However, due to the variety of local building regulations, your plan may need to be modified to comply with local requirements — snow loads, energy loads, seismic zones, etc. Do check them fully and consult your local building officials.

A few states require that all building plans used be drawn by an architect registered in that state. While having your plans reviewed and stamped by such an architect may be prudent, laws requiring non-conforming plans like ours to be completely redrawn forces you to unnecessarily pay very large fees. If your state has such a law, we strongly recommend you contact your state representative to protest.

The rendering, floor plans, and technical information contained within this publication are not guaranteed to be totally accurate. Consequently, no information from this publication should be used either as a guide to constructing a home or for estimating the cost of building a home. Complete blueprints must be purchased for such purposes.

the Garlinghouse company

---

## Order Form

Plan prices guaranteed until 2/15/01— After this date call for updated pricing

Order Code No. **CHP16**

Foundation _____

_____ set(s) of blueprints for plan # _____    $_____

_____ Vellum & Modification kit for plan # _____    $_____

_____ Additional set(s) @ $30 each for plan # _____    $_____

_____ Mirror Image Reverse @ $50 each    $_____

_____ Right Reading Reverse    $_____

_____ Materials list for plan # _____    $_____

_____ Detail Plans @ $19.95 each    _____

_____   ❏ Construction   ❏ Plumbing   ❏ Electrical    $_____

_____ Bottom line ZIP Quote @ $29.95 for plan # _____    $_____

Additional Bottom Line Zip Quote

     @ $14.95 for plan(s) # _____    $_____

Zip Code where you are building _____

Itemized ZIP Quote for plan(s) # _____   $_____

Shipping (see charts on opposite page)   $_____

Subtotal   $_____

Sales Tax   (CT residents add 6% sales tax, KS residents add 6.15% sales tax) (Not required for all states)   $_____

**TOTAL AMOUNT ENCLOSED**   $_____

Email address _____

Send your check, money order or credit card information to:
(No C.O.D.'s Please)

**Please submit all United States & Other Nations orders to:**

Garlinghouse Company
P.O. Box 1717
Middletown, CT. 06457

## ADDRESS INFORMATION:

**NAME:** _____

**STREET:** _____

**CITY:** _____ **STATE:** _____ **ZIP:** _____

**DAYTIME PHONE:** _____

### Credit Card Information

Charge To:    ❏ Visa      ❏ Mastercard

Card # | | | | | | | | | | | | | | | | |

Signature _____ Exp. _____ / _____

## ORDER TOLL FREE — 1-800-235-5700
Monday-Friday 8:00 a.m. to 8:00 p.m. Eastern Time
_or FAX your Credit Card order to 1-860-343-5984_
_All foreign residents call 1-800-343-5977_

**BEST PLAN VALUE IN THE INDUSTRY!**

**Please have ready: 1. Your credit card number 2. The plan number 3. The order code number ⇨ CHP16**

## arlinghouse 2000 Blueprint Price Code Schedule

Additional sets with original order $30

| PRICE CODE | A | B | C | D | E | F | G | H |
|---|---|---|---|---|---|---|---|---|
| 8 SETS OF SAME PLAN | $405 | $445 | $490 | $530 | $570 | $615 | $655 | $695 |
| 4 SETS OF SAME PLAN | $355 | $395 | $440 | $480 | $520 | $565 | $605 | $645 |
| 1 SINGLE SET OF PLANS | $305 | $345 | $390 | $430 | $470 | $515 | $555 | $595 |
| VELLUMS | $515 | $560 | $610 | $655 | $700 | $750 | $795 | $840 |
| MATERIALS LIST | $60 | $60 | $65 | $65 | $70 | $70 | $75 | $75 |
| ITEMIZED ZIP QUOTE | $75 | $80 | $85 | $85 | $90 | $90 | $95 | $95 |

## Shipping — (Plans 1-84999)

| | 1-3 Sets | 4-6 Sets | 7+ & Vellums |
|---|---|---|---|
| Standard Delivery (UPS 2-Day) | $25.00 | $30.00 | $35.00 |
| Overnight Delivery | $35.00 | $40.00 | $45.00 |

## Shipping — (Plans 85000-99999)

| | 1-3 Sets | 4-6 Sets | 7+ & Vellums |
|---|---|---|---|
| Ground Delivery (7-10 Days) | $15.00 | $20.00 | $25.00 |
| Express Delivery (3-5 Days) | $20.00 | $25.00 | $30.00 |

## International Shipping & Handling

| | 1-3 Sets | 4-6 Sets | 7+ & Vellums |
|---|---|---|---|
| Regular Delivery Canada (7-10 Days) | $25.00 | $30.00 | $35.00 |
| Express Delivery Canada (5-6 Days) | $40.00 | $45.00 | $50.00 |
| Overseas Delivery Airmail (2-3 Weeks) | $50.00 | $60.00 | $65.00 |

## Our Reorder and Exchange Policies:

If you find after your initial purchase that you require additional sets of plans you may purchase them from us at special reorder rices (please call for pricing details) provided that you reorder within 6 months of your original order date. There is a $28 reorder processing fee that is charged on all reorders. For more information on reordering plans please contact our Customer Service Department.

Your plans are custom printed especially for you once you place your order. For that reason we cannot accept any returns.

If for some reason you find that the plan you have purchased from us does not meet your needs, then you may exchange that plan for ny other plan in our collection. We allow you sixty days from your original invoice date to make an exchange. At the time of the exchange ou will be charged a processing fee of 20% of the total amount of your original order plus the difference in price between the plans (if pplicable) plus the cost to ship the new plans to you. Call our Customer Service Department for more information. Please Note: eproducible vellums can only be exchanged if they are unopened.

## Important Shipping Information

Please refer to the shipping charts on the order form for service availability for your specific plan number. Our delivery service must ave a street address or Rural Route Box number — never a post office box. (PLEASE NOTE: Supplying a P.O. Box number _only_ will elay the shipping of your order.) Use a work address if no one is home during the day.

Orders being shipped to APO or FPO must go via First Class Mail.

For our International Customers, only Certified bank checks and money orders are accepted and must be payable in U.S. currency. or speed, we ship international orders Air Parcel Post. Please refer to the chart for the correct shipping cost.

**Thank you**

Legend: ML = Materials List Available · ZQ = Zip Quote Available · RR = Right Reading Reverse · DP = Duplex Plan

| Plan# | Page# | Price Code | Square Footage | Notes |
|---|---|---|---|---|
| 10492 | 55 | F | 4441 | ML |
| 90406 | 92 | B | 1737 | ML |
| 90409 | 65 | B | 1670 | ML |
| 90410 | 147 | C | 1997 | ML |
| 90412 | 201 | A | 1454 | ML |
| 90413 | 166 | D | 2440 | ML |
| 90420 | 214 | D | 2473 | ML |
| 90421 | 125 | C | 1940 | ML |
| 90423 | 70 | B | 1773 | ML |
| 90433 | 34 | A | 928 | ML |
| 90436 | 83 | C | 2181 | ML |
| 90439 | 188 | D | 2562 | ML |
| 90440 | 115 | B | 1764 | ML |
| 90441 | 337 | C | 1811 | ML |
| 90443 | 107 | E | 2759 | ML |
| 90444 | 182 | D | 2301 | ML |
| 90450 | 218 | D | 2398 | ML |
| 90451 | 39 | C | 2068 | ML |
| 90454 | 247 | D | 2218 | ML |
| 90458 | 261 | D | 2263 | ML |
| 90461 | 311 | D | 2485 | ML |
| 90465 | 120 | C | 1990 | ML |
| 90467 | 139 | D | 2290 | ML |
| 90469 | 163 | C | 2162 | ML |
| 90470 | 289 | E | 2714 | ML |
| 90476 | 36 | C | 1804 | ML |
| 91105 | 246 | C | 1908 | |
| 91109 | 61 | E | 2747 | |
| 91111 | 95 | E | 3034 | |
| 92207 | 171 | E | 3156 | |
| 92209 | 185 | F | 3292 | |
| 92218 | 256 | C | 1920 | ZQ |
| 92219 | 303 | F | 3335 | ZQ |
| 92220 | 72 | C | 1830 | |
| 92237 | 173 | F | 3783 | ZQ |
| 92238 | 222 | B | 1664 | |
| 92239 | 133 | A | 1198 | |
| 92248 | 49 | F | 3921 | ZQ |
| 92257 | 179 | D | 2470 | |
| 92265 | 86 | F | 3818 | |
| 92268 | 187 | B | 1706 | |
| 92269 | 302 | E | 2835 | |
| 92273 | 147 | F | 3254 | |
| 92274 | 121 | F | 3870 | |
| 92275 | 181 | E | 2675 | |
| 92277 | 78 | E | 3110 | ZQ |
| 92279 | 54 | E | 3079 | |
| 92281 | 308 | A | 1360 | |
| 92283 | 97 | B | 1653 | |
| 92284 | 176 | D | 2261 | |
| 92286 | 155 | A | 1415 | |
| 92289 | 168 | D | 2354 | |
| 92400 | 278 | A | 1050 | |
| 92404 | 338 | D | 2275 | ML |
| 92405 | 57 | B | 1564 | |
| 92501 | 88 | F | 2727 | ML |
| 92502 | 24 | B | 1237 | ML |
| 92503 | 29 | B | 1271 | ML |
| 92504 | 236 | F | 3813 | ML |
| 92505 | 164 | F | 3504 | ML |
| 92508 | 159 | F | 2951 | ML |
| 92509 | 269 | E | 2551 | ML |
| 92514 | 148 | D | 2045 | ML |
| 92515 | 138 | D | 1959 | ML |
| 92516 | 228 | D | 1887 | ML |
| 92517 | 53 | D | 1805 | ML |
| 92520 | 200 | B | 1208 | ML |
| 92523 | 32 | B | 1293 | ML |
| 92525 | 108 | B | 1484 | ML |
| 92527 | 294 | C | 1680 | ML |
| 92528 | 286 | B | 1363 | ML |
| 92531 | 153 | C | 1754 | ML |
| 92535 | 306 | F | 2965 | ML |
| 92536 | 64 | D | 1869 | ML |
| 92537 | 240 | E | 2539 | ML |
| 92538 | 177 | F | 2733 | ML |
| 92539 | 194 | D | 2033 | ML |
| 92542 | 180 | D | 1866 | ML |
| 92543 | 192 | D | 1858 | ML |
| 92544 | 319 | D | 1987 | ML |
| 92546 | 225 | E | 2387 | ML |
| 92549 | 315 | E | 2490 | ML |
| 92550 | 334 | F | 2735 | ML |
| 92552 | 129 | D | 1873 | ML |
| 92555 | 189 | C | 1668 | ML |
| 92556 | 96 | C | 1556 | ML |
| 92557 | 23 | B | 1390 | ML |
| 92560 | 26 | C | 1660 | ML |
| 92562 | 134 | C | 1856 | ML |
| 92576 | 42 | E | 2858 | ML |
| 92902 | 89 | E | 2787 | |
| 93000 | 126 | C | 1862 | |
| 93004 | 85 | A | 1260 | |
| 93006 | 175 | A | 1163 | |
| 93013 | 159 | D | 2463 | |
| 93015 | 158 | A | 1087 | |
| 93017 | 209 | A | 1142 | |
| 93018 | 187 | A | 1142 | |
| 93021 | 47 | A | 1282 | |
| 93026 | 145 | A | 1402 | |
| 93027 | 216 | A | 1500 | |
| 93030 | 221 | C | 1955 | |
| 93034 | 283 | E | 2838 | |
| 93035 | 67 | D | 2545 | |
| 93041 | 196 | E | 3034 | |
| 93042 | 207 | E | 2995 | |
| 93048 | 298 | A | 1310 | |
| 93056 | 208 | D | 2517 | ML |
| 93059 | 168 | D | 2559 | |
| 93061 | 231 | B | 1742 | |
| 93073 | 128 | A | 1202 | |
| 93075 | 38 | A | 1170 | |
| 93200 | 204 | F | 5730 | |
| 93202 | 14 | A | 1447 | ML |
| 93205 | 15 | D | 2588 | ML |
| 93206 | 103 | E | 2645 | ML ZQ |
| 93208 | 21 | D | 2421 | |
| 93209 | 141 | D | 2464 | ML ZQ |
| 93210 | 18 | D | 2394 | |
| 93212 | 205 | C | 2091 | ZQ |
| 93213 | 6 | C | 2085 | |
| 93216 | 188 | C | 1918 | ML |
| 93219 | 252 | B | 1668 | ML ZQ |
| 93220 | 167 | B | 1749 | ML ZQ |
| 93222 | 329 | A | 1292 | ML ZQ RR |
| 93230 | 148 | B | 1764 | |
| 93231 | 151 | B | 1781 | |
| 93235 | 155 | C | 2005 | |
| 93240 | 291 | D | 2454 | ML |
| 93243 | 180 | F | 3302 | |
| 93247 | 195 | F | 3840 | |
| 93254 | 21 | D | 2509 | |
| 93255 | 191 | C | 2192 | ML |
| 93261 | 229 | B | 1778 | ML ZQ |
| 93263 | 43 | B | 1625 | |
| 93265 | 242 | A | 1325 | |
| 93267 | 199 | D | 2336 | ML |
| 93269 | 59 | B | 1735 | ML |
| 93270 | 4 | F | 3656 | |
| 93279 | 123 | A | 1388 | ML ZQ |
| 93280 | 152 | B | 1553 | ML |
| 93283 | 106 | D | 2364 | ML |
| 93287 | 149 | C | 2024 | ML ZQ |
| 93294 | 8 | D | 2560 | ML |
| 93297 | 140 | B | 1704 | ML |
| 93298 | 257 | B | 1683 | |
| 93410 | 98 | C | 1854 | ML |
| 93411 | 56 | B | 1780 | |
| 93413 | 197 | C | 1808 | |
| 93432 | 50 | C | 1833 | ML |
| 93436 | 81 | C | 2073 | |
| 93439 | 16 | E | 3013 | |
| 93602 | 184 | D | 2411 | |
| 93603 | 156 | E | 3029 | |
| 93608 | 130 | C | 2060 | |
| 94202 | 176 | F | 3216 | ML |
| 94203 | 12 | B | 1772 | |
| 94204 | 192 | B | 1764 | |
| 94206 | 80 | D | 2214 | |
| 94208 | 223 | B | 1795 | |
| 94214 | 196 | D | 2569 | ML |
| 94220 | 2 | F | 3477 | |
| 94228 | 19 | F | 3980 | |
| 94229 | 17 | F | 3748 | |
| 94230 | 93 | F | 4759 | |
| 94231 | 285 | E | 2891 | |
| 94233 | 35 | D | 2527 | |
| 94239 | 288 | F | 4106 | |
| 94240 | 60 | B | 1647 | |
| 94242 | 305 | E | 2978 | |
| 94246 | 330 | F | 3792 | |
| 94247 | 20 | E | 2875 | |
| 94248 | 290 | C | 1853 | |
| 94600 | 211 | D | 2333 | |
| 94602 | 191 | B | 1704 | |
| 94603 | 227 | B | 1737 | |
| 94609 | 111 | C | 2060 | |
| 94613 | 336 | D | 2357 | |
| 94614 | 212 | D | 2533 | |
| 94615 | 162 | E | 2665 | |
| 94622 | 213 | E | 3149 | |
| 94640 | 255 | D | 2558 | |
| 94641 | 73 | D | 2400 | |
| 94713 | 172 | C | 1939 | ML |
| 94715 | 204 | E | 3012 | ML |
| 94716 | 45 | B | 1770 | ML |
| 94721 | 223 | E | 2832 | ML |
| 94729 | 219 | A | 1417 | ML |
| 94800 | 322 | B | 1199 | ML |
| 94801 | 277 | B | 1300 | ML |
| 94803 | 198 | B | 1752 | ML |
| 94804 | 10 | C | 1855 | ML |

| Materials List Available | Zip Quote Available | Right Reading Reverse | Duplex Plan |

| Plan# | Page# | Price Code | Square Footage | ML | ZQ |
|---|---|---|---|---|---|
| 4805 | 318 | C | 2079 | X | |
| 4810 | 321 | E | 2690 | X | |
| 4811 | 170 | D | 2165 | X | |
| 4812 | 41 | D | 1985 | X | |
| 6402 | 124 | D | 2027 | X | |
| 6403 | 58 | E | 2832 | X | |
| 6404 | 91 | D | 2301 | X | |
| 6405 | 132 | D | 1903 | X | |
| 6406 | 325 | D | 2023 | X | |
| 6407 | 202 | E | 2772 | X | |
| 6408 | 282 | D | 2164 | X | |
| 6411 | 333 | E | 2596 | X | |
| 6413 | 217 | D | 2349 | X | ↻ |
| 6414 | 219 | D | 2196 | X | |
| 6417 | 28 | C | 1561 | X | ↻ |
| 6418 | 31 | B | 1452 | X | |
| 6419 | 309 | C | 1541 | X | |
| 6421 | 249 | D | 2045 | X | |
| 6423 | 295 | D | 2218 | X | |
| 6427 | 160 | C | 1794 | X | |
| 6430 | 238 | C | 1988 | X | |
| 6435 | 100 | E | 2526 | X | |
| 6436 | 74 | C | 1622 | X | |
| 6437 | 172 | C | 1858 | X | |
| 6438 | 112 | D | 2130 | X | |
| 6439 | 234 | D | 2308 | X | |
| 6440 | 135 | C | 1713 | X | |
| 6442 | 75 | D | 2182 | X | |
| 6448 | 46 | D | 2301 | X | |
| 6449 | 157 | D | 2211 | X | |
| 6452 | 190 | B | 1475 | X | |
| 6456 | 193 | C | 1639 | X | |
| 6457 | 84 | C | 1843 | X | |
| 6459 | 208 | D | 2370 | X | |
| 6461 | 250 | C | 1838 | X | |
| 6462 | 264 | C | 1846 | X | |
| 6465 | 212 | D | 2050 | X | |
| 6468 | 297 | C | 1864 | X | |
| 6471 | 271 | D | 2190 | X | |
| 6472 | 254 | C | 1989 | X | |
| 6476 | 276 | C | 1823 | X | |
| 6478 | 116 | D | 2203 | X | |
| 6479 | 327 | C | 1883 | X | |
| 6483 | 179 | D | 2057 | X | |
| 6484 | 215 | B | 1246 | X | |
| 6487 | 258 | C | 1669 | X | |
| 6490 | 301 | E | 2682 | X | |
| 6491 | 284 | D | 2250 | X | |
| 6493 | 66 | C | 1770 | X | |
| 6500 | 227 | E | 3011 | X | |
| 6503 | 104 | D | 2256 | X | |
| 6504 | 211 | C | 2162 | X | |
| 6505 | 33 | D | 2069 | X | |
| 6506 | 241 | B | 1654 | X | |
| 6509 | 316 | A | 1438 | X | |
| 6510 | 160 | A | 1372 | X | |
| 6512 | 224 | D | 2276 | X | |
| 6513 | 268 | B | 1648 | X | |
| 6519 | 262 | A | 1243 | | |
| 6522 | 232 | B | 1515 | X | |
| 6529 | 183 | C | 2089 | X | |
| 6530 | 215 | D | 2289 | X | |
| 3211 | 251 | E | 3063 | | |
| 3231 | 226 | E | 2980 | | |
| 98400 | 68 | F | 3262 | X | |
| 98402 | 118 | F | 3027 | X | |
| 98403 | 44 | F | 3395 | X | |
| 98404 | 156 | F | 4362 | X | |
| 98405 | 154 | F | 3039 | X | |
| 98406 | 87 | B | 1600 | X | |
| 98407 | 253 | C | 2052 | X | |
| 98408 | 82 | C | 1856 | X | |
| 98410 | 293 | D | 2389 | X | |
| 98411 | 122 | A | 1373 | X | |
| 98414 | 150 | B | 1575 | X | |
| 98415 | 186 | A | 1429 | X | |
| 98416 | 235 | B | 1619 | X | |
| 98417 | 267 | D | 2600 | X | |
| 98419 | 307 | E | 2425 | | |
| 98421 | 184 | C | 2094 | X | |
| 98422 | 203 | A | 1436 | X | |
| 98423 | 324 | B | 1671 | X | |
| 98425 | 300 | C | 1845 | X | |
| 98426 | 273 | E | 2622 | X | |
| 98427 | 244 | C | 2051 | X | |
| 98429 | 101 | C | 1906 | X | |
| 98430 | 169 | C | 1884 | X | |
| 98431 | 137 | B | 1675 | X | |
| 98432 | 199 | B | 1670 | X | |
| 98434 | 113 | A | 1346 | X | |
| 98435 | 312 | C | 1945 | X | |
| 98437 | 220 | F | 3949 | X | |
| 98438 | 110 | F | 3525 | X | |
| 98439 | 335 | F | 4125 | X | |
| 98441 | 131 | B | 1502 | | |
| 98443 | 76 | A | 1359 | | |
| 98445 | 259 | C | 1913 | | |
| 98446 | 152 | B | 1800 | | |
| 98447 | 265 | C | 2155 | X | |
| 98449 | 171 | B | 1700 | X | |
| 98451 | 175 | E | 2267 | | |
| 98452 | 287 | E | 3083 | X | |
| 98454 | 48 | C | 1874 | X | |
| 98455 | 69 | D | 2349 | X | |
| 98456 | 51 | B | 1715 | X | |
| 98457 | 105 | E | 2686 | X | |
| 98460 | 136 | B | 1544 | | |
| 98462 | 279 | B | 1750 | | |
| 98463 | 165 | B | 1505 | | |
| 98473 | 280 | C | 1862 | | |
| 98474 | 326 | B | 1744 | | |
| 98503 | 260 | C | 1876 | | |
| 98508 | 239 | F | 3480 | | ↻ |
| 98510 | 224 | C | 1840 | | |
| 98511 | 263 | D | 2445 | | |
| 98512 | 292 | C | 2167 | | |
| 98513 | 317 | F | 3352 | | |
| 98514 | 331 | F | 3381 | | ↻ |
| 98518 | 63 | D | 2455 | | ↻ |
| 98519 | 79 | D | 2524 | | |
| 98522 | 99 | B | 1528 | | |
| 98524 | 146 | E | 2902 | | |
| 98525 | 313 | E | 2685 | | |
| 98528 | 203 | E | 2748 | | |
| 98533 | 178 | D | 2567 | | |
| 98534 | 210 | E | 2959 | | ↻ |
| 98535 | 151 | F | 3512 | | |
| 98536 | 243 | F | 3423 | | ↻ |
| 98538 | 164 | F | 4082 | | |
| 98539 | 274 | F | 3936 | | ↻ |
| 98540 | 332 | D | 2464 | | |
| 98904 | 167 | D | 2614 | X | |
| 98912 | 299 | A | 1325 | X | |
| 98915 | 77 | A | 1208 | X | |
| 99800 | 320 | C | 1663 | X | |
| 99801 | 52 | D | 2188 | X | ↻ |
| 99802 | 22 | C | 1576 | X | ↻ |
| 99803 | 71 | C | 1977 | X | ↻ |
| 99804 | 117 | C | 1815 | X | ↻ |
| 99805 | 143 | C | 1787 | X | ↻ |
| 99806 | 161 | B | 1246 | X | |
| 99807 | 233 | C | 1879 | X | ↻ |
| 99808 | 248 | C | 1832 | X | ↻ |
| 99809 | 127 | B | 1417 | X | ↻ |
| 99810 | 30 | C | 1685 | X | ↻ |
| 99811 | 245 | B | 1699 | X | |
| 99812 | 272 | B | 1386 | X | ↻ |
| 99813 | 296 | C | 1959 | X | |
| 99814 | 310 | C | 1800 | X | ↻ |
| 99815 | 323 | D | 1912 | X | ↻ |
| 99821 | 216 | E | 2916 | X | |
| 99824 | 40 | D | 2121 | X | |
| 99825 | 90 | E | 2869 | X | |
| 99826 | 25 | B | 1346 | X | |
| 99829 | 114 | C | 1972 | X | |
| 99830 | 144 | B | 1372 | X | ↻ |
| 99831 | 237 | C | 1699 | X | |
| 99834 | 266 | C | 1575 | X | |
| 99835 | 281 | C | 1515 | X | |
| 99836 | 314 | C | 1792 | X | |
| 99838 | 328 | D | 2192 | X | |
| 99840 | 200 | C | 1632 | X | |
| 99843 | 37 | E | 2563 | X | |
| 99844 | 62 | C | 1737 | X | |
| 99845 | 94 | C | 1954 | X | ↻ |
| 99849 | 31 | B | 1322 | X | |
| 99851 | 13 | C | 1861 | X | |
| 99852 | 109 | C | 1898 | X | |
| 99853 | 119 | E | 2692 | X | ↻ |
| 99855 | 163 | C | 1817 | X | |
| 99856 | 102 | B | 1310 | X | |
| 99857 | 270 | C | 1865 | X | |
| 99858 | 27 | B | 1253 | X | ↻ |
| 99859 | 142 | C | 1831 | X | ↻ |
| 99860 | 174 | B | 1498 | X | |
| 99864 | 183 | C | 1426 | X | |
| 99868 | 207 | B | 1350 | X | |
| 99871 | 206 | C | 1655 | X | |
| 99873 | 275 | C | 1778 | X | |
| 99874 | 220 | C | 1936 | X | |
| 99878 | 304 | C | 1864 | X | ↻ |
| 99884 | 167 | C | 1689 | X | |
| 99895 | 230 | D | 2435 | X | |

# CREATIVE HOMEOWNER®

# How-To Books for...

## REMODELING BASEMENTS, ATTICS & GARAGES

Cramped for space? This book shows you how to find space you may not know you had and convert it into useful living areas. 40 colorful photographs and 530 full-color drawings.

BOOK #: 277680          192pp.          8½"x10⅞"

## BASIC WIRING
(Third Edition, Conforms to latest National Electrical Code)

Included are 350 large, clear, full-color illustrations and no-nonsense step-by-step instructions. Shows how to replace receptacles and switches; repair a lamp; install ceiling and attic fans; and more.

BOOK #: 277048          160pp.          8½"x10⅞"

## BATHROOMS: Design, Remodel, Build

Shows how to plan, construct, and finish a bathroom. Remodel floors; rebuild walls and ceilings; and install windows, skylights, and plumbing fixtures. Specific tools and materials are given for each project. Includes 90 color photos and 470 color illustrations.

BOOK #: 277053          192pp.          8½"x10⅞"

## The Smart Approach to BATH DESIGN

Everything you need to know about designing a bathroom like a professional is explained in *this book*. Creative solutions and practical advice about space, the latest in fixtures and fittings, and safety features accompany over 150 photographs.

BOOK #: 287225          176pp.          9"x10"

## BUILD A KIDS' PLAY YARD

Here are detailed plans and step-by-step instructions for building the play structures that kids love most: swing set, monkey bars, balance beam, playhouse, teeter-totter, sandboxes, kid-sized picnic table, and a play tower that supports a slide. 200 color photographs and illustrations.

BOOK #: 277662          144 pp.          8½"x10⅞"

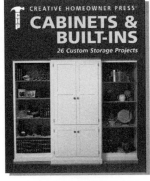

## CABINETS & BUILT-INS

26 custom cabinetry projects are included for every room in the house, from kitchen cabinets to a bedroom wall unit, a bunk bed, computer workstation, and more. Also included are chapters on tools, techniques, finishing, and materials.

BOOK #: 277079          160 pp.          8½"x10⅞"

## DECKS: Plan, Design, Build

With this book, even the novice builder can build a deck that perfectly fits his yard. The step-by-step instructions lead the reader from laying out footings to adding railings. Includes three deck projects, 500 color drawings, and photographs.

BOOK #: 277180          176pp.          8½"x10⅞"

## FURNITURE REPAIR & REFINISHING

From structural repairs to restoring older finishes or entirely refinishing furniture: a hands-on step-by-step approach to furniture repair and restoration. More than 430 color photographs and 60 full-color drawings.

BOOK #: 277335          240pp.          8½"x10⅞"

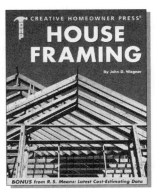

## HOUSE FRAMING

Written for those with beginning to intermediate building skills, this book is designed to walk you through the framing basics, from assembling simple partitions to cutting compound angles on dormer rafters. More than 400 full-color drawings.

BOOK #: 277655          240pp.          8½"x10⅞"

# the Home Planner, Builder & Owner

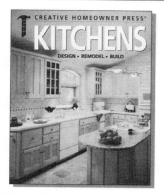

## KITCHENS: Design, Remodel, Build

This is the reference book for modern kitchen design, with more than 100 full-color photos to help homeowners plan the layout. Step-by-step instructions illustrate basic plumbing and wiring techniques; how to finish walls and ceilings; and more.

BOOK #: 277065          192pp.          8½"x10⅞"

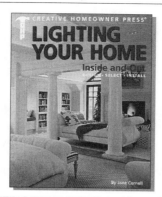

## LIGHTING YOUR HOME: Inside and Out

Lighting should be selected with care. This book thoroughly explains lighting design for every room as well as outdoors. It is also a step-by-step manual that shows how to install the fixtures. More than 125 photos and 400 drawings.

BOOK #: 277583          176pp.          8½"x10⅞"

## MASONRY: Concrete, Brick, Stone

Concrete, brick, and stone choices are detailed with step-by-step instructions and over 35 color photographs and 460 illustrations. Projects include a brick or stone garden wall, steps and patios, a concrete-block retaining wall, a concrete sidewalk.

BOOK #: 277106          176pp.          8½"x10⅞"

## The Smart Approach to KITCHEN DESIGN

Transform a dated kitchen into the spectacular heart of your home. Learn how to create a better layout and more efficient storage. Find out about the latest equipment and materials. Savvy tips explain how to create style like a pro. More than 150 color photos.

BOOK #: 279935          176 pp.          9"x10"

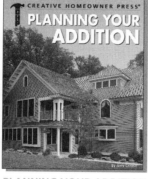

## PLANNING YOUR ADDITION

Planning an addition to your home involves a daunting number of choices, from choosing a contractor to selecting bathroom tile. Using 280 color drawings and photographs, architect/author Jerry Germer helps you make the right decision.

BOOK #: 277004          192pp.          8½"x10⅞"

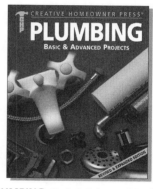

## PLUMBING: Basic & Advanced Projects

Take the guesswork out of plumbing repair and installation for old and new systems. Projects include replacing faucets, unclogging drains, installing a tub, replacing a water heater, and much more. 500 illustrations and diagrams.

BOOK #: 277620          176pp.          8½"x10⅞"

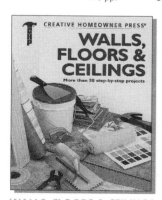

## WALLS, FLOORS & CEILINGS

Here's the definitive guide to interiors. It shows you how to replace old surfaces with new professional-looking ones. Projects include installing molding, skylights, insulation, flooring, carpeting, and more. Over 500 color photos and drawings.

BOOK #: 277697          176pp.          8½"x10⅞"

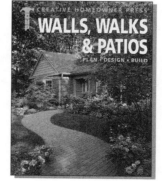

## WALLS, WALKS & PATIOS

Learn how to build a patio from concrete, stone, or brick and complement it with one of a dozen walks. Learn about simple mortarless walls, landscape timber walls, and hefty brick and stone walls. 50 photographs and 320 illustrations, all in color.

BOOK #: 277994          192pp.          8½"x10⅞"

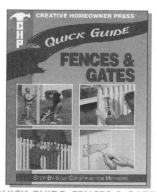

## QUICK GUIDE: FENCES & GATES

Learn how to build and install all kinds of fences and gates for your yard, from hand-built wood privacy and picket fences to newer prefabricated vinyl and chain-link types. Over 200 two-color drawings illustrate step-by-step procedures.

BOOK #: 287732          80pp.          8½"x10⅞"

# Place your Order ....

### WORKING WITH TILE
Design and complete interior and exterior tile projects on walls, floors, countertops, shower enclosures, patios, pools, and more. 425 color illustrations and over 80 photographs.

BOOK #: 277540     176pp.     8½"x10⅞"

### COLOR IN THE AMERICAN HOME
Find out how to make the most of color in your home with ideas for analyzing, selecting, and coordinating color schemes. Over 150 photographs of traditional and contemporary interiors.

BOOK #: 287264     176pp.     9"x10"

### The Smart Approach to HOME DECORATING
Learn how to work with space, color, pattern, and texture with the flair of a professional designer. More than 300 color photos.

BOOK #: 279667     256pp.     9"x10"

## CREATIVE HOMEOWNER®

## BOOK ORDER FORM          *Please Print*
SHIP TO:

Name:

Address:

City:                State:                Zip:                Phone Number:

*(Should there be a problem with your order)*

| Quantity | Title | Price | CH # | Cost |
|---|---|---|---|---|
| | 380 Country & Farmhouse Home Plans | $9.95 | 277035 | |
| | 400 Affordable Home Plans | 9.95 | 277012 | |
| | 408 Vacation & Second Home Plans | 8.95 | 277036 | |
| | 450 One-Story Home Plans | 9.95 | 277014 | |
| | 450 Two-Story Home Plans | 9.95 | 277042 | |
| | 600 Most Popular Home Plans | 9.95 | 277029 | |
| | Adding Value to Your Home | 16.95 | 277006 | |
| | Basic Wiring | 14.95 | 277048 | |
| | Bathrooms: Design, Remodel, Build | 16.95 | 277053 | |
| | Better Lawns, Step by Step | 14.95 | 274359 | |
| | Bird Feeders | 10.95 | 277102 | |
| | Build a Kids' Play Yard | 14.95 | 277662 | |
| | Cabinets & Built-Ins | 14.95 | 277079 | |
| | Color in the American Home | 19.95 | 287264 | |
| | Complete Guide to Wallpapering | 14.95 | 278910 | |
| | Complete Guide to Water Gardens | 19.95 | 274452 | |
| | Complete Home Landscaping | 24.95 | 274615 | |
| | Creating Good Gardens | 16.95 | 274244 | |
| | Custom Closets | 12.95 | 277132 | |
| | Decks: Plan, Design, Build | 14.95 | 277180 | |
| | Decorating with Paint & Paper | 19.95 | 279723 | |
| | Decorative Paint Finishes | 10.95 | 287371 | |
| | Drywall: Pro Tips for Hanging & Finishing | 14.95 | 278315 | |
| | Easy-Care Guide to Houseplants | 19.95 | 275243 | |
| | Fences, Gates & Trellises | 14.95 | 277981 | |
| | Furniture Repair & Refinishing | 19.95 | 277335 | |
| | Gazebos & Other Outdoor Structures | 14.95 | 277138 | |
| | Home Landscaping: Mid-Atlantic Reg. | 19.95 | 274537 | |
| | Home Landscaping: Midwest Reg./S Can. | 19.95 | 274385 | |
| | Home Landscaping: Northeast Reg./SE Can. | 19.95 | 274618 | |
| | Home Landscaping: Southeast Reg. | 19.95 | 274762 | |
| | House Framing | 19.95 | 277655 | |
| | Kitchens: Design, Remodel, Build (New Ed.) | 16.95 | 277065 | |
| | Lighting Your Home Inside & Out | 16.95 | 277583 | |
| | Masonry: Concrete, Brick, Stone | 16.95 | 277106 | |
| | Mastering Fine Decorative Paint Techniques | 27.95 | 279550 | |
| | Planning Your Addition | 16.95 | 277004 | |
| | Plumbing: Basic and Advanced Projects | 14.95 | 277620 | |
| | Remodeling Basements, Attics & Garages | 16.95 | 277680 | |
| | Smart Approach to Bath Design | 19.95 | 287225 | |
| | Smart Approach to Home Decorating | 24.95 | 279667 | |
| | Smart Approach to Kitchen Design | 19.95 | 279935 | |
| | Smart Approach to Window Decor | 19.95 | 279431 | |
| | Trees, Shrubs & Hedges for Home Landscaping | 19.95 | 274238 | |

| Quantity | Title | Price | CH # | Cost |
|---|---|---|---|---|
| | Walls, Floors & Ceilings | $16.95 | 277697 | |
| | Walls, Walks & Patios | 14.95 | 277994 | |
| | Working with Tile | 16.95 | 277540 | |

***Quick Guide Series***

| Quantity | Title | Price | CH # | Cost |
|---|---|---|---|---|
| | Quick Guide - Attics | $7.95 | 287711 | |
| | Quick Guide - Basements | 7.95 | 287242 | |
| | Quick Guide - Ceramic Tile | 7.95 | 287730 | |
| | Quick Guide - Decks | 7.95 | 277344 | |
| | Quick Guide - Fences & Gates | 7.95 | 287732 | |
| | Quick Guide - Floors | 7.95 | 287734 | |
| | Quick Guide - Garages & Carports | 7.95 | 287785 | |
| | Quick Guide - Gazebos | 7.95 | 287757 | |
| | Quick Guide - Insulation & Ventilation | 7.95 | 287367 | |
| | Quick Guide - Interior & Exterior Painting | 7.95 | 287784 | |
| | Quick Guide - Masonry Walls | 7.95 | 287741 | |
| | Quick Guide - Patios & Walks | 7.95 | 287778 | |
| | Quick Guide - Plumbing | 7.95 | 287863 | |
| | Quick Guide - Ponds & Fountains | 7.95 | 287804 | |
| | Quick Guide - Pool & Spa Maintenance | 7.95 | 287901 | |
| | Quick Guide - Roofing | 7.95 | 287807 | |
| | Quick Guide - Shelving & Storage | 7.95 | 287763 | |
| | Quick Guide - Siding | 7.95 | 287892 | |
| | Quick Guide - Stairs & Railings | 7.95 | 287755 | |
| | Quick Guide - Storage Sheds | 7.95 | 287815 | |
| | Quick Guide - Trim (Crown Molding, Base & more) | 7.95 | 287745 | |
| | Quick Guide - Walls & Ceilings | 7.95 | 287792 | |
| | Quick Guide - Windows & Doors | 7.95 | 287812 | |
| | Quick Guide - Wiring, Third Edition | 7.95 | 287884 | |

Number of Books Ordered _____ Total for Books _____

NJ Residents add 6% tax _____

*Prices subject to change without notice.*     Subtotal _____

Postage/Handling Charges _____
*$3.75 for first book / $1.25 for each additional book*

Total _____

*Make checks (in U.S. currency only) payable to:*
### CREATIVE HOMEOWNER®
P.O. BOX 38, 24 Park Way
Upper Saddle River, New Jersey 07458-9960

Please visit us at our Web site: **www.creativehomeowner.com**